OTHER TITLES IN THE GREENHAVEN PRESS LITERARY COMPANION SERIES:

THE GREENHAVEN PRESS

Literary Companion

TO BRITISH LITERATURE

OLIVER TWIST

Jill Karson, *Book Editor*

Bonnie Szumski, *Series Editor*

Greenhaven Press, San Diego, CA

Every effort has been made to trace the owners of copy-righted material. The articles in this volume may have been edited for content, length, and/or reading level. The titles have been changed to enhance the editorial purpose. Those interested in locating the original source will find the complete citation on the first page of each article.

Library of Congress Cataloging-in-Publication Data

Readings on Oliver Twist / Jill Karson, book editor.
    p.   cm. — (The Greenhaven Press literary
companion to British literature)
    Includes bibliographical references and index.
    ISBN 0-7377-0444-6 (lib. bdg. : alk. paper) —
    ISBN 0-7377-0443-8 (pbk. : alk. paper)
    1. Dickens, Charles, 1812–1870. Oliver Twist.
I. Title: Oliver Twist. II. Karson, Jill. III. Series.

PR4567 .R43   2001
823'8—dc21   00-048374
                                                          CIP

Cover photo: Editorial Photocolor Archives/Art Resource
Library of Congress, 14

Copyright © 2001 by Greenhaven Press, Inc.
PO Box 289009
San Diego, CA 92198-9009
Printed in the U.S.A.

> **66** *I wished to show, in little Oliver, the principle of good surviving through every adverse circumstance, and triumphing at last.* **99**
>
> **Charles Dickens**

CONTENTS

Oliver's experiences reflect traumatic events in Dickens's past, including his separation from his family and banishment to a blacking factory.

FOREWORD

The story's bare facts are simple: The captain, an old and scarred seafarer, walks with a peg leg made of whale ivory. He relentlessly drives his crew to hunt the world's oceans for the great white whale that crippled him. After a long search, the ship encounters the whale and a fierce battle ensues. Finally the captain drives his harpoon into the whale, but the harpoon line catches the captain about the neck and drags him to his death.

A simple story, a straightforward plot—yet, since the 1851 publication of Herman Melville's *Moby-Dick*, readers and critics have found many meanings in the struggle between Captain Ahab and the whale. To some, the novel is a cautionary tale that depicts how Ahab's obsession with revenge leads to his insanity and death. Others believe that the whale represents the unknowable secrets of the universe and that Ahab is a tragic hero who dares to challenge fate by attempting to discover this knowledge. Perhaps Melville intended Ahab as a criticism of Americans' tendency to become involved in well-intentioned but irrational causes. Or did Melville model Ahab after himself, letting his fictional character express his anger at what he perceived as a cruel and distant god?

Although literary critics disagree over the meaning of *Moby-Dick*, readers do not need to choose one particular interpretation in order to gain an understanding of Melville's novel. Instead, by examining various analyses, they can gain numerous insights into the issues that lie under the surface of the basic plot. Studying the writings of literary critics can also aid readers in making their own assessments of *Moby-Dick* and other literary works and in developing analytical thinking skills.

The Greenhaven Literary Companion Series was created with these goals in mind. Designed for young adults, this unique anthology series provides an engaging and comprehensive introduction to literary analysis and criticism. The essays included in the Literary Companion Series are chosen for their accessibility to a young adult audience and are expertly edited in consideration of both the reading and comprehension levels of this audience. In addition, each essay is introduced by a concise summation that presents the contributing writer's main themes and insights. Every anthology in the Literary Companion Series contains a varied selection of critical essays that cover a wide time span and express diverse views. Wherever possible, primary sources are represented through excerpts from authors' notebooks, letters, and journals and through contemporary criticism.

Each title in the Literary Companion Series pays careful consideration to the historical context of the particular author or literary work. In-depth biographies and detailed chronologies reveal important aspects of authors' lives and emphasize the historical events and social milieu that influenced their writings. To facilitate further research, every anthology includes primary and secondary source bibliographies of articles and/or books selected for their suitability for young adults. These engaging features make the Greenhaven Literary Companion series ideal for introducing students to literary analysis in the classroom or as a library resource for young adults researching the world's great authors and literature.

Exceptional in its focus on young adults, the Greenhaven Literary Companion Series strives to present literary criticism in a compelling and accessible format. Every title in the series is intended to spark readers' interest in leading American and world authors, to help them broaden their understanding of literature, and to encourage them to formulate their own analyses of the literary works that they read. It is the editors' hope that young adult readers will find these anthologies to be true companions in their study of literature.

INTRODUCTION

Charles Dickens learned about poverty in the worst possible way—by being a poor youth. Clearly, the material deprivations and emotional isolation endured by the young Dickens were indelibly imprinted in the writer's mind, and the die was cast for Dickens's brilliant literary legacy. Yet while the threads of his own childhood suffering created the fabric of much Dickensian literature, *Oliver Twist* stands out as one of the most penetrating accounts of the deplorable social conditions plaguing Dickens's England.

In many ways *Oliver Twist* represents Dickens at his finest: The richly textured descriptive passages, combined with snatches of humor and deep psychological insights, are testament to Dickens's enormous creative genius. Perhaps most importantly, in *Oliver Twist*, Dickens not only tackles the grim conditions of his own boyhood, but addresses the plight of all downtrodden, isolated individuals.

Readers across the globe recognize the scene in which the diminutive orphan Oliver who, "desperate with hunger and reckless with misery," asks his astonished keepers for "more." This volume invites readers to look beyond the surface plot and contemplate the work's many layers of meanings. To this end, *Readings on* Oliver Twist gathers a number of critical views from a broad range of critics. Several essays examine thematic material and Dickens's social purpose; others consider the design and structure of *Oliver Twist;* still others include analyses of Dickens's broad cast of colorful characters. Each essay begins with a brief introduction that highlights the author's main ideas. A chronology and biography provide information about Dickens and lend historical background to *Oliver Twist.* Additional research tools include a list of characters, a plot synopsis, a detailed bibliography, and an annotated table of contents. Together, these features aid comprehension and appreciation of this multifaceted work, making the reading of *Oliver Twist* a richly rewarding and enjoyable experience.

CHARLES DICKENS: A BIOGRAPHY

Charles Dickens exuded an energy and determination that awed friends and overwhelmed relatives. His temper flared at slights to himself and his work; his generosity and compassion extended to children and the working poor. He was a pessimist who doubted that government and the upper class would ever pass reforms to help poor people, but who optimistically believed in the goodness of the lower class and championed their cause throughout his life. He made his mark in nineteenth-century England with humor, creating a cast of characters that exemplified all that he loved and satirized all that he hated about his society. Biographer Edgar Johnson says in the preface to his biography of Dickens:

> Dickens was himself a Dickens character, bursting with an inordinate and fantastic vitality. The world in which his spirit dwelt was identical with the world of his novels, brilliant in hue, violent in movement, crammed with people all furiously alive and with places as alive as his people. "The Dickens world" was his everyday world.

Scholars attribute much of the formation of Dickens's personality and, consequently, his achievements to two phases in his boyhood years. The first, happy phase gave him hope and optimism; the second, sad phase instilled his spirit for social reform.

Charles John Huffman Dickens was born on February 7, 1812, in the southwestern English town of Landport in Portsea, the second of eight children born to John and Elizabeth Barrow Dickens. John Dickens, a clerk in the Navy Pay-office, and Elizabeth, a pretty, educated woman, belonged to the middle class, but were not prosperous enough to withstand the extravagant spending and entertainment they enjoyed. John Dickens enjoyed a house full of party guests and rehearsed little Charles and his sister to entertain them. In *Charles Dickens: A Critical Study,* G.K. Chesterton says:

> Some of the earliest glimpses we have of Charles Dickens show him to us perched on some chair or table singing comic

songs in an atmosphere of perpetual applause. So, almost as soon as he can toddle, he steps into the glare of the footlights. He never stepped out of it until he died.

In 1814 John was temporarily sent to the London office before being transferred to the naval dockyards in the south-eastern town of Chatham in 1817, when Charles was five. There John rented a large house for his family, two servants, and Aunt Fanny, his wife's widowed sister, but soon found it beyond his means and moved his family to a smaller Chatham home.

A HAPPY AND SAD CHILDHOOD

In a family that felt financially secure, Charles enjoyed his years in Chatham, five years that permanently affected his outlook on life. He played games with friends, put on magic-lantern shows (an early form of slide projector), and continued to sing duets with his sister Fanny. Mary Weller, the maid who cared for the children, told bedtime stories and hummed evensong, or evening worship, hymns. Dickens investigated the town, recording in his mind the sights of its shipwrights, convict laborers, guild hall, cathedral, and castle on the hill and the smells of rope and wood and canvas down by the docks. Because he was often sick, Charles never played sports well, but he loved to read, saying later, "When I think of it, the picture always arises in my mind of a summer evening, the boys at play in the churchyard, and I sitting on my bed, reading as if for life." In addition to reading the family books, such as *Peregrine Pickle, Don Quixote,* and *Robinson Crusoe,* Aunt Fanny's suitor, Dr. Matthew Lamert, and his son James took Charles to farces, melodramas, and to *Richard II* and *Macbeth.*

Dickens attended the school of William Giles, a Baptist minister in Chatham. A precocious child, Charles fully expected to attend both school and college and enter a profession. These early, happy years laid the groundwork for his lifelong hope and vitality.

His hopes for a bright future were dashed, however, when his father, now heavily in debt, was transferred back to London in 1822, when Charles was ten. John Dickens settled his family in Camden Town, a poor section of London, in a four-room house that held Dickens's parents as well as six children, one maid, and James Lamert, who lived with them. No arrangement was made for Charles to go to school, though Fanny had won a scholarship to the Royal Academy of Music.

Charles did chores at home, and just as curiously as he had done in Chatham, he wandered the streets of Camden Town, observing its noisy vehicles, small factories, taverns, cooked-food stalls, and rubbish dumps and watching chimney sweeps, muffin-boys, and apprentices at work—all sounds, sights, and smells that imprinted themselves on his mind.

Not long after moving to London, Charles learned what it meant to be poor. One sad day his family sold his beloved books from Chatham days to pay debts, after which he borrowed copies of the newspapers *Spectator* and *Tatler* for his reading. His mother rented a room and started a school, but not one pupil came. James Lamert, who managed a boot-blacking factory, suggested that Charles work there to help with the deteriorating family finances. At twelve, Charles worked from eight A.M. to eight P.M. for six shillings a week in the tumbledown warehouse tying and labeling pots of blacking. Two weeks after Charles started at the blacking factory, John Dickens was arrested for not paying his debts and sent to Marshalsea, a debtors prison, or workhouse for the poor, with meager food and hard labor. Charles was sent out to pawn household goods, and when only beds, chairs, and the kitchen table were left, the rest of the family moved to Marshalsea (which admitted groups in family quarters) with the father.

Charles Dickens

John Dickens, who still drew a small naval salary, paid for lodgings so that Charles could continue his job at the blacking factory. Now that he had to feed himself on six shillings a week, he divided his money into packages, one for each day, occasionally splurging the whole day's allotment on a sweet or a good ale; when he had no money, he walked to the Covent Garden market and stared at food. Alone in the lodging house with no companion but the boys from the blacking factory, who mocked him because he was small and shy and different, Charles suffered greatly. In an unpublished autobiography, he later wrote of this time in his life:

> No words can express the secret agony of my soul, as I sunk into this companionship; compared these everyday associates

with those of my happier childhood; and felt my early hopes of growing up to be a learned and distinguished man, crushed in my breast.

The deep remembrance of the sense I had of being utterly ne-glected and hopeless; of the shame I felt in my position; of the misery it was to my young heart to believe that, day by day, what I had learned, and thought, and delighted in, and raised my fancy and my emulation up by, was passing away from me, never to be brought back any more; ... even now, famous and caressed and happy, I ... wander desolately back to that time of my life.... That I suffered in secret, and that I suf-fered exquisitely, no one ever knew but I.

Following a quarrel with John Dickens, Lamert fired Charles after twenty weeks that seemed to Charles like twenty years. The experience of the blacking factory made an indelible impression on him, setting in him a hard deter-mination, but through his suffering he developed an equally permanent sensitivity from which he created in his novels a host of suffering children and other innocent victims of in-justice and pain.

After three months in Marshalsea, John Dickens's mother died and John inherited £450, enough to get him out of prison, and John went back to his job with the navy. From 1824 to 1826, he sent Charles to Wellington House Academy, where Charles studied English, French, Latin, writing, mathematics, and dancing. When John lost his job and took work as a reporter for the *British Press*, he was again deep in debt, and Charles had to drop out of school. He took a job at the law office of Ellis and Blackmore, which he found so boring that he determined never to be a lawyer who spent his life "splitting hairs slowly and growing rich on the dis-tress of others." Dickens then set out to educate himself. He taught himself shorthand in eighteen months, went to acting school, and procured a pass to the Reading Room in the British Museum (the national library) where he spent hours reading, the "usefullest [days] of my life."

While working at the law office, Dickens had met and fallen in love with Maria Beadnell, a banker's daughter a year older than he. Dickens pursued her diligently, but her parents disapproved. The disappointment of losing Maria re-newed old feelings of despair and shame felt so vividly dur-ing the days of the blacking factory. At his twenty-first birth-day party, Maria rejected him, after which Charles returned her letters, but she kept up a teasing relationship that fed his hopes. When Maria's parents sent her to Paris to finishing school, Charles realized he had no chance to win her love after four years of trying. He vowed he would never again be anyone's plaything. Lacking family wealth or prestige, he would need independent success, and from then on he was determined to have his way.

DICKENS BEGINS AS A JOURNALIST

Four years after taking a law-clerk job, Dickens began his writing career as a reporter. Once he had mastered shorthand, he set himself up as a freelance reporter near the law courts and waited to be hired as a recorder of court cases. He acquired a job on the *Mirror of Parliament,* a paper that reported the daily transactions of the lawmakers, and worked his way to an advanced position hiring and supervising other reporters. He earned a reputation for accuracy and speed in recording speeches of members of Parliament, and was invited to join the staff of another paper, the *True Sun.* As a reporter observing the workings of Parliament, he was unimpressed with its red tape; he saw that a few reforms benefited the middle class, but that lawmakers did nothing for the masses of poor whose lives were, as he described, "misery, starvation, unemployment and cholera." Of particular interest to Dickens, Parliament, in 1832, appointed a Royal Commission to examine legislation concerning the poor—and reform the system of providing relief. The events centering on these poor laws—and the history that led to them—made an indelible impression on Dickens.

THE POOR LAWS

For many years, England had grappled with supporting its swelling class of paupers. Since the time of Queen Elizabeth, direct relief alleviated some of the problem. As the number of paupers continued to increase, however, so, too, did the cost of public relief, which reached staggering heights. Parish taxes were imposed, not only to provide direct relief but also to supplement starvation wages. This system, inevitably, invited widespread abuse. In response, Parliament passed the Poor Law of 1834, which required that all able-bodied paupers enter a workhouse. To discourage people from living at public expense, living conditions in the workhouse were deliberately made intolerable: Workhouses were usually overcrowded, filthy facilities where food was meager and medical aid almost nonexistent. As one of Dickens's contemporaries observed: "The principle upon which relief is administered under the law appears to be to make the help rendered so distasteful, that they must be far gone indeed in wretchedness who will apply for it; and the high-hearted poor will starve rather than take it, will die instead of coming on the rates."

Dickens found the Poor Law of 1834 reprehensible. Though Dickens himself had acquired some professional and economic success, he still remembered the days in the blacking factory and had compassion for those who worked hard and had almost nothing. Several years later, when Dickens embarked on the serial that was to become *Oliver Twist*, he lashed out at the pitiable condition of the poor and, even more specifically, the harsh tenets of the Poor Law of 1834. Indeed, the treatment of the poor was to become a common—and passionate—theme in Dickens's writing.

THE ROAD TO SUCCESS

After 1833 Dickens's determination and hard work brought results. The *Morning Chronicle* hired him as a full-time reporter and soon after added him to the staff of its affiliate, the *Evening Chronicle*. When the *Monthly Magazine* printed, without his name and without paying him, a sketch Dickens had submitted, he was thrilled to see his writing in print. The editors asked for more sketches, which he signed "Boz" for the first time in 1834. Dickens took the name Boz from his family; his little brother Augustus, nicknamed Moses but unable to pronounce the word, called himself Boz. When Dickens was covering plays for the *Evening Chronicle*, he discovered that some of the Boz sketches had been adapted for the stage. Dickens's "sketches" were entertainingly written anecdotes about London people and places. Since the *Monthly Magazine* did not pay him, he quit and wrote street sketches for the *Evening Chronicle*. In addition, he wrote twelve sketches for *Bell's Life in London*. His new success brought him to the attention of writer William Harrison Ainsworth, who introduced Dickens to artist George Cruikshank and publisher John Macrone. In 1836, on Dickens's twenty-fourth birthday, Macrone published *Sketches by Boz*, a two-volume collection of sketches illustrated by Cruikshank.

George Hogarth, Dickens's editor on the *Evening Chronicle*, often invited Dickens to join family gatherings and introduced Dickens to his daughters, all of whom Dickens found charming. On April 2, 1836, he married the oldest daughter, Catherine, called Kate, at St. Luke's Church, Chelsea. When the couple was settled, Catherine's sixteen-year-old sister, Mary, came to live with them; unmarried sisters or brothers living with a married couple was common practice in Dickens's day. Later, Dickens's brother Fred also lived in their home. Charles and Mary, who had a sweeter disposition than Catherine, developed a close friendship with more understanding than existed between Charles and his wife, who nevertheless bore ten children, seven boys and three girls, between 1837 and 1852.

FROM SKETCHES TO NOVELS

When *Sketches by Boz* brought good reviews, publishers Chapman and Hall invited Dickens to write, for £14 a month, twenty monthly installments about an imaginary sports club, the Nemrod Club, sketches to be illustrated by Robert Seymour. Dickens, knowing nothing about sports, renegotiated the proposal to focus instead on the travels and investigations of Mr. Pickwick and the imaginary Pickwick Club, illustrated by Hablôt Knight Browne, called Phiz, who became Dickens's illustrator for other works. The first installments from the Pickwick Club were poorly received, until Dickens added the character of Sam Weller in the fourth installment. The addition changed the fortunes of the series from sales of four thousand to forty thousand copies. Biographer Wolf Mankowitz describes the popularity of Pickwick:

> It was read upstairs and downstairs [by all classes], by judges on the bench and the cleaners after them. . . . Critics spoke of Dickens as another Cervantes, poor people shared a shilling copy and read it aloud in groups. A clergyman, having consoled a sick man, heard him mutter behind his back, "Well, thank God, Pickwick will be out in ten days anyway!"

Chapman and Hall sold back issues by the thousands, and they more than doubled Dickens's salary. The installments were published as a book, entitled *Pickwick Papers,* in 1837. Dickens was "the sudden lion of the town," and offers poured in for children's books, novels, and more sketches.

Dickens accepted an offer to edit the monthly *Bentley's Miscellany* and include in it installments of *Oliver Twist,* to be illustrated by Cruikshank, the illustrator of Boz. The first February 1837 installment garnered great reviews and sold many copies even though it had a more serious tone than *Pickwick.* In *Pickwick,* Dickens presented prison with humor and a mild view; in *Oliver Twist,* he wrote about prison in grave, realistic language. While he was writing the installments for the novel, Mary Hogarth died suddenly. Because Dickens loved Mary as a close friend, he felt such grief he had to take time off. He coped with the loss by taking long walks and horseback rides with John Forster, who had become his friend and agent. Dickens's sadness over Mary's death further strained his relationship with Catherine, who, though she mourned the loss of her sister, was jealous of her husband's affection for Mary. Determined to continue writing, he finished the installments, after which Bentley published *Oliver Twist* in a three-volume book in 1838, the first book to have Dickens's name, not the anonymous "Boz," on the title page.

Before Dickens completed *Oliver Twist* he was already thinking of his next novel, and he traveled with his illustrator Phiz to Yorkshire to research the conditions of boarding schools there. He found maggots, fleas, beatings, and ignorance, schools where illegitimate children were hidden for low fees. At Bowes Academy, run by one-eyed William Shaw, boys were sick, some went blind, and on average one died each year. These schools became the model for Dotheboys Hall in *Nicholas Nickleby*, whose first installment was published in April 1838 while Dickens was still drawing praise from critics for *Oliver Twist*. Of *Nicholas Nickleby*, biographer Edgar Johnson says, "it mingles the sunlight of *Pickwick* with the darkness of *Oliver*," and "fuses the inexhaustible laughter of *Pickwick* with the somber themes of *Oliver Twist*." These two books, *Oliver Twist* and *Nicholas Nickleby*, Johnson says, "were clarion peals announcing to the world that in Charles Dickens the rejected and forgotten and misused of the world had a champion." The first installment of *Nicholas Nickleby* sold fifty thousand copies on the first day.

The success of Dickens's books brought him enough earnings to move up in social class. He bought a house with a gate on Doughty Street in London and traveled within England and abroad. He was invited to join social clubs and literary societies and met other writers—essayist Leigh Hunt and novelists William Thackeray and Edward Bulwer-Lytton. Invitations came to Dickens from the city's cultured elite on the west end of town, but not to Kate, not known for charm or wit. Dickens was greeted by footmen and led up grand staircases to attend breakfasts and dinners at which the educated and famous displayed their skills and amused one another. Mankowitz describes Dickens's reaction to this social class:

It was a strictly mannered, often cruel world, but Dickens had already learned self-assurance, was a practised mimic of any tone, and felt confident in his intelligence and great gifts: gifts, he soon came to realize, that few of these privileged people had even a tiny part of. That awareness defended him against their insolence or patronization. He was acute enough to see behind the social masks.

As Mankowitz says, Dickens's novels harshly satirize the "masters of material gain and the parasites of materialism, in law courts, the factories and workhouses," but they seldom attack the aristocratic and intellectual elite. He became adviser to one of its members, Angela Burdett Coutts, an heiress who wanted to use money from her two fortunes for social improvement. She took Dickens's advice to fund slum clearance and homes for "fallen women."

Though Dickens's social relations went smoothly, his relations with critics and publishers were often rancorous. Writing about *Oliver Twist,* one critic said that Dickens wrote so much and so fast that he was likely to decline in quality and popularity unless he slowed down. Dickens, angered, vowed, "They shall eat their words." G.K. Chesterton thought perhaps the critics misunderstood Dickens and said, "Dickens has greatly suffered with the critics precisely through this stunning simplicity in his best work," but his disputes with publishers usually involved money and contracts, not the quality of his work. Dickens was inclined to sign a contract that seemed good at the time, then demand more money than the original contract stipulated when sales and the publisher's profits were much larger than expected. In one dispute with the publisher Bentley, Dickens wanted both money and a change in the work contract. Bentley had published *Oliver Twist,* and contracted with Dickens for two additional novels. Dickens wanted to consider *Oliver Twist* one of the two and then jump to the publishers Chapman and Hall. When the dispute reached a stalemate, Dickens's friend and agent Forster negotiated for him. The determination Dickens had learned from the days at the blacking factory got him what he wanted but left hard feelings with the publisher that Forster was unable to smooth over.

LITTLE NELL SAVES A WEEKLY

Dickens wanted to be free of the contract with Bentley because he had an idea for a weekly that he wanted Chapman and Hall to fund. Dickens intended *Master Humphrey's Clock* to include a variety of short sketches written by a number of contributors. Responding to the sale of seventy thousand copies of the first issue, Dickens said, "What will the wiseacres say to weekly issues *now*? And what will they say to any of those ten thousand things we shall do together to make 'em writhe and stagger in their shoes." Sales, however, dropped markedly when the public discovered the weekly had no installments by Dickens. Within two weeks, Dickens was serializing *The Old Curiosity Shop,* a travel story about an odd collection of characters. In *The World of Charles Dickens,* Angus Wilson says that this novel

> shows up alarmingly to modern readers the degree of oddity then accepted in a supposedly realistic story—a devilish, fire-drinking dwarf, a little child, an undersized servant maid, a woman (Sally Brass), who is reported as having enlisted as a guardsman or gone down to the docks in male attire, a small boy who stands on his head in mudflats.

It was, however, sweet Little Nell, persecuted by the dwarf Quilp and loved by the honest boy Kit Nubbles, who captured readers' hearts and sent weekly sales above a hundred thousand copies. When Nell neared death, readers deluged the paper with letters pleading that Dickens not let her die. Die she did, nonetheless, in an installment that prompted an outpouring of emotion, as Mankowitz describes:

> Scottish critic Lord Jeffrey was found weeping in his library. 'I'm a great goose to have given way so', he sobbed, 'but I couldn't help it.' [Actor William] Macready, [playwright and poet Walter] Landor, Thomas Carlyle and Edgar Allan Poe were all moved to a similar plight. So was [member of Parliament] Daniel O'Connell, reading on a train journey; he groaned, 'He should not have killed her', and threw the story out of the window.

Dickens's hold on the attention and sentiment of the public loosened with the weekly installments of his next novel written for *Master Humphrey's Clock.* A historical novel, *Barnaby Rudge* recounts the riots of the poor against Parliament, but Dickens gives the story a more anti-Catholic than anti-Parliament emphasis. The strain of producing weekly installments of two books took a toll on Dickens's health, and he took a year's rest, which publishers Chapman and Hall funded with a salary.

DICKENS'S VISIT TO AMERICA

During his year off, Dickens and Catherine visited America. They sailed on January 2, 1842, and arrived in Boston to huge crowds wanting to know why Little Nell had to die. He and Catherine visited Boston, Niagara, Philadelphia, St. Louis, and New York City. Wherever he went, crowds surrounded him, cheered, stared, wrung his hand, and clipped fur souvenirs from his coat. He had invitations from every state, from universities, Congress, and all kinds of public and private bodies. He visited orphanages, schools for the blind, reform schools, prisons, and industrial mills. New York published a special edition, the *Extra Boz Herald*, and held a Boz Ball in a ballroom decorated with characters from his books. In a letter to Forster, Dickens wrote:

> I can do nothing that I want to do, go nowhere where I want to go, and see nothing that I want to see. If I turn into the street, I am followed by a multitude. If I stay at home, the house becomes, with callers, like a fair. . . . If I go to a party in the evening, and am so enclosed and hedged about by people, stand where I will, that I am exhausted for want of air. I go to church for quiet, and there is a violent rush to the neighbourhood of the pew I sit in, and the clergyman preaches at *me*. I take my seat in a railroad car, and the very conductor won't leave me alone. I get out at a station, and can't drink a glass of water, without having a hundred people looking down my throat when I open my mouth to swallow. . . . I have no peace, and am in a perpetual worry.

In Washington, D.C., Dickens attended a session of Congress and visited President Tyler, who said little and sat beside a spitoon. To Dickens's amazement, people everywhere—in offices of the state, in courts of law, at parties, in bars, on trains—chewed large wads of tobacco and spit everywhere, "all squirted forth upon the carpet a yellow saliva which quite altered the pattern." Dickens's patience gradually ran out. At one dinner in his honor, after being introduced as a moral reformer and a champion of the downtrodden, Dickens began speaking in the manner expected of him, but midway in his remarks, he switched to the topic of American copyright laws and railed against the unfairness of Americans who made a profit from his works and those of Sir Walter Scott without paying the authors anything. The audience applauded politely, but the next day's papers criticized him for insulting those who had come to honor him. American authors remained silent on the subject, a situation that baffled and rankled Dickens. G.K. Chesterton comments on the English misunderstanding of Americans:

> America is a mystery to any good Englishman; but I think Dickens managed somehow to touch it on a queer nerve. There is one thing, at any rate, . . . that while there is no materialism so

crude or so material as American materialism, there is also no idealism so crude or so ideal as American idealism. America will always affect an Englishman as being soft in the wrong place and hard in the wrong place.... Some beautiful ideal runs through this people, but it runs aslant.

After four months of tours, crowds, and little privacy, Dickens left New York harbor on June 7, 1842, to sail for home, his children and friends, and his writing.

Before beginning his next novel, Dickens recorded his impressions of his American visit in *American Notes.* In polite tones, he praised many features of American life (and remained silent about copyright laws). America had, however, failed to live up to Dickens's expectations; its slavery, its business practices, its sensational journalism, and the manners of its people offended him. The book brought Dickens £1,000 toward the cost of the trip, but it brought him an array of adjectives in American newspapers—"coarse, vulgar, impudent, superficial, narrow-minded, conceited cockney, flimsy, childish, trashy, contemptible." He was less polite in his next book. After several installments of *Martin Chuzzlewit* sold poorly, Dickens hoped to increase sales by sending Martin to America. With none of the polite restraint shown in *American Notes,* Dickens expressed his impatience with America in harsh humor through the character of Mrs. Gamp, a brutalized victim of the society in which Mr. Pecksniff rules with unctuous hypocrisy. The Americans were angry, the British disappointed by its bitter tone, and Dickens's publishers reduced his year-off salary.

RESTLESSNESS AND TRAVEL

The year following his American visit, 1843, began a period of restlessness for Dickens. In a row with Chapman and Hall over salary, Dickens lost his temper and threatened to find a new publisher, but Christmas was coming soon and he did not act. Instead, with financial pressures mounting—*Chuzzlewit* sales had been disappointing and household expenses were growing—Dickens threw himself into writing a Christmas story. Working at a feverish pace, he completed the manuscript, originally titled *A Christmas Carol, In Prose, Being a Ghost Story of Christmas,* by the end of November. It was published shortly before Christmas 1843. With its attractive gold-lettered cover and hand-colored interior illustrations, six thousand copies were sold the first day. It was not just the physical beauty of the book that drew praise.

Like readers today, Dickens's contemporaries were deeply moved by the story's message that Christmas can and should spread love and brotherhood among humanity.

Dickens was exceedingly pleased with his Christmas story and its huge sales. Yet the book didn't generate as substantial an income for Dickens as he had hoped. With its colored plates, the book was costly to produce. At the same time, the selling price was fixed at only five shillings, leaving little profit for the author. Dickens was incensed. Although he never used color plates again, he would go on to write in the new genre that he had created: the Christmas book.

During this time, Georgina Hogarth, daughter of George Hogarth, who was as sweet as Mary had been, came to live in the Dickens home. After the holidays, Dickens took his family and servants to Italy, stopping first in Genoa and renting a house from which he could hear Genoa's constantly chiming bells. He used the opportunity to write another Christmas story, entitled "The Chimes," which became the second in a series of annual Christmas stories. In the following years, he wrote "The Cricket on the Hearth," "The Battle of Life," and "The Haunted Man" for publication just before the holidays. Before returning to England, he and Kate toured southern Italy, where he came to appreciate the manners and language of the Italians but grew to dislike the Catholic Church, which was, he thought, "a political arm against the poor and ignorant." Unlike his American trip, this trip was private and much more satisfying. When he returned to England in 1846, he started a new liberal paper, *Daily News,* during a political turmoil over the Corn Laws. When the first issue came off the press, ten thousand Londoners wanted to see what Dickens had said, as did thousands around the rest of the country. But once the paper was successfully established, Dickens lost patience with the details of publication and turned it over to Forster after seventeen issues.

Dickens became a familiar figure in London and a comic but difficult character in his home. A man of medium height who appeared small, he had thick brown hair, a mustache and beard, a large expressive mouth, and bright, active eyes that darted back and forth, taking in the details around him. His nervous and delicate manner belied a rather steely personality. He wore flashy waistcoats and velvet coats in public and liked to be looked at if the looks were admiring. Personally, he fussed over little things and directed his whims to be acted on instantly: If the house was too quiet at night, everyone had to get up; if it was too noisy, all had to be quiet. G.K. Chesterton said of Dickens, "His private life consisted of one tragedy and ten thousand comedies." His marriage was a failure, but he loved his children, and filled their home with energy, with daily pranks and practical jokes.

PERSONAL AND PROFESSIONAL TURNING POINTS

The mid-1840s marked a turning point both in Dickens's personal life and in his novels. Unhappy in his marriage, he developed undisciplined and unhealthy habits in his daily routines. His discontent spurred him to go to Lausanne, Switzerland, to start a new novel, *Dombey and Son,* his last farce. Like all of Dickens's first novels, which are primarily farces, *Dombey* is filled with caricatures who could not exist anywhere; the novels that followed have more realistic characters who could live everywhere. *Dombey* attacks the class system and moral pestilence that Dickens believed corrupted English society. He believed that the aristocracy perpetuated itself by taking advantage of "the pure, weak good nature" of the people.

If *Dombey* is the last of the first novels, *David Copperfield* is the transition novel. Dickens got the idea for the title by reversing his initials. It is his most autobiographical book and his favorite, about which he said, "I really think I have done it ingeniously and with a very complicated interweaving of truth and fiction." He tells the story of David in the first person and makes memory an important part of the theme, memories so personal that at one point he temporarily stopped writing because he felt sick and weak and shed tears for days. Writing *David Copperfield* helped to heal some of Dickens's wounds: "I can never approach the book with perfect composure it had such perfect possession of me when I wrote it." From the first installment in May 1849, the book was a success with the public. Novelist William Thackeray said, "By jingo it's beautiful. . . . Those inimitable Dickens touches which make such a great man of him. . . . There are little words and phrases in his book that are like personal benefits to his readers. . . . Bravo Dickens." And yet after the successful completion of this novel, Dickens was still restless and filled with nervous energy, which he directed toward production of plays.

As early as 1836, Dickens was interested in plays, but he had little success as a dramatist. His interest continued, however, in the form of amateur theatricals, farces Dickens and his family performed for friends at annual Twelfth Night celebrations in his home. Each year these productions became more elaborate until he offered them publicly and used the profits for charity. In 1847 he organized a theatrical company for his charity plays, arranged a benefit tour of the play *Every Man in His Humour,* and gave the profits to a budding but poor playwright. The next year the company produced *The Merry Wives of Windsor* to buy Shakespeare's birthplace in Stratford-on-Avon as a national monument. As the production of charity plays grew and audiences increased, Dickens hired professional actresses Mary Boyle and Ellen Ternan. In 1852 the company performed in thirteen cities and put on a performance for Queen Victoria, all profits going to the Guild of Literature and Art.

Amid his busy schedule of writing books and producing plays, Dickens leased a larger house in Tavistock Square in a more fashionable area of London, but first contracted to reconstruct, redecorate, and refurnish it before the family moved in. While waiting for the work to be done, he was too agitated to work; he said, "I sit down between whiles to think of a new story, and, as it begins to grow, such a torment of desire to be anywhere but where I am . . . takes hold of me, that it is like being *driven away.*" He settled down, however, after he had moved into the Tavistock home and started *Bleak House.* The first novel of the second, more realistic phase, *Bleak House* centers around a legal issue that typified the way the courts handled cases for prisoners of Chancery. Dickens parallels the slow pace of the courts to the coming and going of the indifferent political parties, satirically called Boodle and Coodle. From the first chapter, fog covers the whole London world of Chancery, the dark, murky atmosphere in which Dickens exposes the corruptions and ineptitudes of government and the courts. The first issue of *Bleak House* exceeded the sales of *David Copperfield* by ten thousand copies.

In 1850 Dickens started and edited a weekly called *Household Words,* a publication of short articles and tidbits written by a variety of contributors. Though Dickens exercised firm control over the editing of contributors' work, he gave many young writers an opportunity for valuable training. Subject matter covered a wide range: public education, campaigns against social abuses, entertainment, fiction, and humor. Two weeks after its first issue, a monthly news supplement was added, the *Household Narrative of Current Events.* The weekly carried explanations of scientific and technological discoveries, brief biographies of many historical figures, reviews of new and old books, travel tips, and Dickens's installments of *A Child's History of England.* Since three out of four people in England could read, Dickens wanted the weekly to appeal to all social classes. When circulation began to decline after more than two years of regular publication, Dickens propped up sales with a new book, *Hard Times,* in which he uses places to portray two opposing views. Coketown represents cold, rational industrialism and the Circus represents warmth, intuition, and humanity; in the end, the natural world of Sissy Jupe and the Circus people is the only hope. Before writing this book about the materialistic laws of supply and demand, the system of high profits and cheap labor preached by utilitarians, Dickens toured the cotton mills of Lancashire and interviewed striking cotton workers in Preston.

PUBLIC SUCCESS AND PRIVATE SADNESS

As a result of the reforms Dickens advocated in *Household Words,* he was sought as a public speaker and lecturer; out of these appearances he developed public readings from his works. He began with readings of "A Christmas Carol" and donated the proceeds to poor workers. He added other works, cut the excerpts and wrote stage directions, and took his readings throughout England, Scotland, and Ireland to audiences up to two thousand. Though he did not need the money and the exertion of performance strained his health, he liked the stimulation he received from the audiences. The next year, he hired a personal valet and an agent to help him with forty-two performances in Birmingham and Ireland. In 1867 he planned a hundred readings for an American tour. He had large, sell-out audiences in Boston, New York, Philadelphia, Baltimore, and Washington. But after seventy-six performances, Dickens's health was failing and he had to go home. In 1868 he went on a farewell reading tour in London, Ireland, and Scotland, but grew more and more exhausted with each performance. His agent Dolby, who urged him to quit, described Dickens as a man with "the iron will of a demon and the tender pity of an angel." At every reading, Dickens insisted that a certain number of good seats be sold for a small amount to the poor, believing that those he had spent his life championing should be able to hear what he said.

For many years, Dickens's public life had been a series of successes, but his private life was marked by numerous sad events. In 1848 his sister Fanny died of tuberculosis, followed by the death of her crippled son. Following the birth of their third daughter, Kate had a nervous breakdown. Shortly after Kate recovered, Dickens's father, John, died, and the baby, Dora Annie, became ill and died before she was a year old. Over the years, Dickens's relationship with Kate had continued to deteriorate, and when Dickens flirted with other women and gave them his attention, Kate, cowed by her famous and brilliant husband, withdrew further. During one of the public-reading tours, Kate left him. Dickens blamed himself:

> It is not only that she makes me uneasy and unhappy, but that I make her so too—and much more so . . . but we are strangely ill-assorted for the bond there is between us. God knows she would have been a thousand times happier if she had married another kind of man, and that her avoidance of this destiny would have been at least equally good for us both. I am often cut to the heart by thinking what a pity it is, for her own sake, that I ever fell in her way.

When Kate left with one of the children, Georgina Hogarth stayed on and ran the household as she had been doing for some years. In addition to his other problems, several of Dickens's brothers, who managed money as irresponsibly as their father had done, asked Dickens for financial help. While personal problems made him impatient and irritable, they never depleted his energy and enthusiasm for his work.

Dickens's whirlwind of plays, readings, serials, family, friends, travels, and new houses never seemed to die down. By chance, Dickens learned that he could buy Gad's Hill, the "castle" from his childhood, when he discovered that one of the contributors to *Household Words,* Eliza Lynn, owned it and wanted to sell. "I used to look at it [Gad's Hill] as a wonderful Mansion (which God knows it is not), when I was a very odd little child with the first faint shadows of all my books in my head," he said. He had it renovated and enlarged and brought his family there for the summer of 1857. Dickens was spending more of his time with younger people now—his children, the staff of *Household Words,* and actors from the charity plays. He particularly enjoyed a friendship with Wilkie Collins, a young writer on the staff, and traveled with him to the Lake District and Paris. And his attraction to young Ellen Ternan, with whom he had acted in many plays, grew to serious infatuation.

NEW NOVELS FOR THE MAGAZINES

Dickens's major accomplishment in the last two decades of his life was the writing of six novels and part of a seventh that constitute the second phase of his career. After *Bleak House* and *Hard Times* came *Little Dorrit*, a serial novel in which Dickens attacks the cynicism, despair, and victim attitude that existed in all levels of society. It has few saints and few villains but many gray characters—bad people with redeeming qualities and good people with sinister motives. Little Dorrit, whose girlhood is affected, as Dickens's was, by a father imprisoned for debts, grows up to lead a useful, happy life. Before writing another novel, Dickens had a fight with his publisher of fourteen years, Bradbury and Evans. In the outcome, Dickens took *Household Words*, renamed it *All the Year Round*, and went back to publishers Chapman and Hall. The first serial novel published in the renamed weekly was *A Tale of Two Cities*, Dickens's story version of Thomas Carlyle's account of the French Revolution and the last book illustrated by Phiz. In this book, Dickens explores the theme of renunciation, redemption, and resurrection through the character of Sydney Carton, who offers to die in a convicted man's place.

A year later, Dickens explores the same theme of renunciation, redemption, and resurrection in *Great Expectations*. The main character, Pip, goes from the country to London and back, during which he meets eccentric characters and discovers that multiple strands of his life are interwoven. During the interim between *Great Expectations* and Dickens's next novel, Chapman and Hall published a collection of pieces from *All the Year Round* entitled *The Uncommercial Traveller*, the same title used for a second collection four years later. The next novel, *Our Mutual Friend*, appeared in monthly installments for a year and a half, beginning in May 1864. It is a modern novel, set in Dickens's mid-Victorian England, in which he anticipates the nature of declining Victorianism. He portrays a society so corrupt that money, which Dickens symbolizes as huge dustheaps, has become the measure of human worth. Angus Wilson says of *Our Mutual Friend*, "What is so extraordinary is that the tired Dickens should so nearly capture this world of the future, this world only glimpsed by a few beneath the seeming-solid surface of the sixties." The last novel, *The Mystery of Edwin Drood*, set in a small cathedral town, involves the upper-middle, professional class. In the six parts that Dickens wrote before he died, there is an unsolved murder, and critics have argued that its theme involves the forces of law against evil.

DECLINING HEALTH AND DEATH

Dickens's health was in decline for the last five years of his life. After a mild stroke in 1865, he drove himself to exhaustion on his reading tours. In March 1870, he gave his final public reading at St. James Hall. At the end, when his voice weakened, two thousand people rose to their feet, and he returned to the stage. Tears falling down his cheeks, he said, "From these garish lights I now vanish for ever more, with a heartfelt, grateful, respectful, affectionate farewell," and he kissed his hands to the audience and was gone. In late spring, he went to Gad's Hill to work on *Edwin Drood,* but he seemed to know the end was near when he told his daughter Katey on her last visit that he had high hopes for the book if he lived to finish it. On June 8, he worked all day rather than following his usual routine of working only in the morning. When he stood up from the dinner table that evening, he collapsed and was put on the sofa. He lay quietly, breathing heavily, until six o'clock the next evening, June 9, 1870, when he died at the age of fifty-eight. On June 14, his body was brought to Westminster Abbey, and after a simple service, he was laid to rest in Poet's Corner, a section of the church where honored writers are buried. Thousands of people filed past the grave left open for the public until it was full to overflowing with flowers.

Characters and Plot

List of Characters

Oliver Twist: A gentle-natured orphan; son of Edwin Leeford and Agnes Fleming.

Sally Thingummy: The old pauper woman who is present at Oliver's birth in the workhouse.

Agnes Fleming: Oliver's mother; daughter of a naval officer; she dies giving birth to Oliver.

Mrs. Mann: An unscrupulous elderly woman who oversees the infants at the workhouse.

Mr. Bumble: The parish beadle.

Gamfield: A chimney sweep.

Mr. Sowerberry: A brutish undertaker.

Mrs. Sowerberry: The undertaker's wife.

Charlotte: The Sowerberry's maidservant.

Noah Claypole: An orphan employed by the Sowerberrys; he joins Fagin's gang using the name Morris Bolter.

Little Dick: Oliver's friend at the workhouse.

Jack Dawkins: Fagin's underling, known as "The Artful Dodger."

Fagin: Ringleader of a gang of criminals.

Charley Bates: A young member of Fagin's gang.

Nancy: A member of Fagin's gang who tries to protect Oliver.

Betsy: A member of Fagin's gang.

Mr. Brownlow: A kind and respectable gentleman.

Mr. Fang: The magistrate.

Bill Sikes: A vicious associate of Fagin and Nancy.

Mr. Grimwig: An elderly friend of Mr. Brownlow.

Tom Chitling: A member of Fagin's gang.

Mrs. Corney: Wife of Mr. Bumble; she resided in the workhouse where Oliver was born.

Monks (Edward Leeford): Son of Edwin Leeford and his wife; Oliver's half-brother.

Rose Maylie (Rose Fleming): Agnes Fleming's sister who is adopted as Mrs. Maylie's niece; Oliver's aunt.

Mrs. Maylie: Rose's aunt.

Harry Maylie: Mrs. Maylie's son.

PLOT SUMMARY

Oliver Twist is born in a workhouse in an unidentified town. Sally Thingummy, an old pauper woman, attends to the birth, explaining to the doctor that Oliver's mother had been found lying in a street the night before. The pale young mother looks upon her child briefly before she dies.

Now an orphan, the baby Oliver is dressed in rags and "badged and ticketed . . . a parish child—the orphan of a workhouse—the humble, half-starved drudge—to be cuffed and buffeted through the world—despised by all, and pitied by none."

Oliver remains in the workhouse for eight or ten months before he is dispatched to a juvenile facility, where the youngsters could roll about the floor all day, "without the inconvenience of too much food or too much clothing." At this "infant farm," the unscrupulous supervisor, Mrs. Mann, "knowing what was good for children," routinely pockets the funds provided for the children's care. Many of the starving, neglected children fail to survive in this abusive environment.

After nine years of this harsh treatment, Oliver is thin, pale, and diminutive. On his ninth birthday, Oliver, along with two other youngsters, is beaten and confined to a coal cellar for "atrociously presuming to be hungry." They are released when Mrs. Mann ushers in Mr. Bumble, the parish beadle who has "a great idea of his oratorical powers and his importance." After drinking Mrs. Mann's gin, the beadle declares that Oliver is to be returned to the workhouse in which he was born. Meanwhile, the authorities have determined that workhouse life—"a regular place of public entertainment for the poorer classes"—encourages a life of pauperism. To remedy this, they adopt a number of callous measures—a starvation regime among them—that make life in the workhouse even more unbearable.

After several months, Oliver—suffering the tortures of starvation—is encouraged by his companions to ask for more gruel. "Desperate with hunger, and reckless with misery," Oliver approaches his fat master and asks for more food. The horrified authorities immediately confine Oliver to a solitary room for this "impious and profane offence." The following morning, a notice is placed offering five pounds to anyone who would take Oliver as an apprentice.

In response, a cruel-looking chimney sweep named Gamfield volunteers to apprentice Oliver. A kind magistrate observes the look of abject fear on Oliver's face and refuses to sign the indenture papers. Consequently, Oliver is apprenticed to Mr. Sowerberry, the undertaker. At this "new scene of suffering," Mrs. Sowerberry offers Oliver scraps that even the dog refuses to eat. Oliver, ravenous, devours the pitiful meal before being conducted to his new sleeping quarters among the coffins.

The next day, Oliver meets Noah Claypole, a charity boy who also works for Sowerberry.

Noah resents Oliver, who is formally apprenticed after a month. As Oliver's experience increases, so, too, does Noah's enmity. Taunting Oliver, Noah goads, "Yer mother was a regular right-down bad 'un." Though normally docile, Oliver explodes into action and delivers a fierce blow to Noah. As punishment, Sowerberry viciously beats Oliver. The next morning at the first sign of light, Oliver takes his few meager possessions and walks away from the Sowerberrys. Leaving town, he passes the workhouse. He lingers long enough to bid farewell to his young friend Dick.

Heading for London, Oliver endures extreme hunger and other discomforts. After seven days, he happens upon "one of the queerest-looking boys" that Oliver has ever seen. The boy's name is Jack Dawkins, or "The Artful Dodger" as he is known by his friends. Dawkins offers to accompany Oliver to London, where he promises to introduce Oliver to his friend Fagin.

Once in London, the two boys make their way to a dark and filthy building. Here, Oliver meets Fagin, "a very old shrivelled Jew, whose villainous-looking and repulsive face was obscured by a quantity of matted red hair." Other young boys mill about the room. Fagin feeds Oliver and gives him a place to sleep.

After a long, deep sleep, Oliver wakes late the next morning. He sees Fagin withdraw a small box from a hiding place in the floor. The dirty old gentleman gloats over the contents of the box until he realizes that Oliver is watching him. He explains to Oliver that the cache of hidden treasures is his savings for old age. Next, the Dodger returns with Charley Bates, a sprightly youth known for his uproarious laughter.

The two practice picking the pockets of Fagin. Later, two girls enter. While Oliver finds the girls, Betsy and Nancy, rather untidy in appearance, he appreciates their amicability. As they leave, Fagin introduces Oliver to the art of picking pockets.

Oliver remains in Fagin's den for many days. Languishing for fresh air, Oliver entreats the old man for permission to go out with the Dodger and Charley Bates. Finally, when Fagin allows Oliver to accompany the two boys out on the streets, the Dodger steals an old gentleman's handkerchief and hands it to Bates. The two flee. Oliver, realizing what has just happened, begins to run. The gentleman's cries alert passersby, who begin to pursue Oliver. The terrified youth is ultimately subdued, taken into police custody, and conducted to a courtroom headed by the odious magistrate Mr. Fang. Oliver is discharged when a witness to the crime testifies to his innocence. Although freed, Oliver remains weak and trembling in the aftermath of the frightening experience. The kindly old gentleman, Mr. Brownlow, takes pity on Oliver and installs the sickly orphan in his stately home.

At Brownlow's home, Oliver recuperates. There, he is mesmerized by a portrait of a woman that hangs on the wall. With a sudden exclamation, Mr. Brownlow notices that Oliver's face closely resembles the woman in the portrait. Oliver faints, and the portrait is removed from the wall.

Oliver continues to thrive in this new and orderly environment. At the same time, Brownlow's tender feelings for the boy intensify. Before Oliver gets a chance to recount the sad events of his past to Mr. Brownlow, the old gentleman is persuaded by a friend, Mr. Grimwig, to send Oliver on an errand to test the youth's honesty: Oliver is given some money and valuable books to convey to the bookseller's shop. Out in the streets, Oliver is overpowered by Nancy and her evil consort, Bill Sikes. The two return the grief-stricken Oliver to Fagin's den, where Oliver begs to be able to return the books.

Back at Oliver's birthplace, Mr. Bumble meets with Little Dick, Oliver's friend who is ravaged with sickness and near death. Bumble banishes Dick to the coal cellar when the dying orphan states that he wishes, before he dies, to communicate his good will to Oliver. Later, in London, Bumble sees an advertisement offering a monetary reward for information about Oliver Twist. Soon thereafter, Bumble makes his way to the Brownlow house and gives an utterly false and ruinous account of Oliver's life, stating that the orphan had, "from his birth, displayed no better qualities than treachery, ingratitude, and malice." Although deeply saddened, Mr. Brownlow does not question the veracity of Bumble's story.

Meanwhile, Oliver is kept locked in Fagin's dilapidated hideout. One stormy night, Fagin meets with Bill Sikes. The two plan a burglary that will include Oliver. Fagin muses that Oliver's participation in a crime will indoctrinate the youth into a criminal lifestyle. Nancy is present while the two plan their endeavor. Even though she cares deeply for Oliver, Nancy does not object.

Following the plan, Nancy takes Oliver to see Bill Sikes the following night. Oliver notices that she is upset. Trembling, she confesses that she has no power to help him and entreats him to keep quiet. When the two reach his house, the malevolent Sikes threatens to shoot Oliver if the boy speaks out.

The next morning at daybreak, Oliver and Sikes set out. They meet up with two accomplices, Barney and Toby Crackit. As the party nears a house, Oliver suddenly realizes that they are about to burglarize the residence. "Well-nigh mad with grief and terror," Oliver begs to be released. His cries in vain, Oliver is hoisted through a small window and instructed to unlock the street door. Oliver, however, resolves to alarm the family. In the following moments, shots are fired. The burglars pull the wounded Oliver out the window and swiftly retreat.

Back at the workhouse where Oliver was born, Mr. Bumble visits Mrs. Corney. An old pauper interrupts the two as they share a kiss. Mrs. Corney is led to the dying Sally Thingummy, the woman who attended Oliver's birth. She relates to Mrs. Corney that Oliver's mother, before dying, had entrusted her with a gold object with clues to Oliver's origins. In her death throes, Sally admits that she stole the object, but dies before she can tell more. Walking carelessly away, Mrs. Corney remarks that the crone had "nothing to tell, after all."

At Fagin's dwelling, Toby Crackit returns. He recounts that after the foiled robbery attempt, the group was chased by dogs. Deciding that each man would fend for himself, they abandoned the wounded Oliver in a ditch. Extremely agitated by Crackit's words, Fagin rushes out. Meandering through the streets, Fagin inquires about Sikes's whereabouts. At a public house, he tells the landlord he wishes to meet with someone named Monks. Next he goes to Sikes's house, where he finds Nancy, who is deeply sorrowful and drunk. Back at home, Fagin lets in Monks. As the two men converse in hushed whispers, Monks perceives a shadow moving along the wall. Fagin assures his frightened companion that it is just his imagination.

Back at the workhouse, Mr. Bumble continues to court Mrs. Corney. The two agree to marry. Mr. Bumble then departs for the Sowerberrys, where he reveals his hypocrisy when he chastises Noah Claypole for asking Charlotte for a kiss.

Meanwhile, Oliver gains consciousness and pulls himself out of the ditch in which he was abandoned. He stumbles to the nearest house, which he recognizes as the house they tried to burglarize. He is dragged inside and taken to the room of Mr. Giles, the butler of the house. Brittles, a handyman, fetches a doctor. When the doctor, Mr. Losberne, has examined the patient, he calls for the lady of the house, Mrs. Maylie, and her niece, Rose. The kindly women take pity on the would-be burglar when they see that he is "a mere child: worn with pain and exhaustion."

When Oliver awakens and relates the unhappy events of his life, the women resolve to care for Oliver. Although Oliver has already been implicated in the attempted burglary, the two women, along with the doctor, strategically handle the investigation so that Oliver eludes arrest.

Oliver flourishes in the care of the benevolent Maylie women. One day, Mr. Losberne takes Oliver out in a carriage. The boy becomes pale and agitated when he recognizes the house in which the thieves live. The doctor storms the house but finds only an old, crippled man, causing Mr. Losberne to doubt, if only momentarily, the truthfulness of Oliver's tale of sorrow. Next, the two proceed to the Brownlow residence, where a "For Rent" sign adorns the window. They learn that Mr. Brownlow left for the West Indies six weeks ago. Oliver is deeply disappointed that he cannot see his old friend and vindicate himself.

Mrs. Maylie and Rose take Oliver to a cottage in the country. Oliver thrives in the fresh air and natural surroundings. As three idyllic months pass, Oliver becomes deeply attached to Mrs. Maylie and her niece. Oliver's happiness is marred, however, when Rose becomes fiercely ill. Just as it becomes clear that Rose will survive, Harry Maylie, Mrs. Maylie's son, arrives. He confesses to his mother that he is deeply in love with Rose. While Mrs. Maylie is devoted to

Rose, she expresses concerns about Rose's "doubtful" origins.

One night, Oliver dozes as he is studying. He awakens to find Fagin and another man looking through the window. Although Oliver screams for help, the two menacing figures vanish without a trace. As the incident is forgotten, Harry declares his ardent love for Rose. She resolutely replies that although she shares his feelings, the "stain upon her name" makes her an unsuitable wife for a man of his status and rank. Before he leaves, he begs Rose for permission to repeat his proclamations in a year's time. He also asks Oliver to write to him every two weeks, while keeping his whereabouts unknown to Rose and his mother.

Meanwhile, Mr. Bumble has married Mrs. Corney. Their union is contemptuous, and Bumble derives little satisfaction from his new post as master of the workhouse. After a quarrel with his wife, Bumble visits a public house where he meets up with a dark, cloaked figure. The man offers to pay Bumble for information about Oliver Twist's birth. Before he leaves, the mysterious man reveals that his name is Monks. The next night, the Bumbles secretly meet with Monks. Mrs. Bumble relates her conversation with the dying Sally. She describes how she procured from the corpse a pawnbroker's ticket, which she has since redeemed for a locket holding a wedding ring inscribed with the name "Agnes." She hands the locket to Monks, who immediately throws it into the river.

The next evening, Monks visits Sikes's dwelling. As the two commence to another part of the house, Nancy ascends the stairs. When she comes back, she is visibly upset and nervous. The next day, Sikes notices the girl's agitation. Nancy uses opium to drug Sikes into a deep sleep so that she can sneak out. She goes to the Maylie residence, where Rose receives Nancy with kindness. Nancy confirms details of Oliver's past and confesses that she has been eavesdropping on Sikes and Monks. Nancy's most shocking revelation follows: Oliver is the half brother of Monks—and the object of Monks's enormous enmity. Eschewing Rose's repeated offers of assistance, Nancy leaves Rose alone to ponder the startling discoveries. Before she sets out, however, she declares that if Rose ever needs her, she can be found on the London Bridge every Sunday night.

The day after, an excited Oliver exclaims to Rose that he saw Mr. Brownlow. Immediately, Rose takes Oliver to see

Brownlow and divulges all that has transpired since he last saw the orphan—including her clandestine conversation with Nancy. Together with Mr. Losborne, Mr. Grimwig, and the Maylies, Brownlow resolves to trap Monks and put an end to his villainous schemes.

Meanwhile, Noah Claypole and Charlotte—now fugitives for robbing from the Sowerberrys—trek to London and end up in the Three Cripples tavern. Here, they link up with Fagin. The old man sends Claypole—who uses the alias Bolter—to report on the trial of the Dodger, who has been charged with pickpocketing.

At Fagin's dwelling, Nancy is burdened with worry. She appears fretful to those around her. When she attempts to go to the London Bridge on Sunday night, Sikes forbids her departure. The next morning, Fagin assigns Bolter to spy on Nancy. The next Sunday, Bolter conceals himself as Nancy meets Brownlow and Rose on the London Bridge. He listens as the three plan Monks's capture. When Nancy begins to describe Monks's physical characteristics, Brownlow mumbles to himself: "It must be he!" Before they leave, Brownlow and Rose offer to assist Nancy, who rebukes their kind gestures.

Bolter hurries home to recapitulate the events on the London Bridge. When details of Nancy's betrayal are made known, Sikes's enormous fury is unleashed. Enraged, he storms home to confront Nancy. As she begs for mercy, Sikes bludgeons her to death. Overcome with the sight of her corpse, Sikes leaves the house with his dog and lingers in the country. As the day progresses, guilt over his evil deed mounts. Nevertheless, he resolves to return to London to procure funds needed for his escape. Fearing that his dog will reveal his identity, Sikes makes an unsuccessful attempt to drown the animal.

At twilight, Brownlow enters his house. Two burly men escort Monks, who was seized earlier. The conversation between Brownlow and Monks illuminates the mystery surrounding Oliver's birth and family: Monks's father, Edwin Leeford, had a sister, a girl engaged to be married to Brownlow. Although she died before they could be married, Brownlow stayed in close contact with her brother, who was forced into an extremely unhappy marriage. This union produced one child—Edward Leeford, or Monks as he called himself. After his parents separated. Monks's father Edwin befriended a retired naval officer who had a beautiful daughter, Agnes Fleming. She and Edwin became engaged before he was summoned to Rome to look after an inheritance. In Italy, however, Edwin died suddenly. Before he made his fateful trip to Italy, Edwin had left a portrait of Agnes with Brownlow. At the time, she was expecting the couple's first child—Oliver Twist. Because of Oliver's uncanny resemblance to Agnes, Brownlow began to search for Monks after Oliver's disappearance. Through Nancy's revelations, Brownlow had learned about Monks's conspiracy against Oliver, including the destruction of Leeford's will by Monks's mother. Faced with the abundant evidence against him, Monks agrees to make restitution to Oliver according to the terms of his father's original will.

Meanwhile, Crackit, a boy named Tom Chitling, and a convict named Kags conceal themselves in an abandoned building on Jacob's Island—an area described as littered with "every loathsome indication of filth, rot, and garbage." Chitling recounts that both Fagin and Claypole were arrested earlier in the day. At the same time, Betsy had identified Nancy's body. As the trio postulates Fagin's fate, Sikes's dog enters their hideout, followed by Sikes. Charley Bates follows and, screaming, attacks Nancy's slayer. The boy's screams alert the police. As a great crowd begins to form outside of the building, Sikes escapes to the roof. Attempting to lower himself with a rope, Sikes slips and accidentally hangs himself.

Two days later, Mr. Losberne, Mrs. Maylie, and Rose take Oliver to the town of his birth. Later, Mr. Brownlow arrives with Monks. Mr. Brownlow begins by stating: "This child is your half-brother," and then restates the details of the brothers' sordid history. Brownlow then fills in a few missing details: Edwin Leeford had left the majority of his fortune to Agnes Fleming and her unborn child. Monks confesses that his mother burned the will. The Bumbles join the party and, faced with evidence against them, admit their part in the conspiracy against Oliver. Finally, Rose's dubious origins are revealed: In reality, she is the younger sister of Agnes Fleming—and thus Oliver's aunt. At this point, Harry again declares his love for Rose, adding that he has become a clergyman, thereby repudiating the social ties that kept the couple apart. Now suitably matched in rank and station, Harry and Rose are joyously betrothed.

Back in London, Fagin's trial commences. The guilty verdict is followed by a sentence of death by hanging. As Fagin

awaits his execution, the old wretch becomes horribly de-
mented. Oliver and Brownlow visit Fagin, who—though utterly depraved and completely insane—whispers the hiding
place of some papers relevant to Oliver.

Within three months, Rose and Harry are married; Mrs.
Maylie lives with them. Brownlow adopts Oliver and they
take up residence in the community surrounding the
Maylies' parsonage. Oliver shares his inheritance with
Monks, who nevertheless returns to a life of crime and per-
ishes while in prison. The Bumbles, after losing their position, become inmates of the workhouse in which Oliver was
born.

CHAPTER 1

Design and Structure

READINGS ON
OLIVER TWIST

Oliver Twist's Chronological Structure

Iain Crawford

In his discussion of *Oliver Twist's* chronological structure, Iain Crawford identifies three ways that Dickens
deliberately uses time as a device to shape plot and
theme. First, Dickens manipulates seasonal details
and the characters' ages to reflect the time scheme of
the novel's literal action. Second, in the Monks plot,
Dickens purposefully uses time to emphasize the sim-
ilarities and contrasts between good and evil characters. Finally, Crawford comments on the novel's historical setting, suggesting that Dickens alludes to a
setting "around or before 1830" but also includes
events with immediate topical relevance. Crawford's
essay originally appeared in *The Dickensian*.

In his valuable study of *The Pickwick Papers*, David M. Bev-
ington has shown the importance of the novel's time-scheme
to the organization of its action. Dickens's second novel reveals a further development of this technique, although the
advance is at times faltering and uncertain. As Professor
Tillotson has remarked, 'no version of the novel gives us a
time-scheme that is completely consistent on the literal
level'. While this is undoubtedly true, what is also apparent
is that Dickens uses time in *Oliver Twist* in a variety of ways,
occasionally uncertain, but often clearly deliberate, to infuse
a degree of unity and momentum into a somewhat laboured
plot. Although he again makes some use of the device of
linking the novel's action with the time of its serial publication, this is a peripheral concern, and it is subordinated to a
more internalized chronological structure. Three aspects of
this stand out: the time-scheme of the action, with corollar-

Reprinted from "Time and Structure in *Oliver Twist*," by Iain Crawford, *The Dickensian*, Spring 1981. Reprinted with permission from the author.

ies in the details of seasonal reference and characters' ages; the Monks plot and the link which is established between the novel's action and the reported events of the past; and the date at which the novel is actually set. It may be seen that Dickens became aware of the possibilities of a chronological organization of the novel only gradually and that there is some disparity between his use of the device in structuring the plot and in achieving more subtle tonal effects.

ACTION OF THE PLOT

Dickens's development of his control of chronological detail is most apparent in the timing of the literal action of the novel. Oliver is evidently born in winter, to judge from the surgeon warming his hands at the fire or, more precisely, from Monks's later remarks to Bumble. The first nine years of his life are passed over until, punctually on his ninth birthday, Bumble takes him back to the workhouse proper. Logically, it should then again be winter, but there is no indication of this and Dickens may well have not given it thought. Oliver's removal apparently coincides with the introduction of the provisions of the Poor Law Amendment Act from which he suffers for six months before making his famous request. This coincidence might seem far-fetched and later in the novel will, in fact, become inconsistent with other indications of the date. The reader, however, does not (and in 1837 did not) notice this, for Dickens's concern is clearly with matters, wider than the effects of this one Act, which he uses only as a starting-point.

No appreciable time passes before Oliver finds himself at Sowerberry's, yet he is able to tell Noah Claypole that he is ten years old. The Gamfield episode occurs within a week of his asking for more and there is little indication of any further passage of time before Sowerberry takes him 'on liking'. There is also some confusion as to how long he stays with the undertaker: he is on trial for a month, apprenticed, and then passes many months at Sowerberry's until the fight with Noah which precipitates his departure. However, these 'many months' are a revision of the original text in *Bentley's Miscellany*, which read 'many weeks'. Professor Tillotson suggests that this and other revisions during the early part of the novel were intended to eliminate the inconsistencies which would otherwise appear and also to make Oliver old enough to be apprenticed. This is very probable, but Dickens does not perhaps achieve all that he had intended. Oliver can only be nine, not ten, by the time of his arrival at Sowerberry's and his age was apparently not at issue when he narrowly escaped being apprenticed to Gamfield. If there is some inconsistency here, at least the timing of the action is rather more carefully organized. The months that Oliver passes at Sowerberry's when added to the six months he spent in the workhouse should bring him at least towards his tenth birthday and another winter. Numerous references in the text bear this out: Oliver is bitterly cold in Sowerberry's kitchen; the pauper's funeral evidently takes place during autumn or winter; and in general it is a 'nice sickly season'. Much of this detail, however, occurs before these months have passed and Dickens would appear to be sacrificing strictly literal accuracy to a chronological telescoping of the action which achieves a powerfully reiterative depiction of this period in Oliver's life.

SEASONAL DETAIL

From this point onwards, however, the chronology of the action becomes more regular and is co-ordinated with the consistent use of seasonal reference to emblemize the tenor of events. Moreover, from Chapter XVII (published in November 1837) to at least Chapter XLI (published in October 1838) this seasonal parallel roughly follows the time of year at publication. This, however, is a subsidiary matter and the pattern of seasonal change has its main importance within the development of the plot.

After leaving Sowerberry's, Oliver survives a week in winter on the road to London and meets with the Dodger and Fagin soon after his arrival. 'Many days' pass before he goes out with the Dodger and Charley Bates, but the 'many' is perhaps to be seen more as a reflection of Oliver's feelings than as indicating any considerable length of time. *Bentley's* has 'eight or ten days' which, if less expressive, seems the right sort of period. 'Many days' pass again while he lies ill at Mr Brownlow's and there may be a submerged hint of returning warmth with Brownlow sitting reading at the window overlooking his garden. The interplay of the literal and the metaphorical is quite delicate here, for the notion of spring is only tentatively evoked and winter soon reasserts itself in the emphasis on gloom and fog after Oliver's recapture. Throughout this phase of the novel winter predominates—almost a complete inversion of Pickwick, where there was a Christmas but virtually no winter. Several of the characters are placed against the seasonal setting and through it are both revealed and arranged in comparison with one another. Bumble is typically selfish in ignoring the suffering of the two paupers he is taking to London, while he sits wrapped in his 'porochial' greatcoat. At this point, seasonal reference and time of publication come into synchronization, but this could only be an ancillary effect since the first references to winter occur in Chapters V and VI published in April 1837. Nancy feels the cold but, even though a fallen angel, she still tends the hearth and is seen building up the fire for both Fagin and Oliver. The merry old gentleman himself may also feel the cold, but far more striking is his identification with the harsh environment:

> The mud lay thick upon the stones; and a black mist hung over the streets; the rain fell sluggishly down: and everything felt cold and clammy to the touch. It seemed just the night when it befitted such a being as the Jew, to be abroad. As he glided stealthily along, creeping beneath the shelter of the walls and doorways, the hideous old man seemed like some loathsome reptile, engendered in the slime and darkness through which he moved: crawling forth, by night, in search of some rich offal for a meal.

The prevailing wintry mood of this section of the novel is surely part of the reason why this is so effective and not as excessively exaggerated as, taken out of context, it might otherwise seem. It is also to be noted that Fagin has no fire to offer Monks and that later, on the night of Nancy's murder, he sits waiting for Sikes by an empty grate. Further references to the weather during the expedition to rob Mrs Maylie's house continue the wintry emphasis, although the sun is up between six and seven o'clock, suggesting early March. (The Chapter appeared in January 1838.) Interestingly, there is still enough subjectivity in the weather for the carter who gives Oliver and Sikes a lift to find it a fine day. . . .

PASTORAL SCENERY

Wounded in the robbery, Oliver lies ill for 'many weeks,' an interval which allows a transition to spring to occur. Both he and the aptly-named Rose Maylie look forward to its 'pleasures and beauties' and Dickens quickly proceeds in Chapter XXXII (published in May 1838) to unfold the seasons through spring to full summer. Joseph M. Duffy Jr. has provocatively discussed Dickens's treatment of pastoral in *Oliver Twist* and the extent to which the period at the cottage forms a moral and emotional centre to the novel. He argues, however, that there is no link between this ideal and the real world other than 'the mechanical sense of transit', but at least an attempt to provide some structural and thematic continuity can be seen in the succession of pastoral summer after urban winter. This effort is reinforced by the further development of motifs that have recurred throughout the earlier parts of the narrative. Oliver, for example, at last grows 'stout and healthy' and his education is finally taken in hand benevolently after the less happy versions that both the workhouse and Fagin had offered.

Despite this insistence on a successful culmination to his progress, reservations can still be felt about it. The depiction of summer is as extreme in its way as had been the earlier image of winter and, while the stylized nature of both accounts is no ground for objection, the contrast thus made is overt and dangerously simplistic. As in *Pickwick*, the pastoral scene is something of a genre-painting with its attention to the peace of nature, the trim little churchyard and the poor but contented villagers. But these disembodied clichés contrast weakly with the vigour of the urban scenes and Dickens's prose is slack and full of that over-insistance which so often betrays his commitment to an experience he has not really had:

> Who can describe the pleasure and delight: the peace of mind
> and soft tranquillity: the sickly boy felt in the balmy air, and
> among the green hills and rich woods, of an inland village!
> Who can tell how scenes of peace and quietude sink into the
> minds of pain-worn dwellers in close and noisy places, and
> carry their own freshness, deep into their jaded hearts!

The contrast between Fagin's world and that of the Maylies, which has been partly developed through the use of seasonal reference, thus comes to a rather hollow conclusion. But this should not lead to the conclusion that Dickens was secretly the devil's advocate, for he never found an ability to write such pastoral descriptions effectively and his only successful accounts of nature tend to be those, such as the storm in *David Copperfield*, in which her more dramatic side is seen. One point of interest which arises out of this pastoral evocation, however, is Dickens's concern with memory. Through an allusion to *Paradise Lost*—'Men who have lived in crowded, pent-up streets, through lives of toil: and never wished for change; men to whom custom has indeed been second nature . . .'—he proceeds to develop a lengthy eulogy of Nature's benign effect upon the dying. Oliver, too, finds the pastoral setting conducive to the evocation of memories of a better, happier life. While this ideal is suggested as vaguely and unsatisfactorily as the pastoral which prompts it, it is notable that what will become one of Dickens's major concerns receives such extended treatment early in his career. The echo of Milton may well be more than incidental, for the language of Dickens's pastoral description is generally reminiscent of the poetic diction of the epic simile. It is perhaps not too fanciful to suggest also that the description of Fagin alludes to Satan's return to Hell and the transformation of the devils into serpents. If such is the case, then Dickens is, consciously or not, enriching the implications of his narrative through this resonance.

This summer interval is only an interlude, however, and again is carefully timed. Three idyllic months pass by, only to be broken (apart from the irrelevant digression of Rose's illness) by Fagin and Monks. With this shattering of the mood of tranquillity, the plot's period of suspended animation comes to an end and, not for the first time, Bumble is an important agent in the transition this time, to the novel's final phase. Marriage has brought him no comfort and he finds summer as cheerless as his empty grate. Then, through him and his shrewish wife, Monks re-enters the action in pursuit of the evidence they hold of Oliver's parentage. The meeting which takes place in the ruined mill is, of course, overshadowed by a storm of melodramatic timing and scale. But, while its externalization of Monks's dark passions is crudely done, it does find at least some justification for its occurance in the wider context of the seasonal setting. For this passage (published in August 1838) is the last direct description of summer, and the plot moves towards an autumnal setting for its final phase. A mood of late summer tranquillity is tentatively evoked in the Maylie group's resolve to go to the coast for a holiday just as Dickens and Kate had gone to the Isle of Wight that September, but in Fagin's world, and with the introduction of Noah Claypole to it, the atmosphere is growing distinctly cooler. The gloom, cold and mist re-appear when Nancy goes to her rendezvous on

London Bridge and, as her death approaches, autumn is announced explicitly. Little more than a week is taken over the final sequence of events—Sikes's flight and death, the unmasking of Monks, and Fagin's trial and death—and the novel closes with a return, this time permanent, to the pastoral world.

It is possible, then, to see a fairly coherent and often carefully detailed scheme for the time-scale of the novel's action. Although there is some degree of confusion in the earlier episodes, even then the seasonal pattern begins to emerge at Sowerberry's. It may be conjectured that the notion of using the natural world to mirror the course of the action in this way only came to Dickens as he was actually writing the novel, but there can be little doubt that it grew to be a conscious purpose—Dickens's revisions alone indicate his awareness of the novel's time-scheme. In this respect, *Oliver* is comparable with *Pickwick*, where Dickens's treatment of time also developed in the course of the writing. But, although Dickens does in the central section of the novel again make some use of the device of paralleling seasonal depiction with the time of publication, his treatment of time in *Oliver Twist* is far more relevant to the novel's internal structure than had been the case with *Pickwick*. This, however, is not to say that it is an unblemished achievement, for this pattern seems to have been developed independently of another important aspect of time in the novel, the Monks plot and the events of the past.

THE CHARACTERS' AGES

Oliver's age provides the first indication of this. According to the action, approximately two years elapse between his removal to the workhouse and the end of the novel (the 'many months' at Sowerberry's make it possible, just, to assume the passing of another year, but this seems unlikely). Oliver is thus in theory approaching his eleventh (or twelfth) birthday at the novel's end. However, to be consistent with his past, he should be fourteen. Grimwig, in fact, says that he is twelve, but the real difficulty stems from Brownlow's remark to Monks, 'I speak of fifteen years ago when you were not more than eleven years old'. This account also reveals the ages of some of the characters at the time of the action: Monks must now be twenty-six (confirming Nancy's impression); Rose, two or three then, is now seventeen, as we know. Oliver's age is more problematic. Brownlow's account is somewhat vague—'fifteen years ago', 'the end of a year', 'at length' are all mentioned. To fit in with this account, Oliver should be at least thirteen and perhaps even older. Clearly, he is not, even if Cruikshank's later illustrations, which Forster and Dickens so disliked, tend to imply otherwise. The detail itself seems trivial; certainly no one stops to worry about it in reading the novel; but it is notable that Dickens was concerned enough with maintaining chronological accuracy to attempt to co-ordinate the main plot with the events of the past. His uncertainty about the novel's ending is testified as late as March 1838:

> I am quite satisfied that nobody can have heard what I mean to do with the different characters in the end, inasmuch as at present I don't quite know, myself.

What may well have happened is that he began the novel without any detailed idea of how it would work out, gave Oliver an arbitrary age and later found that this involved him in some inconsistency as he developed other characters and events.

This, however, does serve to draw attention to another pattern of chronological contrasts that emerges as the novel progresses. It is perhaps surprising how many of the characters' ages the reader is told or may infer. Both the Dodger and the rest of Fagin's pupils are the same age as Oliver, although in appearance and experience they are far older than him. Moreover, there is little doubt of the nature of that experience nor of their future prospects, and it is notable that an image that will constantly recur in Dickens's novels makes its first appearance here:

> Several rough beds made of old sacks, were huddled side by side on the floor; and seated round the table were four or five boys: none older than the Dodger: smoking long clay pipes, and drinking spirits, with the air of middle-aged men.

These prematurely aged children, with only transportation or the gallows before them, contrast strongly with Oliver's naïve innocence. Nancy can be seen as approximately seventeen, the same age as Rose, and this reinforces the contrast between them that Dickens clearly intended. His softened attitude towards Nancy is also evident in the change in Bill Sikes's age, from forty-five in *Bentley's* to thirty-five in later editions, a revision which Professor Tillotson links with other small alterations of detail in Nancy's depiction. Harry Maylie, of whom we know very little apart from his age, is twenty-five and is contrasted with the twenty-six-year-old Monks. Fagin, 'a very old shrivelled Jew', is opposed by Brownlow, an 'old gentleman', and to a lesser extent by Grimwig, Mrs Maylie and Losberne. It seems clear, then, that Dickens wanted to make a series of closely paralleled contrasts between the good and evil characters through reference to their age, almost as if he were creating the different generations of two opposing families within the novel. Oliver, of course, is asked to consider himself one of several families between the workhouse and the end of a novel whose entire plot hinges on his familial past. This may account for Brownlow's reference to fifteen years ago as a necessary contrivance to make the series of contrasts possible. Moreover, this pattern, although somewhat contrived, is not obtrusive and gives the novel another, subtle form of unity. Ronald Paulson has shown the importance of such a device in eighteenth-century fiction, particularly in *Tom Jones,* and it may be conjectured that Dickens owes a debt here to Fielding. Both Oliver and Tom follow similar courses and belong to a wider narrative pattern of movement from rural paradise out into the wilderness of the world and finally back to the paradise—in Oliver's case, of course, the initial setting is hardly a paradise, but the threefold structure to his story is clearly similar to Tom's. Both find out the truth of their parentage only after their parents have died yet gain a substitute father in an avuncular figure (with, in Oliver's case, also an aunt). But, while adhering to this broad outline and retaining Fielding's basic contrasts of rural paradise and urban world, Dickens has chosen to put far more emphasis on the depiction of the city than had his predecessor. Moreover, this familial structure works not so much to present a didactic contrast between the two worlds but rather a series of mirror images. The interaction of good and evil in the novel has received some discussion, and the hold that Fagin exerts over Oliver is clearly of some importance here. While the resolution of the plot shatters Fagin's world completely, does not the seasonal parallel also imply that his winter must come again? This, however, is to extend the implications of the novel farther than Dickens allows, yet the subtlety of effect he achieves from a simple device is readily apparent.

HISTORICAL SETTING

Finally, and most uncertain is the question of the date of the novel's setting. Keith Hollingsworth has attempted to place this, with reservations, fairly exactly between 1828 and 1831, but to do so requires an uncritical explanation of Dickens's statements about Oliver's age and is to look for a precision alien to his spirit. Indeed, the action seems to occur at a number of different dates: the policeman who arrests Oliver implies 1828 or later, yet the old Watch, which according to T.W. Hill was abolished by the Police Act, is still in existence. The workhouse scenes imply a depiction of the new, post-1834 system, but might easily refer to the earlier, often equally inhuman one. A transitional period must undoubtedly be allowed for in attempting to date these changes, yet this imprecision itself emphasizes the difficulty of pinning down the novel's action to external events Dickens's concern is evidently more general in nature. The reference to the street improvements and slum clearances that had failed to eradicate ugly sores just across the road from his homes in Furnival's Inn and then Doughty Street was applicable several years before, and indeed after, the novel's publication. Yet Dickens's allusion also has a specifically topical relevance since in February 1838 a Select Committee had been set up to consider plans for the improvement of London's streets. Its conclusions were to present a picture very similar to what Dickens shows and are summarized by Percy J. Edwards:

> There were districts in London through which no great thoroughfares passed, and which were wholly occupied by a dense population composed of the lowest class of persons who being entirely excluded from the observation and influence of better educated neighbours, exhibited a state of moral degradation deeply to be deplored.

But its report, along with those of the eleven or twelve other committees set up between 1832 and 1851, was not followed by any action. In this light, Dickens's reference to 'improvement' may be sardonic in tone but, whatever the case, it is noteworthy that his well-known later concern with public health makes a first, tentative appearance here. Elsewhere, he goes out of his way not to give the date, first at Oliver's birth and then at Mrs Corney's interview with old Sally on her deathbed. In the latter case, Dickens altered the original 'name' to 'year', perhaps deliberately emphasizing the vagueness of the dating. The action in general tends, as so often with Dickens, to suggest a setting around or before 1830 and yet also to have the immediacy of topical relevance. There is little to suggest that he intended any exact historical dating for the novel and it is perhaps more profitable to consider its internal chronological structure.

The degree to which chronological precision is deliberately controlled and subordinated to larger significance is remarkably complete. But even to say this should not imply any conscious, pre-meditated design on Dickens's part, for it is clear that such was not the case. What can be seen, however, is that in writing the novel his awareness of both the problems and possibilities of its time-scheme developed gradually. Clearly, he gave it the same detailed attention he gave statistics of juvenile delinquency and was concerned to create a plausible time-scheme for this first novel of his own. But he also discovered the value of chronological detail in giving an unsteady plot both unity and momentum and in developing its apparently simple contrasts into something far more effective. There were, of course, limitations to this achievement and in his later novels Dickens would develop quite different notions of time. Yet for *Oliver Twist* he surely chose an appropriate form: the combination of the haphazard and the careful, the specific and the more general, played a vital part in his creation of a story that has attained almost mythic power in English culture.

Fictional Modes in *Oliver Twist*

Michael Slater

Michael Slater calls *Oliver Twist* "an extraordinary mixture of satire, nightmare, documentary, farce, melodrama and near-tragedy." For example, in the first part of the novel, Dickens satirizes with "devastating economy" the ineffectual social institutions that were created to protect the weak and poor. From chapter eight on, however, the novel ceases to be satirical and instead becomes a mix of the fabular and documentary. Slater goes on to show how Dickens used these various fictional modes to create a strangely evocative and cohesive narrative. Slater contributed the following critical essay to *The Dickensian.*

Oliver Twist was the first Dickens novel I ever read (at the age of eleven) and, not long afterwards, I sat shuddering and laughing through a showing of David Lean's wonderful film of the story. Ever since, this book—such an extraordinary mixture of satire, nightmare, documentary, farce, melodrama and near-tragedy—has haunted and fascinated me.

SATIRE

It begins as satire in the Swiftian tradition ('my glance at the new poor Law Bill'). Just as the insanely sane *Modest Proposal* resulted from Swift's rage at the English Government's policy towards Ireland so the presentation of the workhouse in *Oliver Twist* results from Dickens's outrage at Malthusian chatter about the 'surplus population' and the Government's 'workhouse-as-deterrent' policy. The 'philosophers' who organise and run these establishments he portrays as deliberate exterminators, 'whose blood is ice, whose heart is iron', out to kill off, by any means short of shooting, the inconvenient hordes of the poor: 'they established the rule, that all

Reprinted from "On Reading *Oliver Twist*," by Michael Slater, *The Dickensian*, May 1974. Reprinted with permission from the author.

poor people should have the alternative . . . of being starved
by a gradual process in the house, or by a quick one out of
it'. Oliver challenges them by actually getting himself born in
a workhouse, thus ironically producing the opposite effect to
that intended. Had he been surrounded, Dickens comments,
'by careful grandmothers, anxious aunts, experienced
nurses and doctors of profound wisdom' he would certainly
have died; but, just because he was born into such a brutal
extermination camp he survived. Moreover, he reaches his
ninth birthday at Mrs Mann's baby-farm perhaps only because his 'good sturdy spirit' gets plenty of room to expand
'thanks to the spare diet of the establishment', and finally
crowns his obstinate defiance of the philosophers by 'asking
for more'. Dickens wonderfully dramatises the famous scene
to make it seem that Oliver's request shakes the whole system to its very foundations: the master of the workhouse
'shrieks' for the beadle and the latter rushes excitedly to the
Board to announce the terrible news that Oliver has asked
for more ('There was a general start. Horror was depicted on
every countenance.'). After this the Board has no option—it
cannot afford to wait for the fulfilment of the gentleman in a
white waistcoat's prophecy that Oliver will eventually be
hanged but must dispose of him more quickly:

> The board . . . took counsel together on the expedience of
> shipping off Oliver Twist, in some small trading vessel bound
> to a good unhealthy port; which suggested itself as the very
> best thing that could possibly be done with him; the proba-
> bility being, that the skipper would flog him to death, in a
> playful mood, some day after dinner; or would knock his
> brains out with an iron bar; both pastimes being, as is pretty
> generally known, very favourite and common recreations
> among gentlemen of that class.

In the event, however, they pay the parish undertaker to take
him away.

The world of the workhouse is embodied in that great
satiric creation, Mr Bumble, whose chief business is to beat
Oliver within an inch of his life, and who dominates the
early part of the novel as Fagin dominates the later part.
Bumble is totally identified with his institutional role; once
he has ceased to be beadle, he dwindles into a stock figure
of farce, the hen-pecked husband (a stock figure hilariously
manipulated by Dickens, though) and an agent of the melodramatic plot. Oliver is the traditional symbolic satiric hero,
like Candide or Byron's Don Juan, the innocent to whom the

things that happen reveal the appalling nature of the world through which he is passing (Martin Chuzzlewit in America fulfills essentially the same role). As such he is the embodiment of the satirist's positive values—humanity, compassion, tenderness, loyalty, love—fiercely defending his dead mother against the taunts of Noah Claypole who, in his relations with Oliver, is a brutal forerunner of Mr Dorrit in his relations with Old Nandy, and very much a documentary or 'realistic' figure, showing us 'what a beautiful thing human nature sometimes is'. Modern readers find little difficulty with this scene because of the vivid realism of Noah but Oliver's parting with Little Dick is less acceptable because both the characters involved lack this kind of realism. Yet it seems to me that this scene effectively makes its point which is to show that no amount of cruelty can altogether dry up the springs of love and tenderness in human nature, to reassure us that, as he leaves Bumble's world, Oliver, humanity's representative, has not, after all, been ground down to that 'state of brutal stupidity and sullenness' that Dickens warns us, in chapter 4, he was 'in a fair way' of being reduced to.

SOCIAL INJUSTICE

In these first seven chapters of the novel Dickens shows with devastating economy the failure, or worse than failure, of the institutions of society—Government, the Law, the Church. Existing to protect the weak against the strong they do nothing of the sort or, if they do, it is quite accidentally. Government, represented by Bumble is, in fact, sheer tyranny; the Church, represented by the clergyman at the pauper funeral, reading 'as much of the burial service as could be compressed into four minutes', is indifferent; and the Law, represented by the 'half blind and half childish' magistrate, saves Oliver from certain death at the hands of Mr Gamfield only by the accident of the ink-pot's not happening to be where the magistrate thought it was. This causes him to look into Oliver's face and see him for a moment as a human being—just as even Bumble is startled into doing in the next chapter—and he then has a human reaction ('Take the boy back to the workhouse, and treat him kindly. He seems to want it'). But, by and large, in this society those in power do not *see* the people they govern; they see only large abstractions such as 'the surplus population' or 'paupers'.

Oliver escapes from this society in chapter 8 only to be decoyed into the criminal underworld of London. A direct cause-and-effect link between social injustice and neglect and crime was always central to Dickens's thinking and the novel's Hogarthian subtitle, 'The Parish Boy's Progress', gives a clear enough hint of the way in which the novel will move. We might recall again the gentleman in the white waistcoat who so perseveringly proclaims his belief that Oliver will come to be hanged; society, Dickens is saying, is a great maker of such self-fulfilling prophecies. It creates and maintains conditions which will drive the poor into crime or, at the very least, encourage the criminal or anti-social tendencies of such a boy as Noah Claypole.

From chapter 8 onwards it seems to me that the novel ceases to be satirical and becomes a strangely powerful mixture of the fabular or visionary, with Oliver as 'the principle of Good surviving through every adverse circumstance', and of the documentary, showing criminals 'as they really are'. The London in which the action takes place is both the actual city of the 1830s—with all the respectable areas left out—and a dark and sinister labyrinth perpetually shrouded in night. The way Dickens describes Oliver's nocturnal entry into the city, escorted by the Artful Dodger, exemplifies this perfectly:

> They crossed from the Angel into St. John's-road; struck down the small street which terminates at Sadler's Wells Theatre; through Exmouth-street and Coppice-row; down the little court by the side of the workhouse; across the classic ground which once bore the name of Hockley-in-the-Hole; thence into Little Saffron-hill; and so into Saffron-hill the Great . . .

One can follow the route on a map but the overwhelming impression that this sentence leaves is not one of topographical exactitude but of the hapless Oliver's being drawn deeper and deeper into a dangerous maze.

FAGIN'S UNDERWORLD

At the heart of this maze is Fagin and indeed he *is* the London of *Oliver Twist.* He incarnates it, just as Bumble incarnates the workhouse and the Poor Law. At one point (chapter 19) he is described as though he were some kind of actual emanation from the black wet streets: 'the hideous old man seemed like some loathsome reptile, engendered in the slime and darkness through which he moved'. Fagin has his documentary aspects such as the way he runs his school for pickpockets, his professional jargon (the 'kinchin lay', etc.) and his Jewishness—as Dickens explained later to Mrs Davis most receivers of stolen property at that time were, in fact, Jewish, like the celebrated Ikey Solomons. But, as has long been recognized, he is differently conceived from all the other thieves in that he is *inexplicably* evil (one could no more imagine an innocent young Fagin than an experienced grown-up Oliver). He is, in fact, the Devil and London is the Devil's city. Confronted with Good in the shape of Oliver he must seek to destroy it as inevitably as Melville's Claggart must seek to destroy Billy Budd. At one point (the end of chapter 19) Fagin is temporarily checked simply by the powerful aura of Oliver's goodness and this is almost like the moment in Milton when Satan is staggered and rendered 'stupidly good' by his first sight of innocent Eve in Paradise. Fagin goes to Oliver to announce his impending delivery over to Sikes to assist in that crime which will make him Fagin's forever ('Once let him feel that he is one of us; once fill his mind with the idea that he has been a thief; and he's ours! Ours for his life!'). But Oliver is asleep and spiritually radiant:

> . . . he looked like death; not death as it shews in shroud and coffin, but in the guise it wears when life has just departed; when a young and gentle spirit has, but an instant, fled to Heaven: and the gross air of the world has not had time to breathe upon the changing dust it hallowed.
>
> "Not now," said the Jew, turning softly away. "To-morrow. To-morrow."

Fagin must be motivated at the level of the plot, however, since this is not overtly a fable, and so he is provided with Monks, a conventional enough melodrama villain and a fit subject for Mr Carey's jesting [Mr Carey observes in his *The Violent Effigy: A Study of Dickens' Imagination* (27) that on the only occasion when Monks attempts to strike Oliver he falls over], though there is some resonance in his relationship to Oliver, I think, the child of socially sanctioned hate bent on destroying the child of socially condemned love.

How is it that Fagin emerges as this terrifying figure, 'the devil with a great-coat on'? By doing so he changes the essential mode of the novel from satire and also from documentary, pushing it towards the fabular mode of the *Christmas Carol* and puzzling even his author (Dickens told Forster that Fagin was 'such an out-and-outer I don't know what to make of him'). The clue to what has happened lies, as John Bayley long ago pointed out, in the character's name:

Dickens himself had been at Fagin's school—the blacking factory—and the boy who chiefly befriended him there was actually called Fagin. No wonder Fagin the criminal is such an ambivalent figure when the real Fagin's kindness had, so to speak, threatened to inure Dickens to the hopeless routine of the wage-slave. So passionate was the young Dickens's desire for the station in life to which he felt entitled, and so terrifying his sense that it was being denied him, that he must have hated the real Fagin for the virtue which he could not bear to accept or recognize in that nightmare world, because it might help to subdue him into it. The real Fagin's kindness becomes the criminal Fagin's villainy.

One can go even further than Mr Bayley does here, I think. Dickens's chief retrospective fear for himself, as it were, was not that he might have become a 'wage-slave' but that 'for any care that was taken of me I might have become a little robber or a little vagabond'. A little robber is, of course, just what Fagin intends to make of Oliver.

In contrast to Fagin, Sikes is essentially a 'documentary' figure. We must accept that he, like Noah Claypole, was once innocent even if he has since eagerly co-operated with society in his own corruption. Dickens says of him (in his 'Preface to the Third Edition'), 'I fear there are in the world some insensible and callous natures that do become, at last, utterly and irredeemably bad'. Notice the word 'become'; Fagin, on the other hand, has not *become* bad, he *is* bad from all eternity. Sikes is treated differently, however, during the description of the murder and its aftermath. Dickens is now attempting the tragic and the housebreaker's status must be raised accordingly to a Shakespearian level (Mr Bayley mentions the echoes of *Macbeth* and, in this number of *The Dickensian*, Professor Senelick draws our attention to the relevance here of *Othello*).

SOCIETY'S VICTIMS

It was essential to Dickens to believe that petty criminals must be miserable (how many suicidal Marthas, moaning low into their shawls, actually arrived at Urania Cottage, one wonders?) since he saw them as victims of society and tended to be rather upset when they appeared to be enjoying themselves—in *Sketches by Boz* he describes the urchins in Newgate as a very 'disagreeable sight' when they merrily show off in front of visitors. Fagin is obviously happy in his work but then he is the Devil (not Milton's Satan, racked with inward torments, but the gleeful Devil of folklore), Nancy and Sikes are appropriately gloomy for most of the time, but what about the Dodger? He, it seems to me, is a case like Mrs Gamp—a marvellous, grotesque exaggeration of a type Dickens had observed (and, in the case of the Dodger, first reportcd on in the sketch called 'Criminal Courts' in *Sketches by Boz*) which soon transcends the author's original intention, whether this be a matter of satire, documentary or moral fable, and ends up as a 'free-standing' Dickens character, exhibited and delighted in for its own sake. The Dodger exits triumphantly from the novel in chapter 43 and one no more believes that that sentence in the last chapter, '. . . far from home, died the chief remaining members . . . of Fagin's gang', applies to him than one believes that Mr Pecksniff degenerated into a 'squalid begging-letter writer' after *his* comparably triumphant exit.

As for Nancy, her 'documentary' aspect ('I will not . . . abate . . . one scrap of curlpaper in the girl's dishevelled hair') is rapidly eclipsed by Dickens's interest in dramatising through her one of his deepest beliefs, that of the beneficent moral influence on us of memories of our own past wrongs and sorrows (cf. *The Haunted Man*). Nancy suddenly sees in Oliver the image of her own past self and pities it: 'I thieved for you when I was a child not half as old as this!' she screams at Fagin, when defending Oliver from his blows, '. . . the cold, wet, dirty streets are my home; and you're the wretch that drove me to them long ago'. Just as Scrooge's heart is unfrozen by being shown a vision of himself as a forlorn and lonely child so Nancy's humanity and goodness is aroused by witnessing a re-enactment of her own undoing. Yet this, and her pathetic loyalty to Sikes, the only object that her sordid and brutal world gives her to love (a love in which she nonetheless takes pride like her prototype in 'The Hospital Patient' in *Sketches by Boz*), leads directly to her murder and brings her closer to true tragic status than any other of Dickens's heroines. Lady Dedlock is too shadowy a figure in comparison though she perhaps comes nearest to Nancy in this kind (essentially a Shakespearian kind) of tragedy whilst Edith Dombey, Louisa Gradgrind and Estella are perhaps closer to George Eliot's kind of tragedy, the sort that the heroine generally survives, a sadder and a wiser woman.

OLIVER'S TWO WORLDS

What continuity is there between the satirically presented social institutions of the first seven chapters and the London of Fagin? They are, I think, thematically linked in a way that, for example, Dotheboys Hall and the London of *Nicholas Nickleby* are not. The society we are shown in the first seven chapters is one in which selfishness dominates everything —each group and individual is out for his own interests but there is a hypocritical pretence at a true society with institutions of government, law and religion. Fagin's anti-society, eating out the heart of the city, occupying ruined old houses deserted by 'respectable' society, is by comparison 'honest' in that 'looking after Number One' is the openly avowed principle on which it rests. It wickedly exploits people by striking devilish bargains with them but it does not want to kill them just for being born. Cruikshank's two plates, 'Oliver asking for more' and 'Oliver introduced to the respectable Old Gentleman' are suggestive here. In each plate the child, in a begging posture, confronts a figure of power presiding over a supply of food. But what is bleak and hostile in the first plate is convivial and welcoming in the second. Fagin and his gang will (for a terrible price) give Oliver that food, warmth, shelter and companionship that 'lawful' society harshly denies him, so forcing him to seek it elsewhere.

The 'good' people in *Oliver Twist*—Brownlow, the Maylies and the rest—belong wholly to the fabular aspect of the book, the story of the 'principle of Good'. Dickens wills them into existence (helped in the case of Rose Maylie by his idealisation of his recently dead young sister-in-law, Mary Hogarth) to counterbalance the nightmare of Fagin, which had so nearly turned into terrible reality for him, and seeks desperately to give them some solidity by providing them with comic attendants such as Mr Grimwig and Dr Losberne. They are identified with a conventionally pastoral countryside (Brownlow's house may be said to be near Pentonville but it is really unlocalised, a state of being—Oliver has only to step outside its doors to be at once reclaimed by Fagin) and they are in no way part of, or responsible for, the atrocious society shown in the early chapters: Brownlow is powerless to cope with Mr Fang. Their only contact with Fagin's world is through the Abdiel-figure of Nancy who meets them in no-man's-land, on London Bridge or in a hotel. Sikes's invasion of their territory is a disastrous failure and Fagin can only leer in at the Chertsey window. At the end of the book they simply withdraw deep into the countryside with little Oliver, 'triumphing at last', leaving the world

(Bumble's Mudfog [Dickens originally gave the town in which Oliver was born the good satirical name of Mudfog, prophetic of the opening of *Bleak House,* but changed it to 'a certain town' for the first volume publication of the story] and Fagin's London) to its fate, and linking themselves together in 'a little society, whose condition approached as nearly to one of perfect happiness as can ever be known in this changing world'. Oliver, in fact, returns to Heaven after his season in Hell. He dies just as surely as Little Nell does at the end of *The Old Curiosity Shop,* even though we see no corpse. Graham Greene's famous description of the abiding impression made on him by *Oliver Twist* still seems to me the truest to my own experience of the book of all the critiques that I have read:

> . . . is it too fantastic to imagine that in this novel, as in many of his later books, creeps in, unrecognized by the author, the eternal and alluring taint of the Manichee, with its simple and terrible explanation of our plight, how the world was made by Satan and not by God, lulling us with the music of despair?

Oliver Twist's Flawed Plot

Arnold Kettle

Arnold Kettle comments on a recurring pattern in many of Dickens's books—and especially in *Oliver Twist:* a protagonist emerges out of squalor into comfort and kindliness. Kettle finds that the first quarter of *Oliver Twist* brilliantly details Oliver's utterly depraved and miserable existence. The artistic effect is diminished in later chapters, however, when the plot takes a turn and Oliver escapes the clutches of Fagin's underworld. By rescuing Oliver, Kettle maintains, Dickens fails to underscore the pattern and struggle established early in the novel: that the poor must struggle against an oppressive bourgeois state. Kettle is the author of *An Introduction to the English Novel,* from which the following is excerpted.

In the twelfth chapter of *Oliver Twist,* Oliver carried insensible by Mr. Brownlow from the magistrate's court, wakes up to find himself in a comfortable bed:

> Weak, and thin, and pallid, he awoke at last from what seemed to have been a long and troubled dream. Feebly raising himself in the bed, with his head resting on his trembling arm, he looked curiously round.

> "What room is this? Where have I been brought to?" said Oliver. "This is not the place I went to sleep in."

> He uttered these words in a feeble voice, being very faint and weak, but they were overheard at once; for the curtain at the bed's head was hastily drawn back, and a motherly old lady, very neatly and precisely dressed, rose as she withdrew it, from an armchair close by, in which she had been sitting at needlework.

> "Hush, my dear," said the old lady softly. "You must be very quiet, or you will be ill again; and you have been very bad—as bad as bad could be, pretty nigh. Lie down again; there's a

dear!" With these words, the old lady very gently placed Oliver's head upon the pillow, and, smoothing back his hair from his forehead, looked so kindly and lovingly in his face, that he could not help placing his little withered hand in hers, and drawing it round his neck.

"Save us!" said the old lady, with tears in her eyes, "what a grateful little dear it is! Pretty creature! What would his mother feel if she had sat by him as I have, and could see him now?"

It is a central situation in the book—this emergence out of squalor into comfort and kindliness—and it is repeated later in the story when once again Oliver, after the robbery in which he has been wounded, wakes to find himself cared for and defended by the Maylies. There is more than mere chance in the repetition and we meet here, indeed, a pattern recurring throughout Dickens's novels. It is worthwhile examining it more closely.

POWERFUL NARRATIVE

The first eleven chapters of *Oliver Twist* are an evocation of misery and horror. We have been drawn straight with the first sentence (of which workhouse is the key word) into a world of the most appalling poverty and ugliness, a world of brutality and violence in which life is cheap, suffering general and death welcome. That the evocation is crude, that it is marred by moments of false feeling and by a heavy-handed irony which weakens all it comments on, is not for the moment the consideration. By and large, the effect is of extraordinary power. No such effect (for good or ill) has emerged from any novel we have previously discussed. It is an effect which is, in the precise sense of a hackneyed word, unforgettable. The workhouse, the parochial baby-farm, Mr. Sowerberry's shop, the funeral, the Artful Dodger, Fagin's lair: they have the haunting quality, but nothing of the unreality, of a nightmare. It is a curious comment on Victorian civilization that this was considered suitable reading for children.

What is the secret of the power? Is it merely the objective existence of the horrors, the fact that such things were, that strikes at our minds? Fairly obviously not or we should be moved in just the same way by a social history. There is a particularity about this world which is not the effect of even a well-documented history. It is not just any evocation of the life of the poor after the Industrial Revolution; when we read the Hammonds' *Town Labourer* or Engels's *Condition of the Working Class in England in 1844* our reaction may not be less profound than our reaction to *Oliver Twist,* but it is different, more generalized, less vivid, less intense.

The most obvious difference between *Oliver Twist* and a social history is, of course, that it deals with actual characters whose personalities we envisage, whose careers we follow, and whose feelings we share. But this difference is not, I think, quite so important as we might assume. For in fact we do not become involved in the world of *Oliver Twist* in the way we become involved in the world of *Emma.* We do not really know very much about any of these characters, even Oliver himself, or participate very closely in their motives and reactions. We are sorry for Oliver; we are on his side; but our feeling for him is not very different from our feeling for any child we see ill-treated in the street. We are outraged and our sense of outrage no doubt comes, ultimately, from a feeling of common humanity, a kind of identification of ourselves with the child in his misery and struggles; but our entanglement in his situation is not really very deep.

In the famous scene when Oliver asks for more it is not the precise sense of Oliver's feelings and reactions that grips us; we do not feel what he is feeling in the way we share Miss Bates's emotion on Box Hill, and in this sense Oliver is less close to us and matters to us less than Miss Bates and Emma. But in another way Oliver matters to us a great deal more. For when he walks up to the master of the workhouse and asks for more gruel, issues are at stake which make the whole world of Jane Austen tremble. We care, we are involved, not because it is Oliver and we are close to Oliver (though that of course enters into it), but because every starved orphan in the world, and indeed everyone who is poor and oppressed and hungry is involved, and the master of the workhouse (his name has not been revealed) is not anyone in particular but every agent of an oppressive system everywhere. And that, incidentally, is why millions of people all over the world (including many who have never read a page of Dickens) can tell you what happened in Oliver Twist's workhouse, while comparatively few can tell you what happened on Box Hill.

That this episode from *Oliver Twist* should have become a myth, a part of the cultural consciousness of the people, is due not merely to its subject matter but to the kind of novel

Dickens wrote. He is dealing not, like Jane Austen, with personal relationships, not with the quality of feeling involved in detailed living, but with something which can without fatuity be called Life. What we get from *Oliver Twist* is not a greater precision of sensitiveness about the day-to-day problems of human behaviour but a sharpened sense of the large movement of life within which particular problems arise. It is pointless to argue whether the way Dickens tackles life is better or worse than the way Jane Austen tackles it. One might just as well argue whether it is better to earn one's living or to get married. Not merely are the two issues not exclusive, they are indissolubly bound up. In a sense they are the same problem—how best to live in society—but, for all their interdependence, one does not tackle them in precisely the same way.

PORTRAIT OF OPPRESSION

What distinguishes the opening chapters of *Oliver Twist* from, on the one side, a social history and, on the other side, *Emma,* is that they are symbolic. It is not a sense of participation in the personal emotions of any of the characters that engages our imagination but a sense of participation in a world that is strikingly, appallingly relevant to our world.

The *Oliver Twist* world is a world of poverty, oppression and death. The poverty is complete, utterly degrading and utterly realistic.

> The houses on either side were high and large, but very old and tenanted by people of the poorest class: as their neglected appearance would have sufficiently denoted, without the concurrent testimony afforded by the squalid looks of the few men and women who, with folded arms and bodies half-doubled, occasionally skulked along. A great many of the tenements had shop fronts; but these were fast closed, and mouldering away, only the upper rooms being inhabited. Some houses which had become insecure from age and decay were prevented from falling into the street, by huge beams of wood reared against the walls, and firmly planted in the road; but even these crazy dens seemed to have been selected as the nightly haunts of some houseless wretches, for many of the rough boards, which supplied the place of door and window, were wrenched from their positions, to afford an aperture wide enough for the passage of a human body. The kennel was stagnant and filthy. The very rats, which here and there lay putrefying in its rottenness, were hideous with famine.

The oppression stems from the "board"—eight or ten fat gentlemen sitting round a table—and particularly (the image is repeated) from a fat gentleman in a white waistcoat; but its agents are the (under) paid officers of the state, beadle, matron, etc., corrupt, pompous, cruel. The methods of oppression are simple: violence and starvation. The workhouse is a symbol of the oppression but by no means its limit. Outside, the world is a vast workhouse with the "parish" run by the same gentleman in a white waistcoat, assisted by magistrates fatuous or inhuman, by clergymen who can scarcely be bothered to bury the dead, by Mr. Bumble. London is no different from the parish, only bigger.

The oppressed are degraded and corrupted by their life (plus a little gin) and either become themselves oppressors or else criminals or corpses. Of all the recurring themes and images of these opening chapters that of death is the most insistent. Oliver's mother dies. "'It's all over, Mrs. Thingummy' said the surgeon . . . ." The note of impersonal and irresponsible horror is immediately struck. It is not fortuitous that Mr. Sowerberry should be an undertaker, presiding over an unending funeral. Oliver and Dick long for death. Fagin gives a twist of new and dreadful cynicism to the theme: "'What a fine thing capital punishment is! Dead men never repent; dead men never bring awkward stories to light.'" The ultimate sanction of the oppressive state becomes the ultimate weapon of its degraded creatures in their struggles against one another.

The strength of these opening chapters lies in the power and justice of the symbols, through which is achieved an objective picture arousing our compassion not through any extraneous comment but through its own validity. The weakness lies in Dickens's conscious attitudes, his attempts to comment on the situation. These attempts are at best (the ironical) inadequate, at worst (the sentimental) nauseating.

> Although I am not disposed to maintain that the being born in a workhouse is in itself the most fortunate and enviable circumstance that can possibly befall a human being . . .

The heaviness of the prose reflects the stodginess and unsubtlety of the thought. So does the reiteration of the "kind old gentleman" as a description of Fagin. (The less satisfactory side of Dickens's treatment of the thieves obviously comes direct from *Jonathan Wild;* the same irony—even to the very words—is used, but because it is not based on Fielding's secure moral preoccupation it becomes tedious far more quickly.) The incursions of "sentiment" (i.e. every reference to motherhood, the little scene between Oliver and Dick) are even more unsatisfactory. After Dickens has tried to wring an easy tear by playing on responses which he has done nothing to satisfy, we begin to be suspicious of the moments when we really *are* moved, fearing a facile trick.

"OBJECTIVE PROFUNDITY"

But the weaknesses—which may be summed up as the inadequacy of Dickens's conscious view of life—are in the first eleven chapters of *Oliver Twist* almost obliterated by the strength. The subjective inadequacy is obscured by the objective profundity. Again and again Dickens leaves behind his heavy humour, forgets that he ought to be trying to copy Fielding or vindicating our faith in the beauty of motherhood, and achieves a moment of drama or insight which burns into the imagination by its truth and vividness. We have already noticed the surgeon's comment on Oliver's mother's death. Most of the Mr. Bumble–Mrs. Mann conversations, the whole of the undertaker section, the meeting with the Artful Dodger, the first description of the thieves' kitchen are on the same level of achievement. So is the moment when Oliver asks for more and the passage when Oliver and Sowerberry go to visit the corpse of a dead woman.

> The terrified children cried bitterly; but the old woman, who had hitherto remained as quiet as if she had been wholly deaf to all that passed, menaced them into silence. Having unloosed the cravat of the man, who still remained extended on the ground, she tottered towards the undertaker.

> "She was my daughter," said the old woman, nodding her head in the direction of the corpse; and speaking with an idiotic leer, more ghastly than even the presence of death in such a place. "Lord, Lord! Well, it *is* strange that I who gave birth to her, and was a woman then, should be alive and merry now, and she lying there, so cold and stiff! Lord, Lord!—to think of it; it's as good as a play—as good as a play!"

> As the wretched creature mumbled and chuckled in her hideous merriment, the undertaker turned to go away.

> "Stop, stop!" said the old woman in a loud whisper. "Will she be buried to-morrow, or next day, or tonight? I laid her out and I must walk, you know. Send me a large cloak—a good warm one, for it is bitter cold. We should have cake and wine, too, before we go! Never mind; send some bread—only a loaf of bread and a cup of water. Shall we have some bread, dear?" she said eagerly, catching at the undertaker's coat, as he once more moved towards the door.

"Yes, yes," said the undertaker, "of course. Anything, every-thing." He disengaged himself from the old woman's grasp, and, drawing Oliver after him, hurried away.

There is no sentimentality here, only horror, and with something of the quality which one associates particularly with Dostoievsky, the strengthening of realism by the mo-ment of fantasy, the blurring of the line between reality and nightmare, a stretching to the ultimate of the capacity of the mind to deal with the world it has inherited.

And then from the desperate horror of the nightmare world Oliver awakes, lying in a comfortable bed, surrounded by kindly middle-class people. He has become all of a sud-den a pretty creature, a grateful little dear. And from that moment the plot of the novel becomes important.

INADEQUACIES OF PLOT

It is generally agreed that the plots of Dickens's novels are their weakest feature but it is not always understood why this should be so. The plot of *Oliver Twist* is very compli-cated and very unsatisfactory. It is a conventional plot about a wronged woman, an illegitimate baby, a destroyed will, a death-bed secret, a locket thrown into the river, a wicked el-der brother and the restoration to the hero of name and property. That it should depend on a number of extraordi-nary coincidences (the only two robberies in which Oliver is called upon to participate are perpetrated, fortuitously, on his father's best friend and his mother's sister's guardian!) is the least of its shortcomings. Literal probability is not an es-sential quality of an adequate plot. Nor is it a damning crit-icism that Dickens should have used his plot for the pur-poses of serial-publication, i.e., to provide a climax at the end of each instalment and the necessary twists and manœuvres which popular serialization invited. (It is not a fault in a dramatist that he should provide a climax to each act of his play, and the serial installment is no more or less artificial a convention than the act of a play.) What we may legitimately object to in the plot of *Oliver Twist* is the very substance of that plot in its relation to the essential pattern of the novel.

The conflict in the plot is the struggle between the inno-cent Oliver, aided by his friends at Pentonville and Chertsey, against the machinations of those who are conspiring from self-interest to do him out of his fortune. These latter stem from and centre in his half-brother Monks. It is not, even by its own standards, a good plot. Oliver is too passive a hero to win our very lively sympathy and Monks is a rather unconvincing villain who is, anyway, outshone in interest by his agents. The good characters are, by and large, too good and the bad too bad. If the centre of interest of the novel were indeed the plot then the conventional assessment of a Dickens novel—a poor story enlivened by magnificent though irrelevant "characters"—would be fair enough. But in fact the centre of interest, the essential pattern of the novel, is not its plot, and it is the major fault of the plot that it does not correspond with this central interest.

THE PLIGHT OF THE POOR

The core of the novel, and what gives it value, is its consideration of the plight of the poor. Its pattern is the contrasted relation of two worlds—the underworld of the workhouse, the funeral, the thieves' kitchen, and the comfortable world of the Brownlows and Maylies. It is this pattern that stamps the novel on our minds. We do not remember, when we think back on it, the intricacies of the plot; we are not interested in the affairs of Rose and Harry Maylie; we do not care who Oliver's father was and, though we sympathize with Oliver's struggles, we do not mind whether or not he gets his fortune. What we do remember is that vision of the underworld of the first eleven chapters, the horror of Fagin, the fate of Mr. Bumble, the trial of the Artful Dodger, the murder of Nancy, the end of Sikes. What engages our sympathy is not Oliver's feeling for the mother he never saw, but his struggle against his oppressors of which the famous gruel scene is indeed a central and adequate symbol.

The contrast of the two worlds is at the very heart of the book, so that we see a total picture of contrasted darkness and light. Often the two are explicitly contrasted in divided chapters. The two worlds are so utterly separate that Oliver's two metamorphoses from one to the other must inevitably take the form of an awakening to a new existence and the root of the weakness as "characters" of both Oliver and Monks is that they are not fully absorbed in either world. Oliver is rather a thin hero because, though he is called upon to play a hero's part, he never becomes identified with the heroic forces of the book; while Monks's stature as the fountainhead of evil is wrecked by his parentage; how can he compete with Sikes and Fagin when he is to be allowed, because he is a gentleman, to escape his just desserts?

The power of the book, then, proceeds from the wonderful evocation of the underworld and the engagement of our sympathy on behalf of the inhabitants of that world. Its weakness lies in Dickens's failure to develop and carry through the pattern so powerfully presented in the first quarter of the novel. It is by no means a complete failure; on the contrary, there are passages in the latter part of the book quite as successful as the early scenes: and in the final impression of the novel the sense of the two worlds is, as has been suggested, the dominant factor. But the failure is, nevertheless, sufficiently striking to be worth consideration.

It is not by chance that the plot and Mr. Brownlow emerge in the novel at the same moment, for their purpose is identical. It is they who are to rescue Oliver from the underworld and establish him as a respectable member of society. It is not through his own efforts that the metamorphosis takes place and indeed it cannot be. For if the whole first section of the novel has convinced us of anything at all it is that against the whole apparatus set in motion by the gentleman in the white waistcoat the Oliver Twists of that world could stand no possible chance.

The introduction of the plot, then, savours from the very first of a trick. It is only by reducing the whole of Oliver's experiences up till now to the status of "a long and troubled dream" that he can be saved for the plot. But we know perfectly well that these experiences are not a dream; they have a reality for us which the nice houses in Pentonville and Chertsey never achieve. Indeed, as far as the imaginative impact of the novel is concerned, it is the Brownlow-Maylie world that is the dream, a dream world into which Oliver is lucky enough to be transported by the plot but which all the real and vital people of the book never even glimpse. The Brownlow-Maylie world is indeed no world at all; it is merely the romantic escape world of the lost wills and dispossessed foundlings and idiotic coincidences which make up the paraphernalia of the conventional romantic plot.

The plot makes impossible the realization of the living pattern and conflict of the book. This conflict—symbolized, as we have seen, by the gruel scene—is the struggle of the poor against the bourgeois state, the whole army of greater and lesser Bumbles whom the gentleman in the white waistcoat employs to maintain morality (all the members of the board are "philosophers") and the *status quo*. The appalling difficulties of this struggle are impressed on our minds and it is because Oliver, however unwillingly, becomes an actor in it that he takes on a certain symbolic significance and wins more than our casual pity.

It is notable that Dickens makes no serious effort to present Oliver with any psychological realism: his reactions are not for the most part, the reactions of any child of nine or ten years old; he is not surprised by what would surprise a child and his moral attitudes are those of an adult. And yet something of the quality of precocious suffering, of childish terror, is somehow achieved, partly by the means by which other characters are presented, with a kind of exaggerated, almost grotesque simplicity, and partly through the very fact that Oliver is—we are persuaded—a figure of symbolic significance. Because he is *all* workhouse orphans the lack of a convincing individual psychology does not matter; it is Oliver's situation rather than himself that moves us and the situation is presented with all of Dickens's dramatic symbolic power.

OLIVER'S TRANSFORMATION

Once he becomes involved in the plot the entire symbolic significance of Oliver changes. Until he wakes up in Mr. Brownlow's house he is a poor boy struggling against the inhumanity of the state. After he has slept himself into the Brownlow world he is a young bourgeois who has been done out of his property. A complete transformation has taken place in the organization of the novel. The state, which in the pattern of the book, is the organ of oppression of the poor and therefore of Oliver, now becomes the servant of Oliver. The oppressed are now divided (through the working of the plot) into the good and deserving poor who help Oliver win his rights and the bad and criminal poor who help Monks and must be eliminated. It is a conception which makes a mockery of the opening chapters of the book, where poverty has been revealed to us in a light which makes the facile terms of good and bad irrelevant.

By the end of the book Nancy can be pigeonholed as good, Sikes as bad. But who can say whether the starving creatures of the opening chapters are good or bad? It is for this kind of reason that the plot of *Oliver Twist* has so disastrous an effect on the novel. Not merely is it silly and mechanical and troublesome, but it expresses an interpretation of life infinitely less profound and honest than the novel itself reveals.

The disaster, happily, is not complete. For one thing, the plot does not immediately, with the entrance of Mr. Brownlow, gain entire ascendancy. The kidnapping of Oliver by Nancy and Sikes and his return to the thieves gives the novel a reprieve. The robbery episode is excellently done. But in this section (Chaps. XII to XXIX) the plot is beginning to seep into the underworld. Monks appears. And the reintroduction of the workhouse (the death of old Sally, the marriage of Mr. Bumble), despite some delicious moments ("It's all U.P. here, Mrs. Corney"; Noah and Charlotte eating oysters; "Won't you tell your own B?"), too obviously serves the contrivances of the plot.

Once, however, the robbery is done with and Oliver awakes for a second time in the respectable world, the plot completely reasserts itself. The third quarter of the book (Chaps. XXIX to XXXIX) is its weakest section. Oliver is here entirely at the mercy of the Maylies and the plot. Monks bobs up all over the place. And our interest is held (if at all) only by the Bumble passages, now completely involved in the plot, and the incidental "characters," Giles and Brittles, Blathers and Duff. And because these characters have no part in the underlying pattern of the book and are therefore, unlike Bumble and Fagin and the Artful Dodger and Noah Claypole, without symbolic significance, they are merely eccentrics, comic relief, with all the limitations the phrase implies.

The basic conflict of the novel is brought, in this quarter, almost to a standstill; the people who have captured our imagination scarcely appear at all. The world of the opening chapters has been replaced by another world in which kindly old doctors like Losberne and crusty but amiable eccentrics like Grimwig are in control of the situation. But after what we have already experienced, we simply cannot believe in this world in the way we believed in the other.

PLOT VERSUS PATTERN

In the final quarter of the book (Chap. XXXIX onwards) plot and pattern, artifice and truth, struggle in a last, violent encounter. The plot wins the first round by extracting Nancy from the clutches of the pattern. The girl's genuine humanity, revealed earlier in the novel by the simple moving language of her moment of compassion for the suffering wretches within the walls of the jail, is debased by the plot into the conventional clichés of cheap melodrama. But Nancy's abduction is countered almost at once by one of the great episodes of the novel, the trial of the Artful Dodger. This scene is irrelevant to the plot except insofar as the Dodger has to be got out of the way before the final dispensing of reward and punishment. It is an interesting instance of the power of Dickens's genius that he should have realized that in the Dodger he had created a figure which the plot was quite incapable either of absorbing or obliterating. And so he is obliged to give the irrepressible boy his final fling, a fling which again raises the book into serious art and plays an essential part in its (by this time) almost forgotten pattern.

The trial of the Artful Dodger (it is a greater because emotionally and morally a profounder scene than Jonathan Wild's dance without music) restates in an astonishing form the central theme of *Oliver Twist*: what are the poor to do against the oppressive state? The Dodger throughout the book is magnificently done: his precosity, the laboured irony of his conversation (which becomes involuntarily a comment on the quality of Dickens's own irony), his shrewdness, his grotesque urbanity, his resourcefulness (gloriously at variance with his appearance), his tremendous vitality, all are revealed without false pathos but with an effect of great profundity.

For what is so important about the Artful Dodger is not his oddity but his normality, not his inability to cope with the world but his very ability to cope with it on its own terms. Oliver is afraid of the world, the Dodger defies it; it has made him what he is and he will give back as good as he got. . . .

EFFECTIVE SYMBOLISM

The final section of the book (the murder of Nancy, the flight and end of Sikes, the death of Fagin and the tying-up of the plot) is an extraordinary mixture of the genuine and the bogus. The violence which has run right through the novel reaches its climax with the murder of Nancy; and the sense of terror is remarkably well sustained right up to the death of Sikes.

Here again Dickens's instinct for the symbolic background is what grips our imagination. The atmosphere of squalid London, powerfully present in so much of the novel, is here immensely effective, especially the description of Folly Ditch and Jacob's Island, sombre and decayed, "crazy wooden galleries common to the backs of half a dozen houses, with holes from which to look upon the slime beneath; windows broken and patched, with poles thrust out on which to dry the linen that is never there . . . chimneys half crushed, half hesitating to fall. . . ." The scene itself ceases to be a mere backcloth and becomes a sculptured mass making an integral part of the novel's pattern. So that in the end it is not Sikes' conscience that we remember but a black picture of human squalor and desolation. Sikes is gathered into the world that has begotten him and the image of that world makes us understand him and even pity him, not with an easy sentimentality, but through a sense of all the hideous forces that have made him what he is.

The end of Fagin is a different matter. It is sensational in the worst sense, with a *News of the World* interest which touches nothing adequately and is worse than inadequate because it actually coarsens our perceptions. It is conceived entirely within the terms of the plot (Oliver is taken—in the name of morality—to the condemned cell to find out where the missing papers are hidden) and the whole debasing effect of the plot on the novel is immediately illustrated; for it is because he is working within the moral framework of the plot—in which the only standards are those of the sanctity of property and complacent respectability—that Dickens *cannot* offer us any valuable human insights, *cannot* give characters freedom to live as human beings.

That is why the struggle throughout *Oliver Twist* between, the plot and the pattern is indeed a life and death struggle, a struggle as to whether the novel shall live or not. And insofar as the plot succeeds in twisting and negating the pattern the value of the novel is in fact weakened. To a considerable degree the novel *is* thus ruined; the loss of tension in the third quarter and the dubious close are the testimony. But the total effect is not one of disaster. The truth and depth of the central vision are such that a vitality is generated which struggles against and survives the plot. Oliver himself does not survive; but the force he has set in motion does. This force—let us call it the sense of the doom and aspirations of the oppressed—is too strong to be satisfied with the dream-solution of Oliver's metamorphosis, too enduring to let us forget the fat gentleman in the white waistcoat who has so conveniently faded from the picture till he is recalled by the Artful Dodger. Confused, uneven, topsy-turvy as the effect of the novel is we would yet be doing it great injustice to discuss it, as it is often discussed, simply in terms of random moments and exuberant caricature. There is pattern behind that power, art behind the vitality, and if we recognize this in *Oliver Twist* we shall not come unarmed to Dickens's later, more mature and greater books: *Bleak House, Little Dorrit, Great Expectations, Our Mutual Friend.*

The Evolving Form of *Oliver Twist*

William T. Lankford

Many modern critics agree that *Oliver Twist* lacks
coherence in theme, structure, and plot. In the following essay, William T. Lankford attempts to resolve some of the novel's inconsistencies by analyz-
ing developments in narrative voice and form.
Lankford maintains, for example, that some of the
novel's thematic confusion is rooted in Dickens's
own ambivalence about some of the issues he explores, such as whether criminals are inherently
corrupt, or whether they are corrupted by an oppressive social order, and also the role Providence plays
in protecting unconditionally good characters such
as Oliver and Rose Maylie. Lankford contributed the
following article to *PMLA,* a publication of the Modern Language Association.

The subtitle of *Oliver Twist—The Parish Boy's Progress—*
indicates that Dickens intended Oliver's story to be representative of a general pattern. The novel begins in the kind
of realistic milieu appropriate to such a concern, but by the
time of the closing chapters, when the mystery of Oliver's
birth has been unraveled and his fortune restored, he has
certainly ceased to be a typical parish boy, and the novel's
realism has been displaced by the stagiest sort of melodrama. Along the way Dickens repeatedly violates convention and consistency, mixing biting satire and insipid
pathos, naturalistic detail and symbolic fable, realistic characters and theatrical stereotypes, coherent plotting and extravagant coincidence, tensely impassioned dialogue and
vapid moralistic platitude. Modern critics have generally
agreed that the novel's moments of unquestionable insight
and power never fit together because of its incoherence of

Excerpted from "'The Parish Boy's Progress': The Evolving Form of *Oliver Twist*," by
William T. Lankford, *PMLA,* January 1978. Reprinted with permission from the Modern Language Association of America.

thought and form. The basic problems have long been established: *Oliver Twist* is inconsistent in theme and conception of character, divided into the two symbolically incongruent worlds of city and countryside, and marred by the melodramatic entanglements of the plot. These difficulties are indeed present, but it is their interplay as the novel develops that is crucial to its problematic form.

The apparent thematic and symbolic confusion is actually a progressive transformation of the novel's mode of representation. *Oliver Twist* begins in one kind of reality and ends in another because Dickens is struggling throughout to evolve a narrative mode adequate to render the compulsions of his imagination and the truth about his society. His effort to assimilate the journalistic accuracy of observation of the *Sketches by Boz* and the emerging social conscience of *Pickwick Papers* into the stagnated framework of the Newgate novel forces him to wrestle with the fundamental conventions by which character, action, and the social world become meaningful in fiction. He labors to create a new kind of novel expressly to reveal an undiscovered truth; the formal problems that he encounters are rooted in deeply felt moral conflicts, both public and personal.

OPPOSING REALITIES

These conflicts are revealed in the troubled ambivalence of Dickens' portrayal of the criminal underworld and his creative uncertainty about the relationship between the thieves and the society on which they prey. In his Preface to the third edition in 1841, Dickens himself addresses the apparent contradictions and inconsistencies in his depiction of the thieves, and his remarks clarify the central tensions in the ideas and attitudes underlying the novel's form. He answers the charges of coarseness and exaggeration that had been raised against his presentation of the thieves by insisting on the verisimilitude of his description: "It was my attempt . . . to dim the false glitter surrounding something which really did exist, by shewing it in all its unattractive and repulsive truth." But Dickens does not defend the truthfulness of his art on the basis of its naturalistic accuracy alone; he finds the value of the truth he presents in its moral purpose: "I wished to shew, in little Oliver, the principle of Good surviving through every adverse circumstance, and triumphing at last." This makes the novel's nominal protagonist an allegorical figure rather than a real boy; he is tested morally, however, not by a set of allegorical vices but by "a knot of such associates in crime as really did exist," ostensibly portrayed "as they really are." Dickens thus defines the opposed forces of the novel as the "principle of Good" and the "miserable reality" of evil, and the conflict of good and evil in the novel is also enacted as a conflict in its mode of representation. Oliver and the thieves represent incommensurate kinds of reality and opposed standards of truth, and the implicit tension between moralizing "principle" and naturalistic "reality" generates the inconsistencies in theme and characterization. In this moralized realism, truth of observation is subordinated to truth of precept, just as in the development of the novel, the realistic representation of the thieves is contained within the moral fable of the triumph of good.

The inconsistencies become coherent when seen as stages in the reorientation and development of narrative form within the evolving context of "The Parish Boy's Progress." The opening chapters bitterly explore the extent to which human nature can be hardened and corrupted by an oppressive society. But the satire gradually dissipates; the moral tensions in Dickens' presentation of the thieves progressively polarize the novel's values and lead to an imaginative impasse halfway through. With the introduction of the Maylies, as James Kincaid has pointed out, the novel "shifts its grounds to a concern with the simplistically defined good and bad." But idealized goodness quickly proves vulnerable; the simplistic morality that briefly dominates in the countryside chapters is shattered by Rose's sickness. When Dickens returns from the countryside to the city in the whirlwind final third of the novel, his suppressed sympathy with the underworld characters erupts to reinvigorate the powerful issues of the opening chapters and to complete the typical pattern that was previously abandoned. While the plot is given over to Brownlow, Monks, and the discovery of Oliver's identity, Dickens' structuring of the action subversively reveals the hidden similarity between the boy and the thieves, and the narrative mode evolves to discover their common inner humanity. "The Parish Boy's Progress" ends at the gallows, but Fagin takes Oliver's place there.

That progress begins in the workhouse "common to most towns, great or small" (Ch. i). At the outset Dickens emphasizes the actuality and typicality of the setting; Oliver is born in "a certain town . . . to which I will assign no fictitious name." The boy is not yet "the principle of Good" but merely an "item of mortality," and the new life begins with "the old story" of an unwed mother. In appearance the unnamed orphan "might have been the child of a nobleman or a beggar," but he is "badged and ticketed" by the workhouse "to be cuffed and buffeted through the world,—despised by all, and pitied by none." His individual nature assimilated into the conventional course of things, the new baby is wrapped in blankets that "had grown yellow in the same service" and is assigned a "fictitious name" by the parish beadle.

SYSTEMATIC OPPRESSION

The following chapters trace how Oliver becomes "the victim of a systematic course of treachery and deception" (Ch. ii). The crucial word is "systematic," for the object of Dickens' attack is the restrictiveness and hypocrisy infusing the social order, the attitudes that sanction the Poor Laws as well as the laws themselves. The brutality of the laws and the callousness of their enforcement become only symptoms of the simpler and broader lack of charity and benevolence throughout the society. The poor are oppressed emotionally as well as economically; the incidents when Oliver asks for more food at the workhouse and when Bumble later chides Mrs. Sowerberry for having "raised a artificial soul and spirit in him" by giving him meat (Ch. vii) have become touchstones, but Dickens' protest is directed more fundamentally at Oliver's desperate need for love than at his physical hunger. Throughout the early chapters the urgent question is whether Oliver can survive, physically and spiritually, when he is repeatedly starved, beaten, and isolated—"in a fair way of being reduced, for life, to a state of brutal stupidity and sullenness by the ill-usage he had received" (Ch. iv). The boy's suffering and endurance take place within a hierarchy of oppression and fear reaching from the "well-fed philosophers" and "the gentleman in the white waistcoat" to the paupers and children. Describing how the shop boys' derision of Noah leads in turn to his abuse of Oliver, Dickens declares that this "shows us what a beautiful thing human nature sometimes is; and how impartially the same amiable qualities are developed in the finest lord and the dirtiest charity-boy" (Ch. v). Dickens is attacking an entire society in which emotional oppression replicates itself into a network of scorn and hatred, corrupting "impartially" the highest and the lowest and shaping the character of children as their "amiable qualities are developed."

This is the system against which Oliver rebels when he strikes back at Noah: "A minute ago, the boy had looked the quiet, mild, dejected creature that harsh treatment had made him. But his spirit was roused at last" (Ch. vi). Intrinsic "spirit" against the effects of "harsh treatment"—for the first time there is something within Oliver that resists oppression, that demands recognition as inalienably human. The eventual discovery that Oliver belongs by "blood" to the genteel classes makes a different matter of his strength of "spirit" and vitiates his typicality, but here he is still "the parish boy," and the original thematic issue is still alive. After Oliver flees to London, Fagin's sustained effort to lead him into crime continues to test the ability of innocence to withstand corruption. But Dickens' interest in this problem is gradually supplanted by a more urgent moral question— whether the thieves themselves are corrupt or corrupted, whether they are irredeemably evil threats to the social order or human victims of the institutions and attitudes that oppress the poor and deny their humanity.

FAGIN'S GANG

The rhetorical and moral equivocations in Dickens' presentation of the thieves redirect his imaginative energies and increasingly obfuscate the novel's thematic progress. When Fagin and his boys are introduced, their place in the system of oppressed and oppressors is not firmly established. Like Gamfield the chimney sweep, Fagin is initially conceived as an evil parasite on the social and legal system that forces homeless boys into dependence on him. Yet his vitality quickly transcends his role; in Fagin's perceptiveness and cunning, his anger and wit, there are signs of his inner emotional life even before the final changes in narrative strategy make his humanity inescapable. He threatens Oliver and attempts to corrupt him, but he is simultaneously patron and protector of the gang of boys, who are victims of the same system that has oppressed Oliver. By the plot's subliminal logic these are the workhouse boys again, grown older, no longer asking for more but taking it, and at least partly justified by the corruption and injustice of the society on which they prey. The Dodger's intransigent truculence and Charley

Bates's irrepressible glee override the moral judgment that would condemn them. James Kincaid has established the effects of the humor in Dickens' depiction of the thieves in the first half of the novel: "The final goal of this technique is to pry us away from the normal identification we make with an aloof society and to force us to enter much more fully into the world of the terrified and alienated individual, who at various times is Oliver, Fagin, Sikes, Bumble, and the Artful Dodger." This deeply antisocial humor disappears from the novel when Oliver knocks at the Maylies' front door, but the identification with the thieves that the laughter engendered forces itself back into consciousness in the final chapters, when the thieves, no longer humorous, become agonizingly human.

OLIVER'S TWO WORLDS

Before the Maylies are introduced, however, the community of the thieves functions as both mirror and parody of the polite society of the suburbs. The two worlds are linked together by a variety of methods, ranging from direct authorial comment on the "strong and singular points of resemblance" between them (Ch. xviii) to the organization of narrative sequence to emphasize this "resemblance" through juxtaposition. Oliver's benevolent patrons are introduced in parallel series with the members of Fagin's gang as Dickens creates the two opposed orders of society: Fagin and Brownlow shelter Oliver and feed him, Sikes and Grimwig mistrust and intimidate him, and Mrs. Bedwin, Nancy, and Rose pity and defend him. The repeated analogies of character and action explore the unresolved relation between genteel society and the criminal underworld, but the underlying similarity between them can be exposed only at the risk of moral disequilibrium. If the two worlds were fully revealed as one, Oliver could find no refuge from loneliness and brutalization, and the liberating humor would harden into bitter grotesque. The corrosive potential of analogy threatens to break out of control when Monks and Harry Maylie concurrently become prominent, paired by age and theatricality of speech: Monks's desire to seduce Oliver into crime makes the analogous threat to innocence in Harry's proposal to deflower Rose seem almost equally criminal.

The gentlefolk and the thieves thus begin as a series of doubles, but, as Dickens attempts to establish a kind of goodness capable of resisting corruption, he is obliged to abandon both the overt pattern of analogy between the two worlds and the quick alternation of narrative focus that enforces it. Brownlow leaves London after Oliver is kidnapped, and when he finally returns he no longer bears any relation either to Fagin or to the "gentleman in the white waistcoat." Meanwhile the Maylies appear, untainted by irony, and in their "bright eyes" Oliver finds a compassion that Dickens labors to represent as a redeeming vision of his fallen world. But the earlier satire so thoroughly anatomized the emotional oppression inherent in the social order that Dickens is compelled to turn away from the city and the public tensions of the present to define an ideal of virtue; Mrs. Maylie is identified with the past, and Rose "seemed scarcely of her age, or of the world" (Ch. xxix). Oliver is purified; as he becomes "the principle of Good" rather than a typical parish boy, his innocence is elevated into an intrinsic moral virtue. The question whether he could resist corruption, which previously provided the motive force and thematic consequence of the plot, disappears, and the struggle of innocence and experience within the boy's mind is reduced to the external machinations of the thieves and the "soft-hearted psalm-singers" for physical possession of him. The conflict between the propertied and the poor, who were shown earlier to be alike except in clothing and experience, is progressively transformed into the melodramatic confrontation of unconditioned goodness and unmitigated evil.

ROSE: WOMAN IDEALIZED

This polarization of values in the novel's evolving morality results largely from Dickens' idealization of Rose. Nothing earlier has prepared the way for the unqualified goodness she represents; from her first appearance she violates the conventions of characterization and conditions of existence established through the previous context of the novel. Dickens acknowledges the problem: "Earth seemed not her element, nor its rough creatures her fit companions" (Ch. xxix). To make Rose plausible, he is forced to build an entirely new system of symbols, thereby altering the values and assumptions that control the novel's representation of reality. Describing the tears that Rose sheds at Harry's proposal, he comments that "When one fell upon the flower over which she bent, and glistened brightly in its cup, making it more beautiful, it seemed as though the outpouring of her fresh young heart, claimed kindred with the loveliest things in nature" (Ch. xxxv). Rose bends over the flower; proximity marks their likeness, as does her name. Her physical beauty likens her to "the loveliest things in nature," but their kinship lies deeper; it is ultimately moral and spiritual as well as physical. For the 1850 edition, Dickens amended the passage to read: "the outpouring of her fresh young heart, claimed kindred naturally, with the loveliest things in nature." The addition of "naturally" makes nature explicitly double in the syntax and the idea of the sentence. Nature is both object and process, both the physical beauty of the tear and the flower and also the generative moral and emotional force of which beauty is the "outpouring"—"her fresh young heart" and the harmonious scheme underlying natural beauty. Fagin is connected metonymically with the city streets; the compound metaphor in Dickens' description of Rose points beyond the appearances of the physical world to the higher order of Providence. As the representation of good in the novel becomes transcendental, evil becomes opaque. Fagin leaves no footsteps outside the window of the Maylies' country cottage, not because he is the devil incarnate, but because within this idealized system of values his existence seems utterly unreal.

This polarization of good and evil and the resulting break in the novel's thematic and causal continuity impose a dangerous direction on the evolving narrative mode. Throughout the early chapters Oliver has been the psychological and moral center of the action. While the other characters are presented almost exclusively in a theatrical mode, their identity established only as it is indicated by their actions and appearance, Oliver's inner feelings are described directly by the narrator. And, although the narrative point of view is never entirely identified with Oliver, we perceive much of the action through the boy's eyes. The effect is to constrain the reader to sympathy with Oliver when the boy's innocent reactions to his experience contradict more sophisticated or worldly perception. As John Bayley describes the technique, "the child is *right*: there is no suggestion that his view of monsters is illusory or incomplete, and the social shock to us is that the child here is right to see things thus —the system is monstrous because he finds it to be so." In the early chapters, Oliver's innocence enables him to perceive emotional truth with a startling immediacy that exposes the hardened insensitivity to injustice and suffering of more experienced observers, both among the novel's other characters and in its assumed audience. But, as Dickens increasingly idealizes Rose and purifies Oliver in the country chapters, innocence becomes a moral authority in itself rather than simply the absence of corruption, and the shift in values threatens to dissolve the reality of the represented world. In a series of discussions of the moral influence of nature, Dickens endows the innocent mind with direct intuition of spiritual order "which no voluntary exertion of the mind can ever recall" (Ch. xxx). The physical world itself begins to become ephemeral and experience to seem an inevitable process of corruption: "The memories which peaceful country scenes call up, are not of this world, nor of its thoughts and hopes" (Ch. xxxii). As nature becomes "a foretaste of Heaven" and the novel's key symbols take on a transcendental reference, Dickens temporarily abandons representation of things "as they really are."

ROSE'S SICKNESS

This is the central imaginative crisis of the novel, and the prevailing values and symbols are challenged when Rose suddenly falls sick in the country. Although her malady has no apparent cause and her recovery only minimal consequence in the development of the plot, the incident is crucial because it marks the major turning point in narrative technique in the novel and a corresponding reorientation of the beliefs and assumptions that govern its surface order. Rose's sickness tests the sentimental trust in Providential protection of the innocent that has increasingly dominated the novel until this point, underlying the use of coincidence in the plot, the dogmatic symbolism of city and country, and the evolving morality of the narrative. The result is a changed conception of order and meaning in the world, which impels Dickens to create a new set of conventions to generate order and meaning in fiction.

The episode is organized as a moral lesson to Oliver. Initially, nature is seen as physically and spiritually beneficent; Rose has already told Oliver, "The quiet place, the pure air, and all the pleasures and beauties of spring, will restore you in a few days" (Ch. xxxii). In his description of the country landscape and the details of Oliver's recovery, Dickens has repeatedly stressed the symbolic and spiritual correspondence between the order of visible nature in the country and human nature, so that the landscape presents the physical signs of its spiritual identity with man. But when Rose suddenly falls sick—after a long walk in the country—the harmonic relationship between nature and the innocent is broken. Mrs. Maylie is nearly overcome with fear that her adopted daughter will die; she and Oliver discuss how and whether Providence will determine the outcome:

> "And consider, ma'am," said Oliver, as the tears forced themselves into his eyes, despite his efforts to the contrary; "oh! consider how young and good she is, and what pleasure and comfort she gives to all about her. I am sure—certain—quite certain—that, for your sake, who are so good yourself; and for her own: and for the sake of all she makes so happy; she will not die. Heaven will not let her die so young."

> "Hush!" said Mrs. Maylie, laying her hand on Oliver's head. "You think like a child, poor boy. But you teach me my duty, notwithstanding. I had forgotten it for a moment, Oliver, but I hope I may be pardoned, for I am old, and have seen enough of illness and death to know the agony of separation from the objects of our love. I have seen enough, too, to know that it is not always the youngest and best who are spared to those that love them; but this should give us comfort in our sorrow; for Heaven is just: and such things teach us, impressively, that there is a brighter world than this; and that passage to it is speedy." (Ch. xxxiii)

Oliver's comments have a calming, restoring effect on Mrs. Maylie, but his reliance on Providence is seen as naïve and must be corrected by a maturer wisdom. "You think like a child," Mrs. Maylie tells him, and in all editions before 1850 she adds, "and although what you say may be natural, it is wrong." His moral notions are "natural" to the innocent mind, but innocence no longer endows Oliver with direct intuition of truth. He is not "wrong" to think that there is a Providential order, but he is mistaken in believing that in the daily affairs of the world Providence necessarily protects and preserves the good. Only experience can correct "natural" morality and enable one to comprehend the moral order. Mrs. Maylie appeals to what she has seen, to the experience that leads her to regard the apparently undeserved deaths of the young and innocent as the revelation of a more distant and obscure kind of Providential order: "Such things teach us, impressively, that there is a brighter world than this." The brightness of the country landscape here is dimmed; the wisdom embodied in the mysterious ways of

Providence is no longer expressed in the harmonious landscape; it exceeds the scope of human reason and perception,
as it may violate the apparent "natural" order and the spontaneous flow of human feeling. The earlier values are now
reversed: the old, rather than the young, are seen as best capable of moral judgment, and experience replaces innocence as a moral guide. In effect, Dickens is here removing
Providence from the surface of his created world, making it
more distant from the development of plot and presentation
of symbol. And, although Rose finally does recover from her
sickness, the simpler morality with which she was earlier
associated never again controls the course of the novel.

Mrs. Maylie's discursive lesson to Oliver is repeated and
confirmed almost immediately in a symbolically dogmatic
event—Oliver witnesses the funeral of a child. Here the relationship of physical nature and human emotion becomes
discordant rather than harmonic. Dickens begins the scene
by directly contrasting the benevolent appearance of nature
and the sorrow caused by Rose's sickness: "The sun shone
brightly: as brightly as if it looked upon no misery or care;
and, with every leaf and flower in full bloom about her: with
life, and health, and sights and sounds of joy, surrounding
her on every side: the fair young creature lay, wasting fast."
The appearances of the physical world have become decep-
tive rather than symbolic; the springtime growth in nature
that engendered Oliver's recovery has no effect on Rose's
sickness and no longer corresponds to human health or
happiness. Rose, with symbols of nature's beneficence "surrounding her on every side," herself representative of the
natural order, is "wasting fast." Dickens is here dismantling
the symbolic system that previously expressed the organizing values of the novel.

OLIVER'S MISGUIDED BELIEFS

The events that immediately follow complete the rejection of
the old pattern. Oliver leaves the house where Rose lies sick
and retreats to "the old churchyard," rather than to the "deep
and pleasant shade" of the trees, which earlier defined the
country landscape. The subsequent funeral modifies both
Oliver's perception of the landscape and the morality based
on it:

> There was such peace and beauty in the scene; so much of
> brightness and mirth in the sunny landscape; such blithe-

some music in the songs of the summer birds; such freedom
in the rapid flight of the rook, careering overhead; so much of
life and joyousness in all; that when the boy raised his aching
eyes, and looked about, the thought instinctively occurred to
him, that this was not a time for death; that Rose could surely
never die when humbler things were all so glad and gay; that
graves were for cold and cheerless winter: not for sunlight
and fragrance. He almost thought that shrouds were for the
old and shrunken; and that they never wrapped the young
and graceful form within their ghastly folds.

A knell from the church bell broke harshly on these youthful
thoughts. Another! Again! It was tolling for the funeral service. A group of humble mourners entered the gate: wearing
white favours; for the corpse was young. They stood uncov-
ered by a grave; and there was a mother: a mother once:
among the weeping train. But the sun shone brightly, and the
birds sang on.   (Ch. xxxiii)

Here again the symbolic correspondence between nature
and human emotion is broken; again Oliver's naïve belief in
such a harmonic pattern is shown to be inadequate. Dickens
moves from description of the "brightness and mirth of the
sunny landscape" through the thoughts it inspires in Oliver
to the event that proves the boy's thoughts and feelings mis-
guided. The sight of the child's funeral demonstrates that the
"blithesome music in the songs of the summer birds" is
delusive; Oliver is wrong to think "that graves were for cold
and cheerless winter." The events recapitulate Mrs. Maylie's
lesson to Oliver earlier in the chapter, and again Dickens or-
ganizes the passage to emphasize the shortcomings of
Oliver's understanding. The crucial idea is that "these youthful thoughts"—Oliver's childish trust that Providence is directly evident in physical nature—are rooted "instinctively"
in his own nature. Earlier in the novel Oliver's instinctive
perception enabled him to perceive spiritual truth analogi-
cally, but his innocence now restricts him to the surface, to
whatever is presently visible in the misleading physical
world. Dickens reverses himself; he is here rejecting not
only Oliver's childish beliefs but also the conception of human character that previously motivated the plot and the
morality of innocence that justified it.

A CHANGING NARRATIVE MODE

Oliver returns from the graveyard to learn that Rose will live,
but the juxtaposition of the unnamed child's death with her
recovery prevents any renewed confidence in the om-

nipresent beneficence of Providence or the sympathetic harmony of man and nature. The relationships of God, nature, and human consciousness within the narrative world have changed irretrievably, and Dickens must now create a new kind of narration to represent this modified conception of truth and the conditions under which it can be understood. The work begins immediately; during Rose's recovery, Oliver's perception of the landscape changes yet again:

> The birds were once more hung out, to sing, in their old places; and the sweetest wild flowers that could be found, were once more gathered to gladden Rose with their beauty and fragrance. The melancholy which had seemed to the sad eyes of the anxious boy to hang, for days past, over every object: beautiful as all were: was dispelled by magic. The dew seemed to sparkle more brightly on the green leaves; the air to rustle among them with a sweeter music; and the sky itself to look more blue and bright. Such is the influence which the condition of our own thoughts, exercises, even over the appearance of external objects. Men who look on nature, and their fellow-men, and cry that all is dark and gloomy, are in the right; but the sombre colours are reflections from their own jaundiced eyes and hearts. The real hues are delicate, and need a clearer vision.   (Ch. xxxiv)

The "blithesome music in the songs of the summer birds . . . careering overhead" is now replaced by the song of the caged birds, "hung out, to sing, in their old places," and the "freedom in the rapid flight of the rook" is sacrificed for the "wild flowers" that are gathered and brought inside. The symbolic congress between man and nature becomes much more limited here; the flowers, cut from their natural setting, no longer grow—they can "gladden" Rose but they do not heal her. Nature is no longer directly responsive to human emotion, and the changing beauty in "the appearance of external objects" now only seems real—it is rooted in the characters' minds rather than in the narrative conventions. Oliver's perception has become unreliable; the narrator must go beyond the limits of what the boy sees or thinks to disclose "the real hues." Robert A. Colby has interpreted this passage as an unsuccessful attempt to resolve the "tension between the tender-minded and the tough-minded Dickens," arguing that "the world of darkness" in the novel is convincing while "The idyllic country scenes remain a roseate blur." Although Colby's view adequately characterizes the first half of *Oliver Twist*, he misreads this passage by overlooking its place in the context of the novel. Dickens does not affirm "delicate hues" against "darkness" in the way that Colby suggests; he acknowledges the presence of both light and dark in "the real hues," which are "delicate" in the sense of subtle, rather than "roseate" or "tender." Dickens here abandons the moral simplifications inherent in the previous course of the novel in both the idealized countryside and the "sombre colours" of the city, in both "bright eyes" and "jaundiced." The passage represents a moral reorientation, which requires a transformation of narrative method. The polarized values produced by the symbolic "principle" of the first half of the novel have broken down, and Dickens now attempts to develop a mode of narration capable of embodying "a clearer vision."

A MORE COMPLEX REALITY

Almost immediately the expository control and moral authority of the narrator are sharply diminished. Harry Maylie's theatrical rhetoric absorbs the occasional exclamatory piety of the narrator's voice, and Noah Claypole is used for several chapters as a mediating observer to stifle the moralizing impulse. But the major changes result from the altered status of the world of appearances—no longer does visible nature provide a system of absolute correlatives to human feeling, and no longer does a character's appearance fully indicate his internal nature or his role in Providential design. So the sources of the narrator's earlier moral and metaphysical certainty have been eroded; the narrative voice is more closely restricted to the limits of human "vision" in a world where "the real hues are delicate" and difficult to perceive. Oliver disappears for almost the entire remaining course of the novel because the earlier mode of narration, based on the moral primacy of innocence, can no longer render the truth in the more complex reality Dickens now presents. The single controlling view of the earlier narrator is relinquished for the numerous more limited perspectives of the characters, which in their diversity define and convey the difficulty of moral judgment in a world where Providence is inscrutable and "our common nature" becomes "a contradiction, an anomaly, an apparent impossibility"— "but it is a truth" (Preface).

The change in narrative mode is accompanied by modification of the organizing principles that shape the progression of the story. After Rose's recovery, Monks's purchase of the locket that establishes Oliver's identity confirms that the boy belongs to another "station in society" by birth. Oliver has entirely ceased to be the parish boy and remains safe with his patrons from this point on; the novel's thematic concern with the impact of social injustice on the poor and homeless is now buried beneath the surface development of the plot. Continuity is no longer supplied by Oliver's movement, but by Nancy, who becomes central to the thematic development; Rose and Sikes contest her loyalty, as earlier Fagin and Brownlow competed for control of Oliver. And while the sustained comparison of Nancy and Rose reinforces the original thematic conflict of nature and experience, the supporting pattern of analogy between their social classes narrows to the two girls alone. The plot degenerates into the melodramatic contrivances necessary to the final revelation of Oliver's identity and "the principle of Good triumphing at last."

The Surreal World in *Oliver Twist*

Mary Rohrberger

Mary Rohrberger quotes the works of various surrealists—and many critics of Dickens—as she describes the surrealistic nature of *Oliver Twist*, in
which good and evil are "inextricably mingled." As
evidence, Rohrberger argues that Dickens uses both
the nightmare and the daydream—symbolized, respectively, by Fagin's filthy and utterly grim underworld and by the peaceful security emblematic of the
Maylie-Brownlow world—as vehicles that structure
the novel and provide cohesion. Rohrberger, a professor of English, has written extensively on various
authors and their fiction.

It is difficult to quarrel overmuch with Taylor Stoehr's argument presented in *Dickens: The Dreamer's Stance* that Dickens is neither "realist nor fantasist, but something in between." Dickens' works, Stoehr says, are not an amalgam of
realism, naturalism and symbolism, but rather his literary
manner is "a kind in itself," a blend that is "dream-like, hal-
lucinatory, super-real." Yet, Stoehr will not call Dickens a
surrealist, because, as he says, "most surrealists consciously
imitate dreams (or think they do) and Dickens rarely does
this." A conscious imitation of dreams, however, is bound to
fail. Stoehr knows this. Dreams, themselves, he says, "are
completely unavailable to conscious thought." Thus, proponents of surrealism, all conscious that they were proponents
of surrealism, tried consciously to tap the unconscious,
some using hunger or drug-induced trances, some automatic writing. A difference seems to be that Dickens unconsciously tapped the unconscious. Stoehr says: "The evidence
for something close to 'automatic writing' in Dickens is quite
full." George Henry Lewes reported that Dickens said to him

Excerpted from "The Daydream and the Nightmare: Surreality in *Oliver Twist*," by
Mary Rohrberger, *Studies in the Humanities*, March 1978. Reprinted with permission.

that every word said by his characters was distinctly heard by Dickens. "He was a seer of visions; and his visions were of objects at once familiar and potent." John Forster quotes Dickens: "I don't invent it—really do not—*but see it,* and write it down." Still, Stoehr insists that Dickens' work is not surrealistic, finally basing his argument in the following:

> But surrealists try to do more than tell their dreams; most often, they want to recreate them. Accordingly, the marked effects of surrealist art reside not so much in the rare successes in producing feelings akin to those we have in dreams, but instead in the failures, which remind us of what dreams are like by a kind of negative implication; the groping work of art seems so strange, so mechanically unreal, rather like our memories of dreams, which never quite suit us though we are at a loss to say why.

I have difficulty in understanding this. It seems as though Stoehr is saying that for a work to be really surrealistic it must be a failure, a proposition certainly antithetical to surrealist goals, which were, as Anna Balakian puts it, to "seize and identify the metaphysical with life *here* and *now* and resituate the imaginary not as the antinomy of the real but as its nucleus. Reality, then, in its dynamic sense proceeding from an interior state, nurtured by what we call imagination, and brought to an exterior existence through the capture of dreams or subconscious verbalization, is what Breton calls the 'surreal.'" The theoretical principle of automatic writing was proposed by Andre Breton as a metaphorical way of suggesting the possibility of multiple means of attaining psychological release and expression, but to a single end: the identification of the esthetic vision with the dream state. It is surely a mistake, as Paul Ilie points out, to refuse to call a writer a surrealist unless he has made a conscious effort to imitate dreams or to imitate other surrealists, especially if, as it seems to me, the work conforms to almost every esthetic pronouncement made by Breton and by subsequent students of the surreal.

But does it really matter whether we call Dickens' work surreal or avoid the term? It is clear, as Stoehr points out, that Dickens' esthetic vision is identified with the dream state. I think it does matter. With the characteristics of surreality in mind, one can avoid judgments that condemn such early works as *Oliver Twist* for inconsistency and bifurcation, or that lead to specious arguments that say, for example, that the coincidences are not coincidences at all since everybody in the novel is related to Oliver and "where there is no accidental population, no encounter can be called a coincidence."

A SURREAL WORK

In this paper I intend to treat *Oliver Twist* as a surreal work, focusing especially on Dickens' use of the daydream and the nightmare as vehicles that structure the novel and provide inner consistency. In doing so, I will make use not only of many of the theories provided by Stoehr and insights presented by such important critics as J. Hillis Miller, Steven Marcus, James R. Kincaid, John Carey, and H.M. Daleski, but also of the writings of Andre Breton, Freud, Ernest Jones, Bergson, and such able students of surrealism as Anna Balakian, Mary Ann Caws, Maurice Nadeau, Paul Ilie, and Nahma Sandrow.

Most critics agree that the major tension in the novel, at least on the surface, is provided by an alternating pull on Oliver by what amounts to two separate worlds—that of the Society of Thieves and what it represents and that of the Maylie/Brownlow group and what it represents—the two forming an apparent duality (the dark and the light), which I here call the nightmare and the daydream. "At the deepest imaginative level," writes J. Hillis Miller, "the London of *Oliver Twist* is no longer a realistic description of the unsanitary London of the thirties but is the dream or poetic symbol of an infernal labyrinth, inhabited by the devil himself. The country world is the reverse of the city world, a place of tranquil repose and order. But Oliver does not get to London until Chapter VIII, and he does not get to the Maylies until Chapter XXVIII. Nevertheless, the tensions have been estab lished and are presaged by Oliver's experiences from the moment of his birth.

The first few paragraphs of the novel establish the terms of the metaphor, which is thereafter used continuously, as images and actions increase and cluster, creating a montage wherein, as Stoehr says, speaking generally of Dickens' rhetoric, "a single image from the cluster can call the whole cluster to mind." In the first paragraph of the novel, Oliver is defined as an "item of mortality," and in the third paragraph, the narrator comments: "The fact is, there was considerable difficulty in inducing Oliver to take upon himself the office of respiration." From these phrases derives the nucleus of one aspect of the metaphor—death, death by lack of air. For some time the infant lies gasping for breath, "poised between this world and the next," until finally the child breathes, sneezes, and sets up a loud cry. At least for a while, then, the life force dominates, and Oliver survives to his ninth birthday which, the narrator tells us, he was keeping in the coal cellar. At this point Oliver enters the world of the workhouse, whose dimensions are similar to those of the coal cellar and whose walls begin to close on him.

Desperate with hunger and reckless with misery, he accepts the lot that falls to him and asks for more food. The response, "That boy will be hung . . . I know that boy will be hung" (Chapter II), picks up the motif begun in the third paragraph of the novel and offers a variation of it that will recur throughout the novel with a constant and rhythmic movement—references to hanging, strangling, suffocation, smothering. Once again, Oliver is confined to a back room where he cries all day and crouches close to the wall, seeking its protection.

NIGHTMARISH IMAGERY

Gamfield, the chimney sweep, is the first to presage Fagin, Sowerberry, the second. Both are associated with death and terrifying confinement. Fire, smoke, and heat imagery surrounds Gamfield. At Sowerberry's Oliver is put to bed among the coffins. The cellar is dank, dark, specter-ridden. It is a miniature of the town outside—a nightmare village whose streets are crowded, narrow, dirty, close. The shop fronts are facades, hiding filth, age, and decay. London, also, is a nightmare city, the streets labyrinths, muddy, odorous. Fagin's lair is bleak with age and dirt, Fagin, an archetypal devil figure with matted red hair. He is seen first tending a fire with a toasting fork in hand, an infernal vision. Later, as the Jew gloats over his treasures, he becomes a personification, raised to a mythical level, of all of Oliver's terrifying experiences. The chase scene that follows, where people pursue Oliver calling, "Stop thief," is the first of many that recur as variations on the same theme. The Society of Thieves is a brotherhood, a family where Oliver picks up a father, a mother/sister, and a host of brother surrogates.

The nightmare presented is that of a strange and disturbing world. Concomitant sensations of uncanniness, incongruity, and absurdity abound. Breton says that it is perhaps childhood that comes closest to "real life," thus delineating a surreal perspective. Seen from Oliver's view, the adults around him are towering grotesques existing on dissimilar planes of reality. Early references to fattening Oliver up so that he may be eaten; Sowerberry's question to Oliver after his first funeral, "Well, Oliver . . . how do you like it?"; the nonsense with Bumble and Mrs. Mann; the combined fantasy of Charlotte, Mrs. Sowerberry, and Noah that Oliver can kick down the dust cellar door and murder them all; the "curious game" played by the "merry old gentleman,"—all of these are among many incidents that create a black humor and an accompanying psychological disassociation, a technique that Dickens continues through the novel. Oliver's passive role throughout is another mark of the nightmare quality. Ernest Jones writes that a typical feature of the nightmare is "the utter powerlessness, amounting to a feeling of complete paralysis, which is the only response of the organism to the agonizing effort that it makes to relieve itself of the choking oppression."

THE DEATH WISH

But the nightmare is not the only dream state that Dickens creates in the opening chapters of the novel. From the beginning there is another condition carefully associated with Oliver—Oliver in a state halfway between dream and reality, desiring death for the peace and order it represents, Oliver seeking the protection of walls, a protection, perhaps, not unlike that his mother provided him before his birth. At Sowerberry's the first overt expression of the death wish occurs: ". . . and he wished, as he crept into his narrow bed, that that were his coffin, and that he could be lain in a calm and lasting sleep in the churchyard ground, with the tall grass waving gently above his head, and the sound of the old deep bell to soothe him in his sleep" (Chapter V). The first morning at Fagin's, Oliver is clearly in a hypnogogic state:

> There is a drowsy state, between sleeping and waking, when you dream more in five minutes with your eyes half opened and yourself half conscious of everything that is passing around you, than you would in five nights with your eyes fast closed and your senses wrapt in a perfect unconsciousness. At such times a mortal knows just enough of what his mind is doing, to form some glimmering conception of its mighty powers, its bounding from earth and spurning time and space, when freed from the restraint of its corporeal associate. (Chapter IX)

Conditions similar to this often accompany Oliver as he passes from one plane of reality to another. The movement from the magistrate's court to Brownlow's house is accompanied by fainting, coma, a prolonged period of restless waking and sleeping, and then a deep and tranquil sleep, "that calm and peaceful rest." This sleep Dickens likens to death, and again the death wish is made manifest: "Who, if this were death, would be roused again?" (Chapter XII). The movement to the Maylies again finds Oliver fainting and brought in unconscious, where he experiences memories of a happier existence—"long gone by . . . which no voluntary exertion of the mind can ever recall" (Chapter XXX). That night Miss Maylie and Rose soothe him. "He felt calm and happy, and could have died without a murmer" (Chapter XXX).

THE DAYDREAM WORLD

With these kinds of transitions Dickens moves Oliver out of the nightmare world to the daydream world, where conditions of wish-fulfillment exist, where Oliver can find his inheritance and live happily ever after in houses large and airy or in the country-side, where he can roam through or work in the garden, where there is enough to eat, and where kind hands soothe and protect him. Here he finds another surrogate family—father, mother, sister, brother. All is apparent peace, order, cleanliness, sweet fragrance.

At first glance it seems there is a clear separation between the nightmare and the daydream worlds. Steven Marcus makes the point: "But *Oliver Twist* cannot be accused of rendering virtue and vice indistinguishable from each other. Rather, it seems to do the reverse, and makes the line of demarcation between them so distinct that goodness and wickedness seem to live in quite separate regions where commerce with each other is at best minimal." There are, nevertheless, ambiguities present that call for reconsideration of such a view. James R. Kincaid, for example, identifies the "bad" people with life and laughter, the "good" people with death and tears. "The one vigorous and persuasive life force in the novel," he continues, "in fact, is centered in Fagin." "The Maylie-Brownlow group are in every way the antithesis of the comic dedication to life." Even Marcus writes: "Nevertheless, this escape from society into an idealized, non-existent little society" a refuge in the country where it is almost impossible to imagine how life goes on, is the least satisfactory part of the novel." But whether one sees a clear line of separation where, as H.M. Daleski says, "the opposed images of home and street are the novel's main analogues," or a situation where the "good" become the "bad," and the "bad," "good," the images are still seen as antithetical. As John Carey says: "It is a leading characteristic of Dickens' mind that he is able to see almost everything from two opposed points of view."

RECONCILIATION OF OPPOSITES

But the basic drive of the surrealist is toward a reconciliation of opposites, toward what Hegel formulated in the thesis-antithesis synthesis and what Bergson spoke of when he said:

> There is hardly any concrete reality which cannot be observed from two opposing standpoints. . . . Hence a thesis and an antithesis which we endeavor in vain to reconcile logically. . . . But from the object, seized by intuition, we pass easily in many cases to the two contrary concepts; and as in that way thesis and antithesis can be seen to spring from reality, we grasp at the same time how it is that the two are opposed and how they are reconciled.

Breton, too, interpreted the surrealistic ideal as the dialectical reconciliation of antitheses and, further, as the reconciliation of perception and representation. it is in this latter area that we must move to perceive the two worlds, not as clearly separate or as separate and reversed, but rather as merged.

In the novel Dickens, speaking to a principle of structure involving a regular alternation of tragic and comic scenes, compares them to "the layers of red and white in a side of streaky bacon," of absurd and apparently unnatural changes and violent transitions, or sudden shiftings of time and place as being part of the "great art of authorship" (Chapter XVII). Miller speaks of past and present being superimposed in the dream episodes and "inextricably mingled." Stoehr says that Dickens' works are each "a cosmos everywhere interdependent"; each is "an interlocking system," "an elaborate structural synecdoche." What it gets down to, I believe, is a vision created by montage, a simultaneity and superimposition of images that juxtapose the nightmare and the daydream in such a way that they are seen to be not opposed but reconciled, not different but the same.

OLIVER'S ROOTS

Oliver is a bastard. As Marcus puts it: "The vindication of his illegitimacy is the event toward which the entire novel is directed." His problem, then, is in being born, in the particular conditions of his birth. A taint is with him from the beginning, and it is a taint deriving from the so-called "good" people, not the "evil" ones. In his youth Oliver's father was coerced into a wretched marriage to satisfy family pride and ambition. From this union comes a son, Monks, whose evil nature seems to be a product of the misery and torment arising from the "unholy" marriage, but a marriage, which, nevertheless, carries with it legal sanction. The later liaison of Oliver's father with Agnes is a union of love, a "holy" contract, but one which has no legal sanction and carries with it society's disapprobation, a condemnation so strong that Agnes' family goes into exile, Agnes leaves home to give birth to Oliver in the situation that begins the novel, and Rose carries with her the stigma of illegitimacy which makes it impossible for her to consent to marry Harry Maylie until after her birthright is established and, even then, after Harry decides to give up his worldly ambitions for life in a peaceful country parsonage. Oliver's father is a close friend of Mr. Brownlow; even more, he is the brother of the woman Brownlow almost married. Brownlow acts as a father surrogate to Oliver and later adopts him. The conditions, then, which give rise to Oliver's predicament are those created by the society in which the Leefords and the Brownlows and the Maylies reside. The "family" that Oliver is left with in the end are remnants of the original group—for father there is Brownlow; for mother, the sister/aunt, Rose; for older brother, Harry. Or, seen in another possible grouping, Mr. Brownlow and Mrs. Maylie become doting grandparents, Rose, the youthful mother Oliver remembers from his infancy, and Harry, the father, untainted by ambition and the need for worldly goods. At the end all are in the country, shielding Oliver, and themselves shielded from any sight of London, whose labyrinthine streets harbor those less fortunate.

But the horror is still there. For the reader it is unabated. It is around a corner, just down the block, at every turn. One need only close one's eyes, and almost by magic Fagin emerges, still alive, and Nancy, and Sikes, and the "artful dodger." More alive. As Kincaid says: "In the end, *Oliver Twist* comes near to making orphans of us all by dislocating us from the world we are comfortable in." "The morally approved people in the novel, including Oliver when he is with them, exist on the edge of the grave." They have shut their eyes, but unlike the reader, they do not see.

FAGIN'S WORLD

Miller says that Fagin and his gang provide for Oliver the parody of a home. But parody or not, it is all they have. The family Oliver gathers here—father, mother/sister, older brother—are multidimensional, existing on several levels of reality simultaneously. On the one hand, they are corrupt men, beasts of the wild, living in dens of sin. Fagin is, also, the archetypal devil, presiding over the darkness and the fire, the motivating force and the first cause of the evil in the souls of men and objectified in the action of Sikes. Still, they are also innocents, orphans of society, living the only way they can on a crazy course from workhouse to the gallows by way of Jacob's Island. And they live their lighter moments with a comic verve and authenticity deriving from a full knowledge of the conditions of life. Their eyes are open and they do see. By means of his fire Fagin feeds them. The "curious game" played by the "merry old gentleman" with Charley Bates and the "artful dodger" is so funny as to cause Oliver to laugh until tears run down his face. Knowingly, they threaten each other with hanging, often acted out in dumb show. The book that Fagin gives Oliver to read, with its pages soiled and thumbed with use, is a history of the lives and trials of great criminals. It suggests the secret guilt of all men, its words sounding in Oliver's ears "as if they were whispered, in hollow murmers, by the spirits of the dead" (Chapter XX).

There is a relationship established between Oliver and Fagin stronger than can be easily explained, one that begins in secret intercourse when Oliver awakens to find Fagin gloating over his treasures and ends with Oliver taking the first few steps with Fagin on his way to the gallows. It is as though somehow Oliver is a part of Fagin and Fagin a part of Oliver, each inhabiting the other's dreams. Fagin's feelings toward Oliver are ambivalent. At the end, his mind wandering, Fagin cries out: "Take that boy away to bed. . . . Take him away to bed. . . . He has been the—the—somehow the cause of all this" (Chapter LII). And, indeed, he has. The child exile, innocent, homeless, he is as they all started, and his presence is a constant reminder of what they were and what they became. "What right have they to butcher me?" Fagin cries out. In a world where criminality is the mode of exchange, people become criminals to survive, but lurking still somewhere within each one is the innocent child, like Oliver, incapable of doing anything for himself, needing a home, love, and care. The woman, Nancy, openly admits the feeling, giving her life to save Oliver. The men fight it. Sikes, beloved of Nancy, murders her to deny it. Fagin goes to his death, alternately a broken and whimpering old man and a fiercely aggressive one. "Strike them all dead," he speaks in rage and terror. As Kincaid points out, at the end Oliver may no longer be a victim, but there are plenty of victims around, and to them the "good" people are enemies.

What we have, then, in *Oliver Twist* is a situation where characters are not "good" or "evil" but where these qualities are inextricably mingled. It is a situation where apparent dualities are seen to merge—not only good and evil, but also the comic and the tragic and life and death. In dying, Fagin lives; in living, Oliver dies. The happy-ever-after world merges with its nether side, the dark and labyrinthine world.

Oliver Twist: A Purposeful Plot

Monroe Engel

Oliver Twist was originally published in monthly serial form in relatively short installments. The result, according to Monroe Engel, is a plot that is purposeful and economical, marked by brisk narrative and bereft of elaborate subplots. Within this concentrated form, writes Engel, Dickens paints a vivid picture of the condemned world inhabited by Oliver Twist, and, more specifically, the connection between poverty and criminal depravity. The following critical essay is excerpted from Engel's book *The Maturity of Dickens*.

In the corpus of Dickens' novels, there is none—with the possible exception of *Hard Times*—more purposeful than *Oliver Twist*, which starts with a birth in a workhouse and ends (excepting the conventional last summary chapter) with the hanging of Fagin. These are the general subjects between which the story moves: poverty and crime, and the connections between them. In its purposeful coherence, *Oliver Twist* is at a far remove from *The Pickwick Papers*. Since it was begun, however, when Dickens was little more than half finished with *Pickwick*, the contrast is peculiarly interesting. But to make sense of the contrast, allowance must be made first for the imposed differences.

SIMULTANEOUS NOVELS

The Pickwick Papers was written for publication in twenty individual monthly parts. This was to become Dickens' favorite and most frequently used form of publication. *Oliver Twist*, however, was to appear serially in *Bentley's Magazine* (a monthly), in relatively short installments, surrounded of course by other fiction and articles. It was to be roughly half the length of *The Pickwick Papers*, and to be published in shortish stretches, and would require special coherence to distinguish it from the other material with which it appeared.

In addition to noting these facts of difference, it is tempting to make certain speculations. Writing two novels simultaneously and at great speed, Dickens might well have required gross difference to keep his own mind and imagination clear. Moreover, he commenced *Oliver Twist* at more or less the time that he was discovering the function of plot in *The Pickwick Papers,* and he may have wished for the chance to make some fuller exploitation of plot, to write a novel whose parts were consequent as well as sequent.

But the form of this shorter novel designed for magazine publication seemed to Dickens himself to impose certain limitations and difficulties. *Hard Times, Great Expectations,* and *A Tale of Two Cities* are written in roughly the same form, and have certain characteristics in common with *Oliver Twist,* but for them the difficulties were even greater because the parts appeared weekly rather than monthly. The 20 part novel Dickens associated with "the large canvas and the big brushes," and he complained once to Forster of the "crushing" difficulty of the shorter-type novel for a writer who had "had an experience of patient fiction-writing with some elbow-room always, and open places in perspective."

But how, specifically, does this difference evidence itself to the reader? In an edition of Dickens in which *The Pickwick Papers* is 968 pages long, *Oliver Twist* is 510 pages long —roughly 2:1. *Pickwick* is divided into 57 chapters averaging 17 pages each. *Oliver Twist* has 53 chapters—only four less —but they average a little under 10 pages each. Since the chapter is, by and large, a genuine unit for Dickens, the difference between a chapter of 17 pages and a chapter of 10 pages suggests a radically different pace of narration.

For example, *The Pickwick Papers* begins with "the perusal of the following entry in the Transactions of the Pickwick Club, which the editor of these papers feels the highest pleasure in laying before his readers, as a proof of the careful attention, indefatigable assiduity, and nice discrimination, with which his search among the multifarious documents confided to him has been conducted." There follows a pompous, windy, circumlocutory account of the resolution to form The Corresponding Society of the Pickwick Club; a florid description of Pickwick himself; an account in indirect discourse of a speech by Pickwick; also of a petty altercation between Pickwick and Mr. Blatton of Aldgate. Everything about this suggests leisure, not least of all the indirect discourse in which a good part of it is cast. The personal qualities that the "editor of these papers" boasts of or lays claim to also promise leisure: the "careful attention, indefatigable assiduity, and nice discrimination" brought to bear on these "multifarious documents."

BRISK NARRATIVE

The chapter of roughly four pages that begins *Oliver Twist* is in marked contrast. Oliver's birth in a workhouse is recorded in the first paragraph. The briskness of the narrative is not so much seen or felt as insisted on when Dickens tells us, for example, that it will be prudent to omit the real name of the town in which the workhouse is located and that he will not bother to assign it a fictitious name, any more than he will bother to give the day and date of the event, since they do not matter; or that he will not take time to repeat Oliver's name, referring to him instead, to save time, as "the item of mortality whose name is prefixed to the head of this chapter." In this first paragraph, more space is spent in talk about saving space than in anything else. Yet, funny as this may be, it does tend to prepare the reader for the genuine speed with which things are to happen. Oliver's mother dies on page 3, and on page 4 we get a suggestion of her general history as an unwed mother. In these four pages, too, we are given an attitude toward the workhouse and public care of paupers, and a considerable amount of specific detail about these facilities. Three pages farther on, Oliver is nine years old. The novel moves swiftly throughout, though not at this pace, of course, or it would be close to the ideal of brevity Dickens suggests on page 1—a novel about a hero who dies at birth.

AN ECONOMICAL PLOT

The plot of *Oliver Twist*, too, is conceived and handled economically, proceeding pretty much on the single strand of Oliver's adventures and misadventures, with no elaborately divergent subplots, and not much more attention to the lives and idiosyncrasies of the other characters than is necessary to bring them into Oliver's story with force. The purposefulness of *Oliver Twist* gives it its power, its unrelenting grasp on what Dickens would have called its "truth," the connection between misery and the criminal life. Oliver Twist begins his life in misery enough—orphaned, underfed, unloved, beaten, apprenticed in time to an undertaking establishment where he is bullied, fed the scraps the dog scorns, and made to sleep in the shop with the coffins at night. Finally, when his mother's memory is insulted, he rebels and runs away to London, carrying with him his total means: the torn clothes on his back, an extra shirt, two pairs of darned stockings, a crust of bread, and a penny. When he reaches the outskirts of London, he is seen by the Artful Dodger, who, being a considerable social philosopher, knows that his starving bedraggled condition makes him a likely candidate for Fagin's gang of pickpockets and thieves. For it is the criminals themselves who—generally without sentimentality, simply as recognition of the way things work —know best the roots and causes of crime. Even Bill Sikes, who is not notably intellectual, knows them in his own way:

> "I want a boy, and he musn't be a big un. Lord! . . . if I'd only got that young boy of Ned, the chimbley-sweeper's! He kept him small on purpose, and let him out by the job. But the father gets lagged; and then the Juvenile Delinquent Society comes, and takes the boy away from a trade where he was arning money, teaches him to read and write, and in time makes a 'prentice out of him. And so they go on, . . . so they go on; and, if they'd got money enough (which it's a Providence they haven't), we shouldn't have half-a-dozen boys left in the whole trade, in a year or two."

Misery is not a matter of conjecture for Dickens, but a terrible presence. It means, for example, the "bleak, dark, and piercing cold," when "the homeless, starving wretch" has little to do but "lay him down and die. Many hunger-worn outcasts close their eyes in our bare streets, at such times, who, let their crimes have been what they may, can hardly open them in a more bitter world." Following Oliver on the job with the undertaker Sowerberry, the reader gets a vivid picture of what Dickens means by misery—the dreadful deprivation of food, shelter, medical care, creature comfort, the deprivation in fact of all the social mitigations that man can muster against the awful, immitigable fact of mortality. Sometimes Dickens' sense of the real situation falters or grows dim in its details and applications, and produces pathos, as when Oliver says farewell to the orphan Dick, or when Dick's dying request is to give his "dear love to poor Oliver Twist." These moments are comparatively few, though, and do not much damage the genuine vision of a misery sufficiently desperate to make a boy wish for the calm sleep of death, or to drive him into depravity.

But it is clear that Dickens does not mean that the depraved are not responsible for their depravity, that they are simply victims of their misery. Oliver, after all, despite his misery and the pressures brought upon him by Fagin and his gang, retains his innocence and even does no wrong, whereas Monks does evil not because he has been forced to evil, but because he is a corrupt man. Dickens believes that there is innate evil and innate goodness, and that true innocence is in some way its own defense. Not even Fagin is unsusceptible to Oliver's innocence, and it is significant for the moral strategy of the novel that Monks and Oliver are half-brothers.

HIDEOUS REALISM

In his Preface to *Oliver Twist,* Dickens says part of his purpose was to paint a picture of criminal life so realistically unattractive that it would throw no false romance about crime, and might even serve as a deterrent to the life of crime:

> It appeared to me that to draw a knot of such associates in crime as really did exist; to paint them in all their deformity, in all their wretchedness, in all the squalid misery of their lives; to show them as they really were, for ever skulking uneasily through the dirtiest paths of life, with the great black ghostly gallows closing up their prospect, turn them where they might; it appeared to me that to do this, would be to attempt a something which was needed, and which would be a service to society. And I did it as I best could.

This statement was made primarily as a defense against the charge that the book's realism was offensive, and as such no modern reader will quarrel with it. The modern complaint is more likely to be that Dickens is not realistic enough. But in any broader context, is this protest of intentions quite convincing? Isn't Dickens, as Edmund Wilson has so illuminatingly argued, fascinated as well as revolted by depravity? The answer to the question at its crudest is quite clear: there is no simple, exclusive revulsion in Dickens' view of criminals. Nor is there much doubt that to some extent at least this ambiguous point of view is prerational or subconscious. But Dickens is a far more rational, controlled writer than is generally allowed, and the ambiguous view and role of the criminal in *Oliver Twist* is in good part rational and intended, and is related to and serves his general view of his society.

The view of institutional society in *Oliver Twist* is clear enough—the view of the police and courts, the workhouse and parish administration, the House of Commons in which Harry Maylie must give up his ambitions in order to marry Rose Fleming. Institutional society is immoral, inefficient, stupid, unfeeling, and—perhaps worst of all, aesthetically—unheroic. Wherever institutions touch, people are corrupted, acquiring a corporate, collective, or administrative view of life, rather than an individual humane view.

THE CRIMINAL WORLD

The criminal in *Oliver Twist* is not simply the enemy of institutional society—of the police, the courts, the lawmakers. He is also in some degree heroic and guided by a peculiar, limited moral code. He is part too of a society whose common members at least are quick, spontaneous, fun-loving, and convivial. To get the significance of this last consideration, compare the mean cheerlessness of the workhouse, or the undertaker's shop, with the first view of the thieves' den with its easygoing, fraternal shelter, and Fagin himself preparing a generous meal of sausage for everybody, of which Oliver is at once invited to partake. The horseplay is rough but largely good-humored. Even Fagin's school for pickpockets is conducted like a stylized game, and his constant and sinister use of the phrase "my dear" has a color of affection to it, perverted though it be, completely lacking from the cold ministrations of Bumble or Mrs. Mann.

The courage of the thieves is at its least a brilliant bravado. This is most immediately apparent in the language of the Artful Dodger, John Dawkins, another one of those brilliant eccentric languages that Dickens creates, reminiscent in originality and energy of the language of the Wellers and Alfred jingle. His bravado before the court, for example, is moving because it is in the face of heavy consequences. The point is not only that the criminals are threatened by death, but that they are all of them, even the most hardened, aware of the imminence of this threat almost all the time. When Sikes and Nancy have abducted Oliver and are hurrying him to Fagin's, they hear the bell sounding from the jail:

> "Eight o'clock, Bill," said Nancy, when the bell ceased.

> "What's the good of telling me that; I can hear it, can't I?" replied Sikes.

"I wonder whether *they* can hear it," said Nancy.

"Of course they can," replied Sikes. "It was Bartlemy time when I was shopped; and there warn't a penny trumpet in the fair, as I couldn't hear the squeaking on. Arter I was locked up for the night, the row and din outside made the thundering old jail so silent, that I could almost have beat my brains out against the iron plates of the door."

"Poor fellows!" said Nancy, who still had her face turned towards the quarter in which the bell had sounded. "Oh, Bill, such fine young chaps as them!"

"Yes; that's all you women think of," answered Sikes. "Fine young chaps! Well, they're as good as dead, so it don't much matter."

Bravado with this consciousness becomes something more profound.

In the Preface, Dickens says too that he does not want to make the thieves' world seem glamorous as it does in Gay's *Beggar's Opera,* and the romantic glamor that Gay employs with Macheath and Polly is certainly absent from *Oliver Twist*—is, specifically, no part of the relationship of Nancy and Sikes. But it is a related world nonetheless that Dickens pictures, where the thieves, in danger from the law and from the leaders in their own hierarchy both, are part of a rapacious society in which every man is alone and there is neither order nor kindness. For Dickens' interest in the thieves' world is at least as much political as neurotic, part of the subversive view of English society that he seems to have held always, and held with increasing strength and consciousness as he grew older. *Oliver Twist* is a novel about society, as all of Dickens' novels that follow are too, and as even *The Pickwick Papers* became before it was finished. We move out from the child in the workhouse in a nameless town to the world at large, and to a picture of the terror of life against which society offers not even the few comforts it could. At the end of *Oliver Twist,* Dickens effects one of those savings of character from type that are his tribute to the complexity of life. For even Fagin, in his cell, is human, mortal, alone, and afraid.

Oliver Twist: Dickens's Portrait of a Cruel World

Edgar Johnson

Edgar Johnson writes that although the plot of *Oliver Twist* is melodramatic and contrived, Dickens's lurid descriptions of the coldhearted workhouse and the depraved criminal underworld are praiseworthy because they convey the hideous reality of Dickens's time. Yet while many passages are indeed drawn from observed reality, Johnson does not consider Dickens an uncompromising naturalist. Rather, Dickens sought to "move the heart rather than turn the stomach." To this end, Dickens toned down the gritty realism in his narrative by fusing realism, drama, pathos, and even laughter into his study of the cruel system compelling paupers to the criminal slum world. The following is excerpted from Johnson's book *Charles Dickens: His Tragedy and Triumph.*

The three novels with which Dickens had now established his literary eminence all glow with his characteristic endowments. They are bursting with vitality. *Pickwick Papers* had swiftly ripened to an affectionate hilarity that made Dickens a master of luminous humor unexampled by any writer since Shakespeare. *Oliver Twist* blazes with a sulphurous melodrama in which horror is fused with angry pathos. *Nicholas Nickleby* mingles the indignation of *Oliver* with the loose, sprawling comedy of *Pickwick.* But their differences are only the flashing facets of a many-sided brilliance. For deep in all three there already runs the vein of social criticism that was to become dominant in Dickens's entire career. They share a unity of viewpoint and of underlying purpose that makes them logically related in the great unfolding of Dickens's powers.

From the sunny landscape of *Pickwick,* no more than dappled with shadow, *Oliver Twist* plunges into a confined world of darkness, an oppressive, lurid intensity from the workhouse to the criminal slum and the jail. In its heart lurks the smoky and fetid thieves' kitchen where the Artful Dodger leers and Fagin grins in mirth through the greasy air. Almost all its interiors are bleak and gloomy: the workhouse where half-starved boys whimper with hunger in the bare stone hall and scrawny hags hang over the beds of the dying, the peep-holed back room of the Three Cripples, the ruined warehouse where Monks terrifies Bumble by night. Even when Oliver rests asleep at Mrs. Maylie's, just beyond the window loom Fagin and Monks, darkening the sunlight like two monstrous demons. The very outdoors huddles under a heavy sky of evil. Nancy lurks in black shadow on the slimy steps of London Bridge, Sikes wanders in horror-haunted flight away from and back to the city, the waving torches glimmer on the mud of Folly Ditch while the murderer clambers over the tiles of the barricaded house. And the end narrows in relentlessly with Fagin cowered in the condemned cell, gnawing his nails and glaring at the close wall.

This progression from the suffering of gaunt and beaten children to the jeering Dodger and the ferocious Sikes and Fagin, foul with evil, is not, of course, merely a piece of melodramatic contrivance. For it was Dickens's bitter conviction that the cold-hearted cruelty that treated pauperism as a crime brought forth its dreadful harvest of criminality and vice. He did not deny the evils of the old system of the dole, nor by any means advocate a return to it. But the intended reform of the new Poor Law, far from accomplishing its purpose, either broke or brutalized the spirit of its victims. If the sturdy pauper gave a wide berth to the workhouse bastille, how often did he drift to the stews of Whitechapel and Saffron Hill? For one Oliver Twist how many Noah Claypoles were there, who gravitated inevitably from the charity school, that taught only idleness and cringing, to the pickpocket school and the training ground for spies and burglars that taught all too well?

THE NEW POOR LAW

During the forty years preceding the enactment of the new Poor Law of 1834 the percentage of paupers had doubled. By the "Speenhamland Act" of 1795 the farm laborer's wages had been fixed at an immovable figure that ignored the rising cost of living and denied him the benefit of bargaining for his services. Instead, he received from the parish for himself and each mouth he had to feed a weekly pittance that varied with the price of a loaf of bread. Meanwhile the landlords were trebling their rents, and agricultural labor, supported by home relief, had been reduced to a state of ragged and hollow-cheeked indigence on the verge of starvation.

Pauperism became, as G.M. Trevelyan says, "the shameless rule instead of the shameful exception." There was no incentive to industry or saving. No matter what they did, a large proportion of laborers were condemned to pauperism for life. And huge families of children were no longer a liability; they even added a trifle to their parents' miserable scale of subsistence. A resulting tide of population eddied into the towns to add its competition to the pool of unemployed factory workers; industrial labor became hardly better off than farm labor. The entire system thus successfully kept wages down, but it also pauperized the laboring class and shattered its self-respect. Under such a dole, shiftlessness was easier and even more profitable for many than industry and personal pride.

The new Poor Law of 1834 was designed to remedy these evils. Its drastic surgery destroyed all encouragement to live in the lap of idleness and pauperism. There was no dole to supplement low wages. The unemployed laborer was no longer allowed to subsist with his family on an allowance from the parish; his home was ruthlessly broken up, father, mother, children, separated and consigned to the workhouse. And the workhouse life and its rations were deliberately made grimmer than the very poorest subsistence he could earn by outside work. For, in addition to discouraging pauperism, economy also was a motive in the new regulations; within three years the cost of poor relief diminished by 36 per cent.

In theory the new Poor Law distinguished between the helpless and the man or woman who could work but wouldn't. In practice, however, it mingled the idler, tramp, drunkard, and prostitute in the same workhouse with the aged, ill, and infirm, and with the foundling children. The children suffered worst of all. Badly educated or left entirely illiterate, branded with the workhouse stigma, associating with men and women of doubtful character, apprenticed at an early age to get them off the rates as quickly as possible —perhaps as chimney sweeps under some master like the Gamfield of *Oliver Twist*—the parish boys were almost predictably doomed to a later career indistinguishable from that which Oliver so narrowly escaped.

Oliver was born under the old Poor Law. But his infancy in the pauper baby farm, "where twenty or thirty other juvenile offenders against the poor-laws rolled about on the floor all day, without the inconvenience of too much food or too much clothing," could equally well have been under the new dispensation. And when, at the age of nine, Oliver returned to the workhouse to be educated by picking oakum from six in the morning on, the Poor Board had the reformed system in full swing. "The members of this Board," Dickens writes, "were very sage, deep, philosophical men; and when they came to turn their attention to the workhouse, they found out at once, what ordinary folks would never have discovered—the poor people liked it! It was a regular place of public entertainment for the poorer classes; a tavern where there was nothing to pay; a public breakfast, dinner, tea, and supper all the year round, a brick and mortar elysium, where it was all play and no work. 'Oho!' said the Board, looking very knowing; 'we are the fellows to set this to rights; we'll stop it all, in no time.' So they established the rule, that all the poor people should have the alternative (for they would compel nobody, not they), of being starved by a gradual process in the house, or by a quick one out of it."

A STARVATION REGIMEN

Dickens's "three meals of thin gruel a day, with an onion twice a week, and half a roll on Sunday," was, of course, an exaggeration, as Humphry House points out. But not a gross one, as he goes on to show by quoting the approved daily ration for an able-bodied man: 12 ounces of bread, $1\frac{1}{2}$ pints of gruel, 5 ounces of cooked meat, $\frac{1}{2}$ pound of potatoes, and $1\frac{1}{2}$ pints of broth. Women and children over nine received slightly less; children under nine were fed "at discretion." "It is fairly plain," House adds, "which way discretion would veer."

These facts explain why the newly apprenticed Oliver's eyes "glistened at the mention of meat" when some scraps that had been put by for the dog were placed before him. "I wish," Dickens bursts out bitterly, "some well-fed philosopher, whose meat and drink turn to gall within him" ("philosopher" is always Dickens's name for the political economist), "whose blood is ice, whose heart is iron; could have seen Oliver Twist clutching at the dainty viands that the dog had neglected. I wish he could have witnessed the horrible avidity with which Oliver tore the bits asunder with all the ferocity of famine. There is only one thing I should like better, and that would be to see the philosopher making the same sort of meal himself, with the same relish."

In the long run, no doubt, the changed order enabled wages to find a natural level and helped to end that artificial depression of earnings that had degraded the working classes. And in a painfully longer run it took the administration of the workhouses out of the hands of people like Bumble, who were holdovers of the days of outdoor relief. But the early reports of the Poor Law Commissioners are severe in their strictures upon unsuitable officers retained from the old system. The typical fault of the old, however, was wasteful and dirty feeding, not underfeeding, whereas it was the calculated intention of the reform to make the diet sparse. And it is specifically the harshness and the starvation regimen of the new that Dickens lashes with all his fury. Bumble illustrates, no doubt, the stupidity of employing the old officers for its administration; but Mrs. Corney symbolizes the frigid brutality of an economic system that condemned the ill, the aged, and helpless children to misery in the name of destroying temptations to idleness.

It is noteworthy that Bumble has some human sympathy in him, and that Mrs. Corney has none. When Oliver weeps in heartbroken loneliness, Bumble is obliged to clear his throat huskily and pretend to a "troublesome cough." On another occasion he says, not unkindly, "don't cry into your gruel; that's a very foolish action, Oliver." "It certainly was," Dickens comments, "for there was quite enough water in it already." But there is never a faltering in the fierce cruelty of Mrs. Corney bullying her starved and cringing victims while the workhouse crones titter in sycophantic delight; "in them, as in many future instances," George Gissing remarks, "Dickens draws strictly from his observation."

HIDEOUS REALISM

He was no less accurate in delineating the foul areas of St. Giles and Saffron Hill and the slums of Whitechapel, Rotherhithe, and Bethnal Green. With hideous realism he painted the squalid shops of Field Lane flaunting the silk handker-chiefs bought from pickpockets, the piles of old iron and bones and stolen, fusty clothes rusting and rotting in grimy heaps. He plunged into tortuous alleys deep in churned-up mud, into dark hallways reeking with odors of decay, rooms blackened with dirt and soot, cellars splotched with green damp. Vividly he revealed the streets of blighted houses, the screaming children, the villainous faces, the drunken men and women wallowing in filth, although even he could not bring himself to say plainly that the filth consisted of offal and the emptyings of chamberpots and privies.

What these places were like was known to those familiar with government reports and the Reports of the Society for the Suppression of Mendicity. For most people, however, they were merely vague unrealities or "mysteriously wicked regions" haunted by thieves, vagrants, and prostitutes, where cholera festered in dirt and vice. But to his readers Dickens gave them a dreadful and concrete reality. Even so, many denied that they could possibly be true; as late as 1850 there were public men who claimed that Jacob's Island was—what it emphatically was not—simply a figment of Dickens's imagination.

His primary objective, in fact, was fidelity to the criminal slum world he was depicting. He would have nothing to do with romanticizing poverty into the picturesque, he would have none of the gallant bandits of romance, gay in crimson coat and lace ruffles, cantering bravely over moonlit heaths or trolling a song with sparkling glass held high, surrounded by a glamorous circle of elegant harlots. Instead, he would show the fatal ease with which a workhouse orphan like Oliver, running away from the harsh master to whom he was apprenticed, might fall into the clutches of a gang of lawbreakers and be subjected to their corrupting influence. That miserable reality Dickens painted in all its deformity—the villainous receiver of stolen goods, the brutal robber and his rum-drinking trull, the ruffian band of boys being trained in crime, with the "great, black, ghastly gallows" al-ways stretching up behind them. He was not writing, Dick-ens said, for those delicate-minded readers who could not bear to hear the truth about crime when it appeared in fust-ian jacket and dirty stockings, and for them he would not abate one hole in the Dodger's coat or one scrap of curlpa-per in Nancy's disheveled hair.

But, despite this note of spirited defiance, Dickens's method was not that of an absolutely uncompromising naturalism. Although Oliver has been brought up in a workhouse, nothing in his vocabulary and accent seems to mark his vulgar background. Dickens deliberately refused to "offend the ear" by reporting all the oaths and indecencies that fell from the lips of Sikes and Fagin. He would make it clear that Nancy was a burglar's drab, but he would not insist on the physical details of their relationship, nor would he suggest the sex-drenched atmosphere in which a gang of young criminals like the Dodger and Charley Bates would live.

OBSERVED REALITY

With the fundamental truth of the facts he was portraying, of course, Dickens never tampered, and Fagin's school for young pickpockets was drawn from observed reality. An autobiographical narrative published later in the century, *Sixty Years of Waifdom,* describes a woman in Whitechapel training boys to sneak a purse from her pocket without tinkling a bell attached to it, and tells of a thieves' tutor who claimed to have taught no fewer than five hundred in twenty years. Even the Dodger's farcical scene in the police court is not fantastically exaggerated. A dozen years after the appearance of *Oliver Twist,* Dickens and Mark Lemon were walking in the Edgware Road when the latter caught a pickpocket feeling in his coat; their captive accused them in court of being "swell mob-men" and Dickens of being a "fence" who had been sentenced to jail. And as accurately based on observation as the cruelty of Mrs. Corney are the sodden ferocity of Sikes and Fagin's readiness to betray his human tools to the gallows after they have outlived their usefulness. But the generalizing epithets in which Dickens described these figures skulking through "cold, wet, shelterless midnight streets" and sprawling in "foul and drowsy dens" where vice lay closely packed, softened and blurred the loathsomest details of dirt and stench.

For it was Dickens's aim not to turn the stomach but to move the heart. So motivated, he always had his eye on how much his readers could stand. If they would turn away in revulsion from the picture of maggoty corpses of dead cats rotting in piles of ordure in the streets, and flies clustered on the festering eyelids of babies, Dickens would not forfeit their attention by thrusting these physical horrors before them. The evil that was being done to the spirits of human beings was more important even than the hideousness and disease in which their bodies were steeped, dreadfully though the two were linked. He had rather, he said, "lead to the unavoidable inference" that a world existed "of the most debased and vicious kind, than to prove it elaborately by words and deeds."

It enhanced rather than detracted from his purpose that he was able to introduce a bitter and pitiful comedy into the workhouse scenes and endow Fagin with a sinister hilarity. His strategy was always to fuse drama, pathos, and laughter with a realism pleading for humane feeling, not to evoke mere nauseated recoil. Of the essential facts he was determined to reveal he would sacrifice not one iota; and these would be more than sufficient to arouse the emotions and stir indignation.

AN ARTIFICIAL PLOT

All these details, however, are woven into a luridly melodramatic plot that poses—in the very process of overcoming them—undeniable problems of belief for the reader. The mystery of Oliver's birth is a complex rigmarole involving the rightful inheritance of an estate and destroyed proofs of identity. Since the illegitimate Oliver will obtain his father's bequest only if his name throughout his minority remains unstained by any act "of dishonour, meanness, cowardice, or wrong," his evil half-brother Monks bribes Fagin to seduce him into crime. (It is significant of Dickens's sympathies with the downtrodden, however, that he reverses the conventional melodramatic formula by making the *legitimate* Monks the vicious one and the bastard Oliver a child whose goodness even the most degraded surroundings have not destroyed.) The cloak-and-lantern villainy of Monks, skulking up dark stairs and slinking to conspiratorial meetings in deserted mills by night, reeks of the stage. No less theatrical are the two chances that bring Oliver, even before his identity is discovered, first under the protection of his father's old friend Mr. Brownlow, and second into the home of his mother's sister, Rose Maylie. Harry Maylie is cut out of the most heroic pasteboard, and Rose Maylie drips a syrupy sweetness transcending patience. That even so unreal a scoundrel as Monks should be foiled by the unworldly Brownlow staggers critical faith no less than the coincidences that prove Oliver to be Rose's nephew and the child of Brownlow's dead friend.

Such flaws in the very reality Dickens has invoked are not to be defended. And yet two things may be said about them. First, that Dickens's own undeviating faith in what he has imagined exerts a magical spell in which we hardly observe the implausibility of these melodramatic embroideries. Second, that the sheer power and speed of the story compel us to intense emotional participation. We believe partly because we want to believe and partly because its rapid intensity gives us no time to stop. Whatever skeptical reservations we may feel about the contrived plot arise only after the story is ended and the light of everyday has melted its fierce, dark hypnosis.

No doubt this is an art inferior to that of *Pickwick*, which is frankly a comic fairy tale with a hero who cannot be destroyed by the dragons of reality. But in *Oliver Twist*, evil men and hideous institutions have a genuine power to harm, and Oliver may really be injured. Its canons of verisimilitude are therefore somewhat different from those that were appropriate to the Pickwick world. Despite the artificiality of its complicated intrigue, however, *Oliver* violates those standards in no significant way. It is guilty of no underlying unreality in the conception of its main characters and no falsification of its criminal world.

So understood, the plot and the stage language are simply the conventions through which Dickens conveys reality. Throughout he knows and insistently emphasizes the fact that even the vilest environment cannot utterly obliterate or corrupt the principle of good in its victims. And if Oliver talks rather more like a little gentleman than is altogether plausible, he has been so drawn that it is not unbelievable to see in him that principle "surviving every adverse circumstance and triumphant at last." And if Nancy's language seems somewhat unnaturally to change from that of the bedraggled whore she is when her sympathies have been aroused by the frail child who has been thrown in her way, the conflict between her devotion to Sikes and her pity for Oliver is wholly convincing. "It is emphatically," Dickens wrote, "God's truth, for it is the truth He leaves in such depraved and miserable breasts; the hope yet lingering behind; the last fair drop of water at the bottom of the dried-up weed-choked well." No less true is Oliver's struggling resistance to the pollutions by which the Dodger is already indelibly stained. It is the wonder but the truth of humanity that it *does* so struggle.

No more are Sikes and merry old Fagin and the cynically high-spirited Dodger fictional distortions. Their corruption sharply portrays the influence of evil surroundings on callous and insensible natures. A masterly vividness bathes the burly thief and the sinister fence. Sikes's bullying speech and sodden silences, his slouching gait, his ferocious hand and murderous rages, give him a physical reality as fiercely menacing as his brutal character. Still more loathsomely memorable is Fagin, now crouching before the fire and glancing over his shoulder with swift and craven suspicion, now dropping soft hints or wheedling hypocritical endearments, again laughing or rushing from the room with a howl of terror. Fagin is one of those nightmare images, often recurrent in his creator's mind, that Dickens regarded with a loathing so fascinated as to be half horrible enjoyment: an image of hilarious evil delighted in cunning self-applause. Daniel Quilp, the deformed dwarf of *The Old Curiosity Shop,* in whom malice boils up into an atrocious playfulness, is a grotesque mutation of the image. Still another—this time a fantastic caricature of false gentility—is Mr. Chester, in *Barnaby Rudge,* consistently appreciating his own duplicity.

POWERFUL NARRATIVE

These figures of brute ferocity and insidious evil embody all the dreadful and lurid power of the book. The grinning knavery of Fagin and the violence of Sikes continually threaten collision. In the end Fagin incites Sikes to the fury that sends him rushing off to murder Nancy and precipitates the book into the wild race of its culminating horrors. "You won't be—too—violent, Bill?" the old villain whispers. Then follow the pistol beaten into the bloody face, the reflection of the pool of gore quivering on the ceiling, the ghastly flight, the peddler's chant that he can remove "pitch-stains, mud-stains, blood-stains," Sikes's desperate escape and delirious wandering.

All this feverish melodrama Dickens conveys with a sharp and sensitive psychological penetration, sometimes startling in its revelation. Sikes tries in vain either to escape or to face the haunting figure always close behind him. "If he shut out the sight, there came the room with every well-known object—some, indeed, that he would have forgotten, if he had gone over its contents from memory—each in its accustomed place." Such a passage shows that Proust was not the first novelist to be aware of the machinery of unwilled memory.

From this wild fury, the closing scenes of Fagin's trial and last night alive plunge us with intensified force into that atmosphere of dark repressive confinement that has dominated the book. All the eyes of the courtroom glaring down hotly upon the villainous old man, his tense listening, his mind wandering over trivia like a snapped pencil point and the broken iron spike before him even while he burns with the terror of death, his beating his hands raw against the door of his cell, his unwashed flesh crackling with fever, the hollow boom of the iron bell reverberating within those narrow walls—all strike the same note. With the arrival of the jailor, speaking his name, comes a detail of extraordinary power: "'That's me!' cried Fagin, falling instantly into the attitude of listening he had assumed upon his trial. 'An old man, my Lord; a very old, old man!'" And then the scene speeds on to its end, Fagin's face retaining no human expression but rage and terror while he struggles with the attendants and sends up cry after cry.

Humor in *Oliver Twist*

James R. Kincaid

According to James R. Kincaid, Dickens purposefully uses laughter as a technique to subvert readers' conventional reactions and combat "comfortable aloofness." Kincaid maintains that by provoking laughter in non-comic situations, Dickens draws the reader not only into Oliver's grim world, but also into closer identification with all of the novel's downtrodden characters: Bumble, Sikes, and Fagin, among others. Further, readers' laughter suggests—if only momentarily—complicity in the attitudes that victimize all of society's alienated individuals. Kincaid is the author of *Dickens and the Rhetoric of Laughter*, from which the following is excerpted.

One of the major questions, then, is how such a dark novel can be so funny. It is probable that most critics often laugh while reading it; it is certain that when they are finished they write essays on its bleak effects. And they are right—in both cases. The reason for the paradoxical reaction is, I think, that Dickens uses laughter here to subvert our conventional reactions and to emphasize more dramatically the isolation of his young hero, indeed, the essential isolation of all men. In denying the possibility of a comic society and yet provoking laughter, the novel continually thwarts and frustrates the reader; for our laughter continues to search for a social basis, "even when there is no longer any support for it in the novel. In other words, laughter is stirred, but the impulses aroused behind it are not allowed to collect and settle. Unlike the convivial atmosphere of *Pickwick Papers*, where our laughter finally provides us a place with Sam and with Mr. Pickwick, here there is no possibility of escape to a society sanctified by the expulsion of all the villains. Instead, laughter is used primarily as a weapon, to suggest that we are the villains. The selfishness and unfeeling cruelty which are a subconscious part of much laughter are here brought to the surface and used to intensify our reaction and our involvement. Laughter is a necessary part of the proper reaction to the novel, but in the end it is used against us, undercutting the comfortable aloofness we had originally maintained and forcing us into conjunction with the lonely and terrified orphan. This suggests that, just as in *Pickwick*, the basic attack is on detachment. But the comparison doesn't go very far. There are no comparable rewards for submitting to the attack in *Oliver Twist* and no comfortably stable scheme of values to which we can attach ourselves. We are left alone in a rootless and threatening world.

There is, of course, an apparently brighter world in *Oliver Twist*, and the plot of the novel seems to point us towards it. Even before the narrative reaches midpoint, Dickens has rescued his hero and placed him firmly in the protection of the Maylie group; the last half of the novel simply reinforces Oliver's 'safe' position, on the one hand, by methodically hunting down the threats to his safety and eliminating them (Fagin and Sikes) or converting them (Charley Bates and Nancy), and, on the other hand, by securing the prospects of wealth for the hero (through Monks's will) and eternal bliss for the rest of the good people (the marriage between Rose and Harry Maylie). Yet most commentators have found themselves untouched by this arrangement of events and have emphasized the novel's predominantly grim effect. This paradox has generally been explained by the argument that Dickens portrayed Fagin and his group with great vividness, that a part of him identified very closely with them, that he treated them with great 'sympathy'. In contrast, even Forster admitted that the Maylie–Brownlow group were so poorly realized, so completely unbelievable as to constitute 'the weak part of the story'. Graham Greene has merged these two contrasting impressions by describing the controlling view of the novel as 'Manichaean'; he argues that the power of the book comes from 'the eternal and alluring trait of the Manichee, with its simple and terrible explanation of our plight, how the world was made by Satan and not by God, lulling us with the music of despair'.

But the problem really goes much deeper, and the novel really does not make such simple distinctions as are implied by these views. The fact is that there are two separate and conflicting dualisms: one social, between the individual and the institution, the second moral, between the respectable and the criminal. Arnold Kettle has described this conflict as that between the pattern and the plot of the novel. For the first eleven chapters the basic pattern of the novel is developed: the evocation of the dark world of the poor and the engagement of our sympathy with them in their struggle against institutions. This pattern, he argues, is most deeply felt and continues throughout, though in the second half of the novel it tends to lose ground to the plot, a relatively superficial and conventionally formulated moralistic conflict. The basic problem, though, is not in the superficiality of the moral theme, but in its conflict with the more deeply-felt theme of institutional oppression. The 'good' people in the second half of the novel sometimes use the hated institution of the first half to fight not only the persecutors but the victims as well.

READER DISCOMFORT

Laughter leads us to Oliver's side, but Oliver soon leaves us and heads for the enemy. As a result we are likely to be stranded. Our laughter has exposed us and isolated us along with Oliver, and it then deprives us of even his alliance. It is our response to this desolation, pushed on us by our laughter, that is at the core of the novel's one undoubted effect: discomfort. We not only have an uneasy aesthetic response to a thematically fractured novel, but an uneasy emotional response at being forced into the same isolation the novel portrays. In the end, *Oliver Twist* comes near to making orphans of us all by dislocating us from the world we are comfortable in, and displaying the full force of Mrs. Thingummy's bitter mockery of consolation.

The most obvious cause of this dislocation is the lack of consistency in the narrative personality. It is impossible to define the characteristics or moral positions of the narrator in this novel, for they are continually shifting. It is true that, as in most Dickens novels, the narrative voice provides a counterpoint to the story and gives oblique directions to the reader. But here the directions are generally misleading. We expect those obtrusive narrative commentaries at least to provide accurate signposts to a comfortable position we can take, but here Dickens exploits this very expectation to attack such smug confidence.

"Tendency Toward Abstraction"

For instance, the narrator is often—though certainly not always—as detached as in *Pickwick Papers,* and this detachment and the 'tendency toward abstraction' [according to Steven Marcus] sometimes work together as a negative object lesson, 'an ironic rhetorical device to generate by negation the outraged sympathy of the reader' [according to J. Hillis Miller]. But moral outrage of this sort is rather a comfortable thing, and *Oliver Twist* never allows us to be comfortable for long; nor does it allow the stability which would come from consistent and obvious irony. The writing with which Dickens begins the novel, for example, certainly does not flatter the reader's sense of moral superiority or reinforce his moral certainty:

> Among other public buildings in a certain town, which for many reasons it will be prudent to refrain from mentioning, and to which I will assign no fictitious name, there is one anciently common to most towns, great or small: to wit, a workhouse; and in this workhouse was born: on a day and date which I need not trouble myself to repeat, inasmuch as it can be of no possible consequence to the reader, in this stage of the business at all events: the item of mortality whose name is prefixed to the head of this chapter.

Certainly there is more than a 'tendency toward abstraction' here; this seems to have been written by the head of the Circumlocution Office. Leisurely, presumably gentle and facetious, the passage throws out humorous barbs in a dozen directions: at authorial egotism ('I' is introduced gratuitously twice), at the reader's concern for trivia ('day and date'), at prudence and care, and so on. Perhaps most obvious, and certainly most important, though, is the attack on the mincing-genteel tone of many novels and, by implication, on the mincing-genteel expectations of many readers. The author parodies our refined concerns by offering mock assurance that he will keep in mind our delicate sensitivities (and the demands on our time) by maintaining an elevated tone. We can be assured, in fact, that no concrete hero will be introduced, simply an 'item of mortality'. The facetiousness of the tone, then, hides the bitterest sarcasm, not an irony which invites our participation in righteous indignation but a covert attack on a trait the narrator caustically assumes we all share: callousness. The narrator simply does not want our company; in fact, he does not allow us any single position. This opening attack dramatically upsets our normally stable position in reference to fiction and tears from us the accustomed comforting shield of a narrative friend and guide.

We might, of course, get used to this sort of attack and gradually assume a defensive but at least constant position. Dickens does not allow even this sort of masochistic stability, however. The appeals of the narrative tone are constantly shifting. Sometimes, in fact, we are invited to share in an easy and removed irony: 'What a noble illustration of the tender laws of England! They let the paupers go to sleep!' (II). Occasionally, the narrator is even chummy in his appeals: Oliver 'was alone in a strange place; and we all know how chilled and desolate the best of us will sometimes feel in such a situation' (v). Even here, though, we are invited to share not the narrator's detachment but Oliver's desolation —but at least we have company. The point is that we can never count on being in any single relationship with the narrative voice for long. Just as we relax in the chumminess or in the comfort of indignation, we are pushed away by an attack on us or by an unsettling sick joke of the kind which heads this chapter—'coffins were looking up'. The end result of the sick joke and of this shifting point of view is that we are made to disavow our accustomed positions in relation to fiction. No novel could be more honest, at least in its rhetorical terms, than is *Oliver Twist*: the reader is never flattered, never comforted. He is pressed to renounce detachment and to enter more completely into the action of the novel, simply because all other outlets are closed. There are no buffers between us and the desolation presented. On the contrary, the rhetoric of attack, based on this radically uncertain narrative tone and on a subversive humour, forces us to share in that desolation. It is an effective, if somewhat vicious, alliance.

EXERCISE IN MALEVOLENCE

Laughter and point of view are, indeed, allied in viciousness, and though the obtrusive narrative passages never help the reader to orient himself, they do reveal an underlying maliciousness which is central to the novel's humour. For instance, early in the novel Dickens comments:

> I wish some well-fed philosopher, whose meat and drink turn to gall within him; whose blood is ice, whose heart is iron; could have seen Oliver Twist clutching at the dainty viands that the dog had neglected. I wish he could have wit-

nessed the horrible avidity with which Oliver tore the bits
asunder with all the ferocity of famine. There is only one
thing I should like better; and that would be to see the
Philosopher making the same sort of meal himself, with the
same relish (iv).

This paragraph embodies the central attack on abstractions,
on treating people from such a distance that they become,
like Oliver, philosophically 'badged and ticketed' (i). But this
passage is more than simply an attack; it is an exercise in
malevolence. Since this is by no means a funny passage and
since there are no disguises for the appeals to vindictive-
ness, we are very likely to resist its aggressive suggestions.
Yet this same unvarnished desire for sadistic revenge is at
the core of much of the humour in the novel; the very fact
that the novel is not satisfied with piercing Bumble's folly,
for instance, in the manner of Fielding or Meredith, but pur-
sues him to the end, defeats him, degrades him, and rubs
him in the mud, alerts us to the cruelty and barbarousness
of this humorous process. We delight in Bumble's fall, but
we are revolted at the extended details of his degradation.
Dickens's subversive humour calls up in us, and presents all
too clearly, the egoistic base from which we had probably
been chuckling. We are likely to resist such exposure, of
course, even to imagine that we didn't laugh at all, and the
book is all the darker for having exposed the potential darkness within us.

The same subversive technique illustrated by the author's
comments and the point of view is utilized more fully and
more subtly in the narrative itself. Though there are other
important humorous appeals, particularly later in the novel,
it is the dominant humour of the first half, focusing on the
conflict between the novel's outcasts and its established society, which is most functional. The laughter called up by
these situations to a large extent determines our reaction to
the general world of the novel and to the social assumptions
on which that world is built.

THE SHOCK OF RECOGNITION

The humour attending these conflicts between the institution and the individual almost invariably calls for an ambiguous response. For example, in the second chapter, Oliver is
told that 'the board had said he was to appear before it forth-
with'. Oliver is confused by this report, 'not having a very

clearly defined notion of what a live board was', and when he is ushered into the august presence of 'eight or ten fat gentlemen' and told to 'bow to the board', 'seeing no board but the table, [he] fortunately bowed to that'. This is both tactful and pointed; it could be very funny. Dickens manages to use Oliver's ignorance to make the point that his confusion is, after all, not so meaningless: the board does have all the flexibility and feeling of a thick plank. Given only these details and this perspective, the humour could well be successful. There are, however, other factors which work against laughter. First of all, the situation is under the control of Bumble, who at this point is an almost unrelieved villain. Second, we are disturbed by Oliver's reaction: he 'was not quite certain whether he ought to laugh or cry'. Finally, however, the boy's conflict is resolved; Bumble gives him so many 'taps' behind that he cries. The scene seems to be devised in such a way as to undercut the aloofness we have originally assumed in order to laugh and to force us into a closer identification with Oliver, adding by the way a penetrating glance into the underlying viciousness of such laughter. In order to laugh in the first place, the reader must remove himself slightly from the situation: he knows what a board is, Oliver does not. Oliver's ambiguous reaction, however, recalls the novel's earlier remarks about institutions, workhouse institutions in particular; and the reference to the possibility of crying similarly recalls us to a position of sympathy for him. When he is finally forced by Bumble to decide against laughing in favour of crying, we too must decide. In order to laugh, we must identify ourselves with the board, and this is clearly impossible. Our probable laughter at the beginning of the scene is cut off, perhaps denied, but we are not likely to escape a recognition of the fact that, for a brief instant, we had allowed ourselves to be members of the board, regarding Oliver as an 'it'. The shock of recognition urges us closer to Oliver and denies us the easy sanctuary of laughter.

EXPOSING BRUTALITY

This same subversive process is used periodically in the novel both to reinforce the reader's feelings for Oliver and to undermine the social assumptions on which laughter is built. In Chapter III, for instance, we are introduced to 'Mr. Gamfield, chimney-sweep', who 'in a species of arithmetical desperation' was 'alternately cudgelling his brains and his donkey'. The zeugma in the last phrase is a witty disguise for the hidden aggression, allowing both the speed and the conciseness necessary to all jokes. Again, we are very likely to laugh. Two paragraphs later, however, we are told that Gamfield gave the donkey's jaw 'a sharp wrench' and that he 'gave him another blow on the head, just to stun him till he came back again'. What happens here is that the wittily disguised 'cudgelling' at which we had been asked to laugh is made repulsively explicit in an entire paragraph devoted to the maltreatment of the donkey. The disguise is removed and the aggression nakedly exposed. When Gamfield then applies to the board in answer to the advertisement offering Oliver as an apprentice, we again sense how perilous is the boy's situation; we are dangerously close to being Gamfields ourselves. In the scene between Gamfield and the board, then, it is hard to miss the point that laughter is being used as a weapon:

> 'Boys is wery obstinit, and wery lazy, gen'lmen, and there's nothink like a good hot blaze to make 'em come down vith a run. It's humane too, gen'lmen, acause, even if they're stuck in the chimbley, roastin' their feet makes 'em struggle to hextricate theirselves.'
>
> The gentleman in the white waistcoat appeared very much amused by this explanation. (III)

Gamfield talks very much like Sam Weller here, but surely his remarks are not funny. Not only is he a brutal man, but he wants to subject Oliver to horrible tortures. We were tempted to laugh at him once before and we certainly won't be victimized again. In case there is any temptation, we are immediately given a picture of the sort of person who is amused: 'the gentleman in the white waistcoat', heartless, stupid, and vicious.

Finally, there is the brilliant scene, perhaps the symbolic centre of the novel, in which Oliver stands for a brief instant against all the institutionalized cruelty and demands that he be allowed to survive. One reason this scene is so memorable is that Dickens controls the humour so as to make us stand with Oliver as he asks for more.

Dickens first, however, tempts us to take a step back from the 'slow starvation' he is discussing by focusing on a threat of cannibalism made to his fellow victims by a cook's son, who 'hadn't been used to that sort of thing'. 'He had a wild, hungry eye; and they implicitly believed him' (II). Notice the traps Dickens sets here for the reader: we are urged to laugh, first, by the camouflage put over the starvation, which becomes 'that sort of thing', second, by the substitution of mock killing for the real institutional murder, and third, by the appeal to our superior experience: the boys may believe him, but we don't. He allows us, by our laughter, to shift our attention and thereby our concern. But, as I said, this shift is a trap meant to expose our callousness. Dickens is fattening us for the kill:

> 'Please, sir, I want some more.'
>
> The master was a fat, healthy man; but he turned very pale. He gazed in stupefied astonishment on the small rebel for some seconds, and then clung for support to the copper. The assistants were paralysed with wonder; the boys with fear. (II)

The reaction of the master is, in one sense, very funny. In one dazzling flash we are told that he is fat and healthy and that he clung to the pot for support. This appeal to our superiority in the absurd causal relationship, a cataclysmic reaction to a trivial event, would certainly satisfy our humorous demands, were it not for the peculiar situation, emphasized by the last sentence. What seems to be a supporting, funny detail, 'The assistants were paralysed with wonder', turns out to be a false lead, for the second part of the sentence, 'the boys with fear', jars us pointedly with the unexpected word 'fear'. We laugh only at the peril of ignoring this fear, and if we do ignore it, we implicitly share in the guilt for the brutality which comes to Oliver as a result of his daring.

These three episodes, similar in effect if not in execution, are all taken from the early sections of the novel. Throughout, however, Dickens subtly reverses even the most conventional humorous situations. For instance, the explosive coughing after drinking liquor is one of the most recurrent pieces of equipment in slapstick comedies. But in the novel Oliver's coughing is almost a threat or a dare, and it is very likely that by the time it takes place we know enough to avoid the trap. At any rate, just before the attempted robbery of the Maylies', the thieves are—rather happily—drinking 'Success to the crack!' Toby Crackit proposes 'A drain for the boy', and Oliver, 'frightened by the menacing gestures of the two men . . . hastily swallowed the contents of the glass, and immediately fell into a violent fit of coughing: which delighted Toby Crackit and Barney, and even drew a smile

from the surly Mr. Sikes' (XXII). By this time, we know instinctively not to be amused by anyone who is 'frightened',
and we identify too strongly with Oliver here to laugh at
him. He is alone and is faced with an adventure which almost kills him. We can't even smile, lest we be associated
with 'the surly Mr. Sikes'.

SIKES'S WORLD

There are, however, times when we *are* associated with
Sikes, or with any other victim, any other man who is
hunted, frightened, or alone. Dickens uses the technique of
subversion so consistently and subtly that, by the end of the
novel, we are asked to react with the same combination of
guilt, insight, and intense association with the victims, even
when there is no 'gentleman in the white waistcoat' to nul-
lify our temptation to laughter and even when the victim is
an equivocal character at best. For instance, during Sikes's
flight through the countryside, he draws near two mail-
coach guards to hear them talk of the murder:

> 'Corn's up a little. I heerd talk of a murder, too, down Spital-
> fields way, but I don't reckon much upon it.'
>
> 'Oh, that's quite true,' said a gentleman inside, who was look-
> ing out of the window. 'And a dreadful murder it was.'
>
> 'Was it, sir?' rejoined the guard, touching his hat. 'Man or
> woman, pray, sir?'
>
> 'A woman,' replied the gentleman. 'It is supposed—'
>
> 'Now, Ben,' replied the coachman impatiently.
>
> 'Damn that 'ere bag,' said the guard; 'are you gone to sleep in
> there?'
>
> 'Coming!' cried the office keeper, running out.
>
> 'Coming,' growled the guard. 'Ah, and so's the young 'ooman
> of property that's going to take a fancy to me, but I don't know
> when. Here, give hold. All ri—ight!'
>
> The horn sounded a few cheerful notes, and the coach was
> gone. (XLVIII)

The joke clashes strongly with an atmosphere which is so
controlled and intense that it allows us no real interest outside Sikes; the brilliant juxtaposition of the guard's slight
and impersonal interest in the sensational aspects of the
crime with Sikes's obsession with the eyes that won't shut is
capped by the final unconsciously brutal witticism about

'the young 'ooman of property'. Since the focus has shifted only very briefly from the killer, the only woman on our minds at the moment is the mangled corpse of Nancy, who has been killed precisely because her 'fancy' for Bill would not allow her to desert him. Two orders of reality, connected only by a startling and accidental relevance of referents, are violently contrasted here: the order which contains the social world, easy jokes and thoughtlessness, and the horribly intense and torturous world of Sikes. By this point, the reader is most likely conditioned by Dickens's technique and has no real choice but to enter into the latter; the social world has consistently been shown to be cruel with the special cruelty of comfortable aloofness. The notes of the horn certainly are cheerful only to those who regard the fact that 'Corn's up a little' as equal in interest to the murder. The continual and subtle rhetorical insistence is that crimes of passion, no matter how brutal, are not nearly so pervasive as crimes of indifference.

The final goal of this technique is to pry us away from the normal identification we make with an aloof society and to force us to enter much more fully into the world of the terrified and alienated individual, who at various times is Oliver, Fagin, Sikes, Bumble, and the Artful Dodger. Laughter, the strongest expression of social identification, is brilliantly used as a weapon against our own safety, quietly urging us to assume, for the moment, the perilous position of the hunted and the trapped. Instead of providing for a comic society, our laughter is meant to deny society altogether and to force us to be as alone as the novel's victims. The novel's humour, in other words, maintains that the real conflict is between the outcasts and the establishment, even after the plot itself has introduced a new theme which seems to provide a sanctified society and which turns against the outcasts.

CHAPTER 2

Important Themes

READINGS ON
OLIVER TWIST

Opposing Worlds in
Oliver Twist

H.M. Daleski

According to H.M. Daleski, *Oliver Twist* presents alternative possibilities of the human condition—the civilized home with its comforts and amenities and, in contrast, the lot of the homeless. The opposing imagery connected to these vastly different worlds, Daleski argues, constitutes the heart of the novel. Using the simple images of home and street—and the workhouse which mediates between the two—Dickens explores his central thematic concerns: the treatment of the homeless in nineteenth-century England. The following critical analysis is excerpted from Daleski's book *Dickens and the Art of Analogy.*

Oliver Twist is . . . an imaginative evocation of a social problem that is consistently presented in terms of two central images. . . .

The action is rooted in the workhouse, with which the book begins; but thereafter it branches out into two areas which have generally been characterized as distinct 'worlds', the underworld of Fagin and his gang, and the middle-class milieu of Mr. Brownlow and of the Maylies. These worlds are only fleetingly brought together by the action in Nancy's surreptitious contacts with Rose and in Brownlow's visit to Fagin in the condemned cell. They are firmly held together, however, by a vision which sees in them alternative possibilities of the human condition, and which projects them throughout in terms of two related images. The images occur together in a passage which may be thought of as at the imaginative centre of the novel:

> The night was bitter cold. The snow lay on the ground, frozen into a hard thick crust; so that only the heaps that had drifted into by-ways and corners were affected by the sharp wind that howled abroad: which, as if expending increased fury on

Excerpted from *Dickens and the Art of Analogy* (New York: Schocken Books, 1970) by H.M. Daleski. Copyright © 1970 by H.M. Daleski. Reprinted with permission from Faber & Faber.

such prey as it found, caught it savagely up in clouds, and, whirling it into a thousand misty eddies, scattered it in air. Bleak, dark, and piercing cold, it was a night for the well-housed and fed to draw round the bright fire and thank God they were at home; and for the homeless starving wretch to lay him down and die. Many hunger-worn outcasts close their eyes in our bare streets, at such times, who, let their crimes have been what they may, can hardly open them in a more bitter world.

In this passage the manifold differences of condition that distinguish the lot of one man from another are starkly narrowed to one fundamental distinction: that between 'the homeless' and 'the well-housed', between poor naked wretches and accommodated man. The distinction is thus between a man's having a 'home', which provides him with shelter, food, warmth and light; and being condemned to be out in the 'bare streets', which means being exposed not only to the cold and the dark but also to starvation. To be out in the streets, moreover, is to move through the darkness of a hell on earth, for those who die in the streets, 'let their crimes have been what they may, can hardly open [their eyes] in a more bitter world'. To have a home, by contrast, is a sign of grace, and the well-housed may duly 'thank God' they are at home.

Opposing Imagery

The opposed images of home and the streets function as analogues of the two opposed worlds of the novel, the worlds of civilized order and of crime. We are adverted to this dimension of the imagery by the curious use of the word 'crimes' in the quoted passage. The use of this word (rather than 'sins', which, in the context, suggests itself as a more natural choice) associates the 'outcasts' not only with the destitute but with the criminal. And indeed the impression of the criminals that we carry away, when we look back on the novel as a whole, is of men who are essentially homeless, who are continually moving from one 'den' to another, who are constantly on the run. Nor need we rely only on such impressions.

In the Preface which he wrote for the third edition of *Oliver Twist* in 1841, Dickens was at some pains to clarify his own moral attitude to the criminals he had depicted. Though he specifically excluded his friend Bulwer Lytton's *Paul Clifford* from having 'any bearing on . . . the subject', it seems clear enough that he was out to dissociate his novel from the genre of the Newgate novel, which *Paul Clifford* might be said to have inaugurated:

> What manner of life is that which is described in these pages, as the every-day existence of a Thief? What charms has it for the young and ill-disposed, what allurements for the most jolter-headed of juveniles? Here are no canterings upon moonlit heaths, no merry-makings in the snuggest of all possible caverns, none of the attractions of dress, no embroidery, no lace, no jack-boots, no crimson coats and ruffles, none of the dash and freedom with which 'the road' has been, time out of mind, invested. The cold, wet, shelterless midnight streets of London; the foul and frowsy dens, where vice is closely packed and lacks the room to turn; the haunts of hunger and disease, the shabby rags that scarcely hold together: where are the attractions of these things? Have they no lesson, and do they not whisper something beyond the little-regarded warning of a moral precept?

It is striking that Dickens, in seeking to describe the habitat of his thieves, should seize first on 'the cold, wet, shelterless midnight streets of London'. And time and again, in the novel, the thieves are typically shown pursuing their way through these streets. Even when 'the sharp wind' seems to have 'cleared' the streets 'of passengers, as of dust and mud', and it is 'within an hour of midnight', Fagin hurries through them 'trembling, and shivering', for 'the weather [is] dark and piercing cold'. Out in the streets on another occasion, he is described in terms which point to the significance of the collocation of street and criminal:

> The mud lay thick upon the stones: and a black mist hung over the streets; the rain fell sluggishly down: and everything felt cold and clammy to the touch. It seemed just the night when it befitted such a being as the Jew, to be abroad. As he glided, stealthily along, creeping beneath the shelter of the walls and doorways, the hideous old man seemed like some loathsome reptile, engendered in the slime and darkness through which he, moved: crawling forth, by night, in search of some rich offal for a meal.

Clearly it befits Fagin 'to be abroad' on such a night not because he is a Jew and a 'hideous old man' but because he is a criminal; and he has his 'being' in the streets because he is produced by them, 'engendered', it seems, in their 'slime and darkness'. The streets are as much the natural home of Fagin and his like as the moors round Wuthering Heights are that of Cathy and Heathcliff. Nancy, indeed, bitterly accuses Fagin of being responsible for the fact that 'the cold, wet', dirty streets are [her] home'. The streets, moreover, are seen to lead the criminals, twist and turn as they may, inexorably in one direction: when Fagin is finally brought to trial, the court is said to be 'paved, from floor to roof, with human faces'; and Fagin makes his last appearance in the streets when he is hanged.

LIFE IN THE UNDERWORLD

But it is, of course, not only the criminals and prostitutes who walk the streets; the 'hunger-worn outcasts' of the previously quoted passage, who, as often as not, 'close their eyes in [the] bare streets', are also the law-abiding poor. Oliver, when he runs away from the undertaker, is one of them; and he reflects that London is 'the very place for a homeless boy, who must die in the streets, unless someone [helps] him'. That a life in 'the cold, wet, shelterless midnight streets' is made to project a life in the underworld is thus not merely a means of countering the 'allurements' of romantic 'canterings upon moonlit heaths'; it is primarily a means of insisting on the connection between poverty and crime. Receiving the efflux of the poor, the streets engender criminals. Implied throughout by the repeated use of the street image, this process—or, at least, the first stage in the process—is dramatized in the case of Oliver. It is precisely when Oliver finds himself in the streets, homeless and starving, that he is approached by the Dodger; and, having been provided by him with a 'hearty meal', Oliver is induced to follow that solicitous youth by his promise to introduce him to 'a 'spectable old genelman . . . wot'll give [him] lodgings for nothink'.

A further feature of life in the underworld is that the thieves' houses have more in common with the street than with a home. Monks, on being received in one of Fagin's dens, complains that 'it's as dark as the grave', and is informed by his host that he and his friends 'never shew lights to [their] neighbours'; Fagin then takes him into a room which is 'destitute of all moveables save a broken armchair, and an old couch or sofa without covering. . . .' After the Chertsey expedition, Bill Sikes takes up his quarters in 'a mean and badly-furnished apartment, of very limited size: lighted only by one small window in the shelving roof, and abutting on a close and dirty lane'; in this apartment there is not only 'a great scarcity of furniture' but a 'total absence of comfort.' Fagin, in the end, like 'all the men he [has] known who [have] died upon the scaffold', comes to '[inhabit]' a condemned cell.

THE CIVILIZED HOME

By contrast the world of civilized order is characterized by the amenities of its homes. Mr. Brownlow takes Oliver home to 'a neat house, in a quiet shady street', where he is 'carefully and comfortably deposited' and 'tended with a kindness and solicitude that [know] no bounds'; a 'motherly old lady' constantly looks 'kindly and lovingly' at him and feeds him broth which is 'strong enough to furnish an ample dinner, when reduced to the regulation strength: for three hundred and fifty paupers, at the very lowest computation'. Mrs. Maylie and Rose are first shown together sitting at 'a well-spread breakfast-table' in 'a handsome room: though its furniture [has] rather the air of old-fashioned comfort, than of modern elegance'. When Oliver goes with them to a cottage in the country, the room in which he works at his lessons is 'quite a cottage-room, with a lattice-window', around which there are 'clusters of jessamine and honeysuckle' that creep 'over the casement' and fill 'the place with their delicious perfume'; the room looks into a garden, and 'all beyond' is 'fine meadow-land and wood'.

These descriptions are not in themselves especially noteworthy, but they are given force by the very vividness of that to which they are quietly opposed. Heaven, even in Milton, is a more prosaic place than Hell. And in *Oliver Twist* Dickens seems to think of home as a heaven as well as a haven. It is not merely, as I have pointed out, that the streets are presented as hell. Harry Maylie tells Rose that 'when the young, the beautiful, and good, are visited with sickness, their pure spirits insensibly turn towards their bright home of lasting rest'. Now that the Clarendon edition of the novel enables us to watch Dickens at work, moreover, we can see how another such identification was originally made explicit— though Dickens finally thought better of it. Oliver is described as sometimes thinking of his dead mother and sobbing unseen, but being comforted when he raises his eyes 'to the deep sky overhead' and ceases 'to think of her as lying in the ground'; in his manuscript Dickens first had Oliver raise his eyes to the sky 'and [remember] that there [is] a home beyond'. The 'long home' of Ecclesiastes is no doubt behind what may well be merely a traditional use of the word 'home' in these two passages, but that does not mean to say that we should brush aside the associations which it gathers in the novel. Certainly Dickens repeatedly suggests that home, like heaven, is a concentration of all good. . . .

When we have registered the significance of the home and street analogues, which are at the heart of the novel, we are better able to appreciate the importance of the workhouse in the narrative. The workhouse is the home which is provided for the poor by the secure; and it is the last refuge of the unhoused poor from a life in the streets. The workhouse, in a word, mediates between the images of home and street, and it thus may also be said to mediate between the two worlds which the images in turn project. Starting life in the workhouse, Oliver—once he has left his birthplace—moves backwards and forwards between the two worlds; and the question posed by the narrative is which world, the respectable or the criminal, he will finally come to inhabit. The main action of the novel, that is to say, is concerned, quite simply, with Oliver's search for a home.

Dickens's social criticism is effective, if limited, because it is conveyed in terms of the two main images of the novel, the striking but simple images of home and street. . . .

THE FAILURE OF THE WORKHOUSE

The indictment of the workhouse in *Oliver Twist* is effective because it is focused on its specific failure to be a home for the indigent: it is a place in which the married man is separated from his family 'and made . . . a bachelor', and the alternative to a life in the streets that it offers is to be 'starved by a gradual process' rather than 'by a quick one'. Far from being made at home, the inmates of the workhouse are depersonalized by it: born in the workhouse, Oliver—an 'item of mortality'—is 'badged and ticketed' a parish child; and is finally put out 'To Let', five pounds being offered 'to anybody who [will] take possession of him'. It is for the midnight streets that he is schooled by the 'want and cold' he suffers at the baby-farm to which he is sent and by 'the gloom of his infant years'.

It is in this light that the most famous incident in the book should, I think, be viewed. J. Hillis Miller maintains that 'the fame of the scene in which Oliver asks for "more" derives . . . from the way it expresses dynamically Oliver's revolt against the hostile social and material world'; but it seems to me that the scene above all dramatizes, in the most direct and simple manner, the extent to which what is taken for granted at home is denied in the workhouse. Hence the enormity of the response to Oliver's request; and hence the power of the scene, which appeals to our own deepest sense of the right to ask for more as a natural perquisite of home and childhood. In this incident Oliver no doubt does revolt against the workhouse system, but it is not as a rebel that he is cast in the novel; indeed, his single act of rebellion against the sort of authority represented by the workhouse even falls to him by lot. He is throughout, rather, the exemplar of a boy without a home; and it is on its failure to provide him with one, to save him from the streets, that Dickens's indictment of the workhouse rests.

Dickens's treatment of the workhouse as the central institution depicted in the novel foreshadows the way in which institutions are presented in later novels such as *Bleak House* and *Little Dorrit,* yet reveals the limitations of his method at this stage of his career. The workhouse is not treated as an isolated social abuse, as Dotheboys Hall is in *Nicholas Nickleby* (which followed *Oliver Twist*); but, at the same time, it is not established as representative of the society that has produced it in the way that the Court of Chancery and the Circumlocution Office are. The structure of the novel, with its polarized worlds, cannot accommodate such an effect, for the workhouse is not part of either. Thus, though the failure of the workhouse is symbolic of the wider failure of society to make adequate provision for the poor, and this failure is fraught with the dangers that are dramatized in Oliver's story; the attitudes that lie behind the failure have no correlative in the world that, we must assume, has brought the workhouse into being. The representative inhabitants of this world are the Brownlows and the Maylies, but there is no indication that they share in a social responsibility for the workhouse. Responsibility is simply attributed, in a kind of limbo, to disembodied 'philosophers' and to fat but insubstantial gentlemen of the board. Dickens's social criticism in *Oliver Twist,* in other words, is limited in force because, though it probes, it does not probe home. The workhouse may mediate between the two worlds of the novel, but it does not link them; whereas in the later novels . . . the institutions that are attacked function as the foci of multifarious worlds that radiate from them, and the analogical method is used to relate public failure and private complaisance.

Domestic Strife in *Oliver Twist*

Kenneth C. Frederick

Kenneth C. Frederick examines domestic scenes in *Oliver Twist,* finding "a vast emptiness where the center of affirmation might be expected to be." Frederick not only finds the Brownlow and Maylie homes "disquietingly empty" but also notes the paucity of married characters. Moreover, the few unions presented stand out for their wretchedness, such as the strife-ridden marriage of the Bumbles. While domestic bliss is presented as an ideal, then, it is never realized. Rather, the orphan Oliver—himself the product of an ill-fated union—must renounce conventional relationships in his quest for a home and family. Frederick contributed the following critical essay to *College English.*

Even in the preface to the Charles Dickens edition of *Oliver Twist,* published thirty years after the novel's first appearance, Dickens felt compelled to account for the dank and squalid scenes depicted therein. Yet nothing he wrote in defense of his purpose can dispel the response of most readers, that the image of evil the book presents is far more forceful than that of the ostensibly triumphant good. Fagin's terrifying detachment during his trial, Nancy's fatal ambivalence toward Sikes, and Sikes's own suicidal guilt—these survive, complex and terrible, in our memory; while Mr. Brownlow's diligent charity and Rose's high-pitched honor dissipate into vapors. On the one side Dickens dramatized emotions, on the other he manipulated attitudes. Still, it is not simply the relative density with which the evil is portrayed that tips the scale so strongly in its direction. It is a matter of proportion as well, for images of deprivation, misery, and malevolence extend across most of the novel, while goodness is subordi-

Reprinted from "The Cold, Cold Hearth: Domestic Strife in *Oliver Twist,*" by Kenneth C. Frederick, *College English,* March 1966. Copyright © 1966 by the National Council of Teachers of English. Reprinted with permission.

nated until the book's closing sections. Charity, solicitude, and good humor maintain a precarious existence through much of the novel and emerge at last somewhat breathless but triumphant. Yet for Oliver none of these virtues is enough in itself; what he seeks is a fixed position in the universe—a home and family. This very goal, however, is rendered distant by the ambiguity with which it is presented.

QUEST FOR A HOME

Oliver Twist is the story of an orphan's search for a home and family. Yet, to examine the picture of family life that the novel presents is to discover a vast emptiness where the center of affirmation might be expected to be. Two striking circumstances can be noted which bear quite directly on Oliver's search: that the households of Mr. Brownlow and Mrs. Maylie, his only contacts with gentleness and peace, provide no real antithesis to Oliver's homeless condition; and that, although the family is founded on marriage, the only marriages dramatized in the book are acutely wretched.

We recognize at once the crucial role of Mr. Brownlow's and Mrs. Maylie's homes as havens in the uncompromisingly dichotomized world of the novel. Only here can Oliver breathe, only here does he know kindness and civility. The rest is viciousness. Graham Greene expresses it well: "We know that when Oliver leaves Mr. Brownlow's house to walk a few hundred yards to the bookseller, his friends will wait in vain for his return. All London outside the quiet, shady street in Pentonville belongs to his pursuers." For Greene, the world of *Oliver Twist* is "a world without God"; Arnold Kettle, whose interests in discussing the novel are less metaphysical, examines that same gulf between good and evil, and its effects on Dickens' technique. He sees the book as a struggle between plot and pattern; yet the starting point of his discussion is that same haven provided by Mr. Brownlow. With a sure sense, Kettle singles out the scene of Oliver's awakening there as "a central situation in the book—this emergence out of squalor into comfort and kindliness," and calls attention to its repetition later when Oliver awakens at the Maylies'.

EMPTY HAVENS

What each critic emphasizes here is that in a universe, if not Manichean, at least abundant in malice, the positive forces find symbolic expression in the two households into which

Oliver passively drifts. These symbols are of course appropriate, since the essential movement of the book is Oliver's quest for a home, a quest that grows out of his very identity as an orphan who, lacking an organic family, is reduced to an abstraction by the "philosophers" of the welfare system; and inducted into the no less organized army of crime that forays ceaselessly into the streets of London. What Oliver seeks, then, is the stability and security of an organic family relationship. Few serious readers, however, are willing to grant that Oliver comes convincingly to the fulfillment of that quest. The fact is that only the criminals exist with psychological solidity while Oliver's helpers are absolutely pure, which is to say that they are absolutely transparent devices of salvation.

Yet if the positive forces do not have the power of the negative ones, it is not simply because the uncomplicated benevolence of the "good" characters is dramatically pallid. Those very havens that give Oliver his only notions of the happy home life he seeks provide no real antithesis to his misfortunes—they are disquietingly empty. If the image of Fagin, the false father, cooking sausages over the fire, is a parody of domestic life, the scenes in the homes of Oliver's benefactors are unfinished pictures of the happy home.

The dominant note in each of the houses is an uneasy silence. At Brownlow's Oliver spends most of his time recovering from his illness. "They were happy days, those of Oliver's recovery. Everything was so quiet, and neat, and orderly—everybody was kind and gentle—that after the noise and turbulence in the midst of which he had always lived, it seemed like Heaven itself" (Chap. 14). Only Grimwig's deceptively hostile bluster breaks the hushed tone. And on the day that Oliver leaves the house in Pentonville our last view of the place is a tableau of Brownlow and Grimwig "sit[ting] in silence, with the watch between them" (Chap. 14). Mrs. Maylie's residences in Chertsey and in the country are no less silent. Here we have not one but two invalids. Rose, who is soon to fall sick herself, describes the cottage to Oliver: "The quiet place, the pure air, and all the pleasures and beauties of spring, will restore you in a few days" (Chap. 32). In the country Oliver is more active, picking flowers, reading the Bible. Yet the three months of Oliver's domestication are reported in panoramic fashion by the narrator, so that they become an idyllic blur. Even here, however, Oliver finds a "little churchyard" whither he may repair to think of his mother and "sob unseen" (Chap. 32).

FRAGMENTED FAMILIES

His benefactors, then, provide retreats, hospitals, and places of meditation, but not homes. It is not only illness that silences them. Rather, each of the households is truncated, each lacks the elements of completeness. Mr. Brownlow is a bachelor, Mrs. Maylie is a widow. Indeed, the entire assemblage of Oliver's friends comprises bachelors, widows, and an orphan. One of the overriding ironies of the novel is that whereas, from the opening scenes in the workhouse, family life is implied as one of the highest goods, Oliver never encounters a complete, happy family; indeed, the family, in so far as it inescapably rests on marriage, seems doomed from the beginning, for the grim fact is that marriage in the book produces not blissful union but strife. The happy family exists only as an ideal, visible for instance in the quivering ethereal nubility of Rose: "The very intelligence that shone in her deep blue eye, and was stamped upon her noble head, seemed scarcely of her age, or of the world; and yet the changing expression of sweetness and good humour, the thousand lights that played about her face and left no shadow there; above all, the smile, the cheerful, happy smile —were made for Home, and fireside peace and happiness" (Chap. 29). How far off, though, are such ends from the world of the book. Oliver knows only fragmentation; he must find solace in partial relationships. The nun-like devotion of Mrs. Bedwin, the eccentricities of Grimwig and Losberne are called upon to fill the void that exists in the homes of Oliver's protectors. The integral domestic bliss which is implied as an end is never dramatized in the novel. If the ultimate union between Harry and Rose is put aside for the moment, the striking fact is that, for a book crowded with characters, *Oliver Twist* presents a panorama singularly deficient in married people, and totally devoid of happy ones.

If Oliver finds only fragmented families among the "good" people, he experiences domestic life quite early in the book during his stay at the Sowerberrys'. Their relationship has a ritualistic quality, the undertaker addressing his wife in terms of endearment and she responding "Ugh, you brute," on occasion accompanying her answers with "an hysterical laugh which threatened violent consequences" (Chap. 5).

Mrs. Sowerberry is of course a witch in a fairy tale. The "short, thin, squeezed-up woman, with a vixenish countenance" treats Oliver even worse than her husband: "There! Get downstairs, little bag o' bones!" she says, pushing him down a flight of stairs into the cellar where she will give him the dog's scraps to eat. Later, she shows him to his bed: "You don't mind sleeping among the coffins, I suppose?" (Chap. 4.). This is Oliver's first experience of domestic life, and it's no wonder he runs away.

THE BUMBLES

But the Sowerberrys are not the only married people in the book. The middle section of the novel contains Mr. Bumble's courting and winning of Mrs. Corney, an episode which parodies the romance of domestic life that so delighted Dickens elsewhere. The beadle, who is detached from the monolith of Oliver's oppressors by virtue of his foolishness, has human qualities, and his response to Mrs. Corney's "cheerful fire" are natural and understandable. Coming in from the bitter cold, Bumble is intoxicated by the warmth and coziness of the apartment. His instincts towards security, if less intense, are as sincere as Oliver's. The difference, of course, is that Mr. Bumble is the servant of mercenary instincts, though they move him to comic not demonic action. The comedy of the situation springs in part from his blending of romance and business: "Oh! Mrs. Corney what a prospect this opens! What a opportunity for a jining of hearts and house-keepings!" (Chap. 27). Though the coziness of the scene is juxtaposed against the misery of the paupers outside, the irony is not driven home harshly—Bumble remains a foolish, not a vicious character.

Yet Dickens has heard the cries of the poor and before the book is over he has ruthlessly administered poetic justice to the pompous beadle, chiefly through the agency of his marriage. Chapter 37 is described thus: "In which the reader may perceive a contrast not uncommon in matrimonial cases." We now see Mr. Bumble musing lugubriously on the loss of his cocked hat, his gold-laced coat and his bachelor's freedom. He reflects, with the lucidity of hindsight: "I sold myself . . . for six teaspoons, a pair of sugar-tongs, and a milk-pot, with a small quantity of second-hand furniture and twenty pounds in money. I went very reasonable. Cheap, dirt cheap!" (Chap. 37). The new Mrs. Bumble systematically strips the former beadle of his power, experimenting half-heartedly with tears and at last resigning herself to brute physical violence, with which she is completely successful. Marriage has brought a remarkable change of fortune to Mr. Bumble: "Two months! No more than two months ago, I was not only my own master, but everyone else's, so far as the porochial workhouse was concerned, and now!—" (Chap. 37). In short, he is thoroughly miserable and begins to feel "that men who ran away from their wives, leaving them chargeable to the parish, ought, in justice, to be visited with no punishment at all, but rather rewarded as meritorious individuals who had suffered much" (Chap. 37). But the worst is still to come. Mrs. Bumble takes the lead in the sinister dealings with Monks and eventually brings ruin upon the family. In the final chapter the wretchedness is complete: "Mr. and Mrs. Bumble, deprived of her situations, were gradually reduced to great indigence and misery, and finally became paupers in that very same workhouse in which they had once lorded it over others. Mr. Bumble has been heard to say that in this reverse and degradation, he has not even spirits to be thankful for being separated from his wife." It is ironically apt that the very last words we hear of Mr. Bumble before he disappears into groan-filled oblivion, are "his wife," the nemesis that has driven him there.

So much for domestic bliss as it is actually dramatized in *Oliver Twist*, no matter how persistently it may hover over the action as an ideal. A convalescent serenity prevails in the foreshortened families of Oliver's protectors, but the only operative unions depicted are full of strife.

The marital blight is not only visited upon the wicked, however. One must remember that the ultimate reason for all of Oliver's troubles is the affair of his mother and father, precipitated by the wreck of the latter's home life. Mr. Brownlow recalls "the slow torture, the protracted anguish of that ill-assorted union. I know how listlessly and wearily each of that wretched pair dragged on their heavy chain through a world that was poisoned to them both" (Chap. 49). As Monks says of Mrs. Leeford and Oliver's father, "she had no great affection for him, nor he for her" (Chap. 51). Thus the panorama of domestic wretchedness extends even into the past. Against this background Oliver's search for a happy home seems a desperately hopeful notion. All his experience seems to confirm the view of the world Oliver learned when working for Sowerberry: "Husbands . . . bore the loss of their wives with the most heroic calmness. Wives, again, put on weeds for their husbands as if, so far from grieving in the garb of sorrow, they had made up their minds to render it as becoming and attractive as possible" (Chap. 6).

An Elusive Goal

One would not like to make too much of a small point. All that can be confidently asserted of the depiction of family life in the novel is that it sharpens the outlines of a world in which evil runs rampant and good is on the defensive, poised for retreat. In a book whose structure is based on an orphan's search for a home and family, the heavily shadowed picture of family life casts considerable doubt on the attainability of this goal. Yet there is a final point to be made which can help us appreciate some of the tensions that are suppressed in the ostensible resolution of Oliver's problem and his achievement of a happy home.

In a world where the family unit seems to be crumbling from within, an outside threat would seem to be superfluous, yet the final irony of this situation is that such a threat exists and is, in fact, embodied in the person of Oliver himself. He is, after all, illegitimate, as his overseers at the workhouse never fail to make clear to him. Passive and feeble, Oliver is time after time reviled by "respectable" members of society. His treatment at the workhouse, the recurrent prophecies of hanging, the taunts of Noah Claypole, "who could trace his genealogy all the way back to his parents" (Chap. 5) are all predicated on the notion that the circumstances of his birth have marked Oliver's character irrevocably for the bad. He is the product of an anti-social act, the rupture of the sacred family unit, and in this role, represents a threat to society itself.

Oliver, the bastard, is naturally good whereas his half-brother Monks, whose credentials are quite legitimate, is depicted in diabolical terms. This reversal of conventional values reverberates throughout the novel in so far as it implicates much of the "respectable" society in the evil that is frankly practiced by the likes of Fagin; and it poses a dilemma: if society itself is corrupt, and that suggestion is strong, where is the outcast of society to turn in his quest for a fixed place? It is in facing this question that one comes to appreciate the importance, perhaps the absolute necessity to Dickens, of Mr. Brownlow and Mrs. Maylie, whose connections with society are so tenuous that they are able to withdraw completely in order to preside over the triumph of the good.

REDEFINING FAMILY

The only possible resolution to Oliver's difficulties is to escape society, to destroy the old family relationships, to create a new society based upon another kind of family. Thus in the eschatological dimension that obtains at the book's close, Oliver and his friends realign society's relationships and reconstruct a family on the basis of love rather than law or blood. The first step is the complete revelation and acceptance of all the socially disgraceful facts about Oliver's (and Rose's) family, and then a conscious, willed transposition of relations. Oliver, the bastard, is accepted by Mr. Brownlow as his son. Oliver himself changes Rose's status: "I'll never call her aunt—sister, my own dear sister, that something has taught my heart to love so dearly from the first" (Chap. 51). Rose, herself an orphan with a "stain" upon her name, achieves a further relation. Mrs. Maylie, upon hearing her story, affirms that Rose is "not the less my niece . . . not the less my dearest child . . . my own dear girl" (Chap. 51). As for Harry, since Rose has considered her family history an impediment to their marriage, he cuts himself off from much of his family; he renounces the world for a country parish. We may be sure that their marriage will work, for it has been purged of the two elements that have caused evil in the other ones: Harry's retirement in the country has removed him from economic competition; and his willingness to choose the "disreputable" Rose at the cost of his political aspirations demonstrates that he is not excessively concerned with his family name—he has no false sense of respectability. Greed had certainly been one of the strongest passions in the homes of Sowerberry and Bumble, and it was "family pride" that forced Oliver's father into the unfortunate marriage that produced all the troubles. Of course, this is a moral and not an artistic victory: the existence of the poor and the wretched in London has not been negated by this idyll, which is simply a turning away from the problem.

Almost all the good people undertake the same symbolic withdrawal from that part of the world of the novel which is most vivid, chiefly symbolized by what Dr. Losberne calls "this confounded London" (Chap. 32). The "good" characters gravitate toward the country retreat, and eventually all of them live there except the eccentric Mr. Grimwig, who nonetheless makes frequent visits. Even Oliver's erring mother is given a posthumous place of honor here. Having totally overturned the world's judgments and relations, Oliver and his friends have created a "little society whose condition approached as nearly to one of perfect happiness as can ever be known in this changing world" (Chap. 53). They constitute, in fact, one happy family.

A World of Evil

Graham Greene

Graham Greene considers *Oliver Twist* a brilliant sketch of "the cold, wet, shelterless midnight streets of London"—and a whole world "made by Satan and not by God." Dickens's hand, writes Greene, "seldom falters" in his descriptions of the demons that haunt Oliver's world after dark, namely Fagin, Sikes, and Monks. According to Greene, these malevolent characters represent Dickens at his finest. Conversely, Greene labels the humane Mr. Brownlow and the sweet-tempered Mrs. Maylie "inadequate ghosts of goodness." The following essay, which originally appeared as an introduction to *Oliver Twist*, is excerpted from Greene's book *The Lost Childhood and Other Essays.*

It is a mistake to think of *Oliver Twist* as a realistic story: only late in his career did Dickens learn to write realistically of human beings; at the beginning he invented life and we no more believe in the temporal existence of Fagin or Bill Sykes than we believe in the existence of that Giant whom Jack slew as he bellowed his Fee Fi Fo Fum. There were real Fagins and Bill Sykes and real Bumbles in the England of his day, but he had not drawn them, as he was later to draw the convict Magwitch; these characters in *Oliver Twist* are simply parts of one huge invented scene, what Dickens in his own preface called 'the cold wet shelterless midnight streets of London.' How the phrase goes echoing on through the books of Dickens until we meet it again so many years later in 'the weary western streets of London on a cold dusty spring night' which were so melancholy to Pip. But Pip was to be as real as the weary streets, while Oliver was as unrealistic as the cold wet midnight of which he formed a part.

Excerpted from *The Lost Childhood and Other Essays* (London: Eyre and Spottiswode, 1951) by Graham Greene. Reprinted with permission from David Higham Associates.

OPPRESSIVE IMAGERY

This is not to criticize the book so much as to describe it. For what an imagination this youth of twenty-six had that he could invent so monstrous and complete a legend! We are not lost with Oliver Twist round Saffron Hill: we are lost in the interstices of one young, angry, gloomy brain, and the oppressive images stand out along the track like the lit figures in a Ghost Train tunnel.

> Against the wall were ranged, in regular array, a long row of elm boards cut into the same shape, looking in the dim light, like high shouldered ghosts with their hands in their breeches pockets.

We have most of us seen those nineteenth-century prints where the bodies of naked women form the face of a character, the Diplomat, the Miser and the like. So the crouching figure of Fagin seems to form the mouth, Sykes with his bludgeon the jutting features and the sad lost Oliver the eyes of one man, as lost as Oliver.

Chesterton, in a fine imaginative passage, has described the mystery behind Dickens's plots, the sense that even the author was unaware of what was really going on, so that when the explanations come and we reach, huddled into the last pages of *Oliver Twist*, a naked complex narrative of illegitimacy and burnt wills and destroyed evidence, we simply do not believe. 'The secrecy is sensational; the secret is tame. The surface of the thing seems more awful than the core. It seems almost as if these grisly figures, Mrs. Chadband and Mrs. Clennan, Miss Havisham and Miss Flite, Nemo and Sally Brass, were keeping something back from the author as well as from the reader. When the book closes we do not know their real secret. They soothe the optimistic Dickens with something less terrible than the truth.'

EVIL VERSUS GOODNESS

What strikes the attention most in this closed Fagin universe are the different levels of unreality. If, as one is inclined to believe, the creative writer perceives his world once and for all in childhood and adolescence, and his whole career is an effort to illustrate his private world in terms of the great public world we all share, we can understand why Fagin and Sykes in their most extreme exaggerations move us more than the benevolence of Mr. Brownlow or the sweetness of Mrs. Maylie—they touch with fear as the others never really touch with love. It was not that the unhappy child, with his hurt pride and his sense of hopeless insecurity, had not encountered human goodness—he had simply failed to recognize it in those streets between Gadshill and Hungerford Market which had been as narrowly enclosed as Oliver Twist's. When Dickens at this early period tried to describe goodness he seems to have remembered the small stationers' shops on the way to the blacking factory with their coloured paper scraps of angels and virgins, or perhaps the face of some old gentleman who had spoken kindly to him outside Warren's factory. He has swum up towards goodness

---

THE LONDON OF *OLIVER TWIST*

In his Introduction to a 1962 edition of Oliver Twist, *J. Hillis Miller writes that the novel is a literal representation of London in the 1830s.*

Oliver Twist is in fact rooted in the reality of the eighteen-thirties. Saffron Hill, Bethnal Green, and the other slums mentioned in *Oliver Twist* were real places in London, notorious in Dickens' day as the dens of thieves and pickpockets. Dickens had seen these places with his own eyes, both as a newspaper reporter and during long walks to every corner of London. The streets through which the Artful Dodger leads Oliver when he first comes to London, the route followed by Sikes when he takes Oliver out in the country to rob the Maylies' house, the wanderings of Sikes after he has murdered Nancy— all these are scrupulously accurate itineraries and can be followed on an old map or retraced in the London of today. And other nineteenth-century reports corroborate Dickens' descriptions of the filth of London, the drunken, brawling crowds in the streets, the sordid rooms, so dark and dirty that they seem far underground, the fog, the mud, the rain, the somber river flowing through the city and bringing more dirt than it takes away. The London of *Oliver Twist*, which seems to a modern reader like the dream of an urban hell, is a literal representation of the city as it was in the early nineteenth century. Mr. Fang, for example, the terrifying magistrate who nearly sentences Oliver to prison, is modelled on a real judge, a Mr. Laing, well known at the time. Dickens had visited his court, and imitates his mannerisms and speech in this novel.

J. Hillis Miller, "Introduction," in Charles Dickens, *The Adventures of Oliver Twist.* New York: Holt, Rinehart and Winston, 1962.

from the deepest world of his experience, and on this shallow level the conscious brain has taken a hand, trying to construct characters to represent virtue and, because his age demanded it, triumphant virtue, but all he can produce are powdered wigs and gleaming spectacles and a lot of bustle with bowls of broth and a pate angelic face. . . .

Turn to the daylight world and our first sight of Rose:

> The younger lady was in the lovely bloom and springtime of womanhood; at that age, when, if ever angels be for God's good purposes enthroned in mortal forms, they may be, without impiety, supposed to abide in such as hers. She was not past seventeen. Cast in so slight and exquisite a mould; so mild and gentle; so pure and beautiful; that earth seemed not her element, nor its rough creatures her fit companions.

Or Mr. Brownlow as he first appeared to Oliver:

> Now, the old gentleman came in as brisk as need be; but he had no sooner raised his spectacles on his forehead, and thrust his hands behind the skirts of his dressing-gown to take a good long look at Oliver, than his countenance underwent a very great variety of odd contortions. . . . The fact is, if the truth must be told that Mr. Brownlow's heart, being large enough for any six ordinary old gentlemen of humane disposition, forced a supply of tears into his eyes by some hydraulic process which we are not sufficiently philosophical to be in a condition to explain.

How can we really believe that these inadequate ghosts of goodness can triumph over Fagin, Monks and Sykes? And the answer, of course, is that they never could have triumphed without the elaborate machinery of the plot disclosed in the last pages. This world of Dickens is a world without God; and as a substitute for the power and the glory of the omnipotent and omniscient are a few sentimental references to heaven, angels, the sweet faces of the dead, and Oliver saying, 'Heaven is a long way off, and they are too happy there to come down to the bedside of a poor boy.' In this Manichean world we can believe in evil-doing, but goodness wilts into philanthropy, kindness, and those strange vague sicknesses into which Dickens's young women so frequently fall and which seem in his eyes a kind of badge of virtue, as though there were a merit in death.

But how instinctively Dickens's genius recognized the flaw and made a virtue out of it. We cannot believe in the power of Mr. Baldwin, but nor did Dickens, and from his inability to believe in his own good characters springs the real tension of his novel. The boy Oliver may not lodge in our

brain like David Copperfield, and though many of Mr. Bumble's phrases have become and deserve to have become familiar quotations we can feel he was manufactured: he
never breathes like Mr. Dorrit; yet Oliver's predicament, the
nightmare fight between the darkness where the demons
walk and the sunlight where ineffective goodness makes its
last stand in a condemned world, will remain part of our
imaginations forever. We read of the defeat of Monks, and of
Fagin screaming in the condemned cell, and of Sykes dangling from his self-made noose, but we don't believe. We
have witnessed Oliver's temporary escapes too often and his
inevitable recapture: *there* is the truth and the creative experience. We know that when Oliver leaves Mr. Brownlow's
house to walk a few hundred yards to the bookseller, his
friends will wait in vain for his return. All London outside
the quiet, shady street in Pentonville belongs to his pursuers;
and when he escapes again into the house of Mrs. Maylie in
the fields beyond Shepperton, we know his security is false.
The seasons may pass, but safety depends not on time but on
daylight. As children we all knew that: how all day we could
forget the dark and the journey to bed. It is with a sense of relief that at last in twilight we see the faces of the Jew and
Monks peer into the cottage window between the sprays of jessamine. At that moment we realize how the whole world, and
not London only, belongs to these two after dark. Dickens,
dealing out his happy endings and his unreal retributions, can
never ruin the validity and dignity of that moment. 'They had
recognized him, and he them; and their look was as firmly impressed upon his memory, as if it had been deeply carved in
stone, and set before him from his birth.'

'From his birth'—Dickens may have intended that phrase
to refer to the complicated imbroglios of the plot that lie outside the novel, 'something less terrible than the truth'. As for
the truth, is it too fantastic to imagine that in this novel, as in
many of his later books, creeps in, unrecognized by the author, the eternal and alluring taint of the Manichee, with its
simple and terrible explanation of our plight, how the world
was made by Satan and not by God, lulling us with the music of despair?

Poverty and Villainy in *Oliver Twist*

Katherine T. Brueck

Many contemporary critics of *Oliver Twist* assert that Dickens renders his villainous characters sympathetic by presenting them as products of an inhumane social system. Katherine T. Brueck charges that this tendency to pity the likes of Fagin, Sikes, and Monks is flawed. Dickens, Brueck contends, reserves his sympathy for Oliver. Thus, when Dickens describes the squalid environment and material deprivations of Fagin's gang, his purpose is to underscore the group's moral ugliness and administer poetic justice—not to elicit sympathy for a gang of miscreants. Brueck contributed the following critical analysis to *Dickens Studies Newsletter*.

A number of recent examinations of *Oliver Twist* endeavor to whittle the Victorian Dickens into a man of twentieth-century sensibilities. These works consistently suggest that Dickens delineates his criminals as victimized products of poverty. Arnold Kettle, for example, maintains that the Artful Dodger's recalcitrant behavior during his trial signifies Dickens's repudiation of the society that relegated the juvenile to slum life. John Bayley, similarly, interprets the cry of outraged defiance uttered by Fagin in his prison cell as the author's ringing appeal for a solution to the ills of the city. In like vein, William T. Lankford claims that Fagin's gang is the sorry fruit of institutions which dehumanize the poor. Zelda Austen, echoing the message of these critics, speaks of Fagin with pity as "a frustrated, shabby old fence, trembling in a cold, ill-lighted, filthy room."

Twentieth-century writers, of course, are infinitely more aware than persons of the previous century that subconscious forces substantially determine human behavior. Thus the reluctance of modern critics to view the criminal in

Reprinted from "Poverty and Villainy in *Oliver Twist:* Unravelling the Paradox," by Katherine T. Brueck, *Dickens Studies Newsletter*, September 1981. Reprinted with permission from *Dickens Studies Newsletter*.

Oliver Twist with facile condemnation is only natural. And yet, regardless of the insights which modern psychology furnishes them, when critics today ascribe to Dickens a social sympathy for the villains in *Oliver Twist*—however careful they might be to label his compassion "implicit"—they disregard an express intention of the author. Dickens purported to write his work not simply in order to formulate a petition for the poor, but, as his preface to the novel directly informs us, also as a means of rendering the criminal repugnant. Upon consideration of the two-fold purpose of Dickens's narrative, it becomes apparent that poverty itself serves two functions in the novel. And through neither use does the fictionist cast a softened eye upon his London scoundrels.

In his major preface to *Oliver Twist*, Dickens attests that he solicited the aid of material setting when he embarked on his attempt to make crime appear repulsive: "The cold, wet, shelterless midnight streets of London; the foul and frowsy dens, where vice is closely packed and lacks the room to turn; the haunts of hunger and disease, the shabby rags that scarcely hold together; where are the attractions of these things? Have they no lesson, and do they not whisper something beyond the little-regarded warning of a moral precept?" Here Dickens specifically maintains that he sketches the poverty of his city thugs in order to sensualize the horror of their crimes, that he might render their gloomy habits obnoxious. This seminal passage is conspicuously uncolored by compassion for the novel's slum dwellers or by outrage against their indigence.

POETIC JUSTICE

Zelda Austen, one critic of late who has become committed to the cause of the poverty-stricken delinquent, claims not only that Dickens identifies with his impoverished n'er-do-wells, but even that the outcasts in *Oliver Twist* "excited both his compassion and his comic genius as the good people could not." An examination of the variance between Dickens's manner of portraying the poverty of the lawless characters and his delineation of the trials of Oliver belies that assertion. Contrary to Austen's contention, the economic need of Dickens's social rejects is a poverty of poetic justice; it is therefore marked neither by humor nor by pathos, but by loathsomeness. Dickens preserves his compassion and his moral irony for his guileless hero; Oliver, to the exclusion of Fagin and his cronies, is the sole object of the author's social concern.

The increasing degree of wretchedness that characterizes Bill Sikes's surroundings as he wades more and more deeply in moral turpitude provides perhaps the clearest evidence that the material deprivation of Fagin's gang is meant to be viewed as a function of poetic justice rather than as a social problem. Significantly, the worldly state of Sikes begins to decline directly after he compels Oliver to participate in the burglary junket at Chertsey. No practical reason for the worsening of the larcener's material condition is given; it can only betoken the degeneration of his soul:

> The room . . . was not one of those he had tenanted, previous to the Chertsey expedition, although it was in the same quarter of the town, and was situated at no great distance from his former lodgings. It was not in appearance, so desirable a habitation as his old quarters: being a mean and badly-furnished apartment, of very limited size: lighted only by one small window in the shelving roof, and abutting on a close and dirty lane. Nor were there wanting other indications of the good gentleman's having gone down in the world of late. . . .

With similar effect, Folly Ditch, the foulest of all sections of London, serves as the backdrop for Sikes's hanging. Dickens plunges his criminal into the most squalid milieu possible in order to make palpable a moral disease which has become truly hideous: "Dirt-besmeared walls and decaying foundations; every repulsive lineament of poverty, every loathsome indication of filth, rot, and garbage; all these ornament the banks of Folly Ditch."

In like vein, Dickens casts the Dodger into a slum and paints there "as dirty a juvenile as one would wish to see" in order to render execrable his moral distortion. To Dickens the muddy visage of poverty particularly suits the Dodger because it is he who seduces Oliver into Fagin's den and who labors most directly to corrupt him. It is highly instructive in this regard that the blighted neighborhood through which the Dodger conducts Oliver, when the thief first leads his captive to Fagin's hideaway, induces the criminal's unsuspecting follower to experience horror rather than compassion: "A dirtier or more wretched place he had never seen. The street was very narrow and muddy; and the air was impregnated with filthy odours. . . . Covered ways and yards, which here and there diverged from the main street, disclosed little knots of houses where drunken men and women were positively wallowing in the filth. . . ."

SYMBOLS OF ETHICAL DECLINE

The vile milieu of Fagin, like that of his henchmen, serves as a metaphorical representation of ethical decline. The walls and ceiling of his room, which "were perfectly black with age and dirt," and Fagin's "greasy flannel gown" symbolize a soul engulfed in moral slime. The emotion manifested by Oliver as he explores his mentor's crumbling house bespeaks strongly the poetic purpose of the arch villain's poverty. Far from being prodded into pity, as Oliver peruses the old man's abode, he indulges in a wistful surmise concerning respectable owners of bygone days.

Similarly, Nancy deplores her moral degradation and her poverty as if they were one and the same condition. Nancy bemoans to Fagin her occupation as thief and prostitute, for example, by bewailing her physical surroundings: "It is my living; and the cold, wet, dirty streets are my home; and you're the wretch that drove me to them long ago; and that'll keep me there, day and night, day and night, till I die!" The guilt-ridden woman reveals to Oliver, in analogous terms, the fits of distraction that have possessed her since the child first fell in league with Fagin: "I don't know what comes over me sometimes . . . ; it's this damp, dirty room, I think." And Nancy strikes the same rhetorical chord as she laments her immoral addictions to the respectable Rose Maylie: "The alley and the gutter were mine, as they will be my death bed."

Thus Dickens couches Fagin and his followers in a loathsome environment in an attempt to underscore the moral ugliness of their pursuits. Dickens combats the contemporary ill-treatment of the poor, on the other hand, to borrow the phrase of Dickens's friend and biographer, John Forster, by means of "the light arms of humour and laughter, and the gentle ones of pathos and sadness." As I will illustrate, the disparity between these "light," "gentle" techniques and the somber ones employed to detail the poverty of Fagin and his company indicates that Dickens wields only Oliver's poverty in the battle for social concern. The destitution of the urban hoods fulfills a separate purpose.

DICKENS'S USE OF HUMOR

Dickens's ironic descriptions of Bumble, the administrator of the workhouse where his pauper-hero first resides, exemplify the novelist's humorous treatment of poverty. In keeping with his desire to arouse social fervor, Dickens's satirical tone simultaneously condemns the perpetrator of human misery, of Bumbles sort, and encourages his readers to believe that even such a callous personality can be reformed. When Dickens maintains that the juvenile inhabitants of Bumble's workhouse subsisted "without the inconvenience of too much food or too much clothing," when he has Bumble remark of a pair of charges whom he is on the point of transferring to London that it is "cheaper to move 'em than to bury 'em," and when the author speaks of the "perverse behaviour of the two paupers, who persisted in shivering, and complaining of the cold," he at one and the same time exposes the prevalent inhumane treatment of the suffering poor, which Bumble typifies, and suggests the ease with which cruelty to the miserable could be remedied by making it look ridiculous.

In the dens of lawlessness, too, Dickens's humor simultaneously unveils the hideous secrets of social abuse and urges a belief that good can vanquish evil. In the following passage, Oliver, who is made vulnerable to the practice of outlaws because he is penniless and alone, reacts with consummate innocence to Fagin's devious encouragement that he practice picking his pocket. Here, again, comedy brightens the dark aspect of social ill in order to induce optimism as well as concern:

> Oliver wondered what picking the old gentleman's pocket in play, had to do with his chances of being a great man. But thinking that the Jew, being so much his senior, must know best, he followed him quietly to the table; and was soon deeply involved in his new study.

Consistent with her fondness for the indigent deliquent, Zelda Austen suggests that the amusing descriptions of Fagin's gang signal the author's warming toward the impoverished malefactors whose society Oliver joins. The irony with which Dickens describes the pursuits of this group however, distinctly indicates that the author himself is no less bewildered by the moral hazards which mine the slum world into which Oliver falls than the boy himself would have been had he been aware that Fagin were not a kind old gentleman but rather a ruthless thief and pimp. Dickens's humor consistently manifests an ingenuous reaction to moral evil which is part and parcel of his social hopefulness. The fact that Dickens exerts his satire invariably in the service of Oliver's poverty and not at all in the rendering of Fagin's illustrates that he articulates a concern for the poor through the innocent youth, but not through the man who seeks his corruption.

A mournful tune interweaves with Dickens's jocular song of compassion for the poor. This doleful melody, like the merry one, absents itself from criminal quarters except when Oliver's poverty is at issue. Dickens suffuses Oliver's leavetaking of the workhouse with a pathos for the rootless pauper that his poetic passages, and his ironic ones, lack by definition. Oliver "burst into an agony of childish grief, as the cottage gate closed after him," for the public institution, although laced with injustice and oppression, afforded the only home he had ever known. Dickens mentions with similar warmth of feeling that when the poor boy readies himself for sleep on the initial night at the shop of his first employer, Oliver's "heart *was* heavy . . . and he wished, as he crept into his narrow bed, that that were his coffin."

Dickens's description of Oliver's arduous journey to London following his expulsion at Sowerberry's is charged with the same notes of pity for the vagabond, whom despair stalks constantly. At one point along the difficult road, wealthy passersby derive amusement from Oliver's adversity. The "outsides" of the stagecoach tease the destitute child with hope of relief from hunger by offering to give him a half-penny if he can run alongside the moving vehicle. Upon observing that the pace of the weak and exhausted Oliver slackens steadily, the onlookers pronounce the boy "an idle young dog," repocket their money, and thence abandon the waif to his fate. Unlike the wretched circumstances of Fagin's gang, Oliver's worldly affliction indisputably softens the heart.

Although current Dickens scholarship maintains that Dickens evokes an implicit lament for the squalid milieu of Fagin and his followers, upon examination it appears that the poverty of the thieves, murderers, and prostitutes in *Oliver Twist* does not in fact elicit heartfelt sympathy of the kind to which Oliver appeals. Nor does the worldly plight of Dickens's scoundrels evince the moral irony that marks his hero's economic difficulties. Recognizing that Dickens enlists the deprivation of his miscreants in the deliberate service of poetic justice minimizes a temptation to grant the villainous slum dwellers in *Oliver Twist* a social compassion that the author does not intend to arouse, however sincerely he may proclaim the message of the downtrodden.

Oliver Twist and Charity

Dennis Walder

In his book *Dickens and Religion,* Dennis Walder describes how the New Poor Law—and Dickens's own purported distrust of public and religious institutions—shaped the novel *Oliver Twist.* In this vein, Walder identifies charity—individual acts of love and goodwill—as the central theme of *Oliver Twist.* Walder notes that Dickens's belief in this Christian virtue crossed sectarian lines. By engaging readers' sympathies with profoundly moving narrative, Dickens attacks prevailing attitudes in society at large.

It is by means of charity that goodness ultimately triumphs in *Oliver Twist.* This is the central theme, explored in both its private and (no less important) public aspects. Dickens expresses the belief that, at the last, acts of individual love, sympathy and goodwill may provide for the suffering poor, if not the thoroughly wicked, and that it is the duty of good Christians to carry out such acts; while the public manifestation of this duty, supposedly encouraged by church and state and embodied in the Poor Laws, he shows to derive from no truly Christian spirit, but rather from the coldly well-meaning, yet inhumane attitudes sponsored by Malthusian and Benthamite 'philosophy'. As John Overs, the working man whom Dickens helped with his literary endeavours, put it: 'Better to sin on the side of sympathy and benevolence than with the ferocious spirit of Utilitarianism and Expedience. *That* is indeed a poisoned valley from which Hope flies, Love enters not; and which Charity and a good honest heart fears and detests.'

A Christian Virtue

Charity is, of course, a Christian virtue, and Dickens treats it as such. In so far as *Oliver Twist* insists upon its importance

Excerpted from *Dickens and Religion* (London: Allen and Unwin, 1981) by Dennis Walder. Copyright © 1981 by Allen and Unwin. Reprinted with permission from Taylor and Francis.

in meeting the needs of the poor, the novel carries a more noticeably Christian hue than most of his fictional works, except perhaps the Christmas books and the last novels. The term means more than the simple human virtue of benevolence, or giving alms to the poor; it implies the more general motive of Christian love, expressed as a love of God and one's neighbour. This distinction has been used to argue that Dickens's charitable characters are not strictly Christian in their performance of benevolent acts towards others, since these seem no more than spontaneous expressions of their good nature, rather than reflections of a will dedicated to God. But Dickens wishes to avoid the premeditativeness of doing good as a duty, as well as any hint of excess—or even merely open—piety, preferring a modest, self-effacing, yet direct goodness which emerges as the natural expression of the personality. He reveals virtue implicitly, in terms of the essential being of a character, rather than in terms of its motivation. If his good people love God—and he often implies that they do—this is revealed only implicitly, through imagery and action, and not by allotting characters overtly Christian motives.

For Dickens, charity is 'the one great cardinal virtue, which, properly nourished and exercised, leads to, if it does not necessarily include, all the others' (*Nicholas Nickleby*, ch. xviii). Nourishing and exercising charity involves other people: it is a social as well as a Christian virtue. St Paul (I Corinthians 13) provides a comprehensive account of it as an impulse directed primarily towards God, but Christ made it clear that we owe it to ourselves, and our neighbours, too, as the objects of God's love (Matthew 22:37–40). Who exactly are our neighbours? Dickens pointedly alludes to the parable Christ used to supply the answer, when he has the parish beadle explain that the 'porochial seal' on the brass buttons embellishing his coat is a representation of the Good Samaritan 'healing the sick and bruised man' (ch. iv). The parable enjoins us to succour him who 'fell among thieves' (Luke 10:29–37). Oliver, plainly, falls among thieves. But his needs are evident before he does so: from the moment of his arrival in the world, a nameless, illegitimate orphan, he is left to 'the tender mercies of churchwardens and overseers' (ch. i). The opening chapters of the novel constitute a fiercely satirical attack upon those public authorities who signally fail to care for the poor in their charge, in direct contradiction to the message of their seal. The social dimension of this has been well accounted for, but the religious dimension has been largely ignored. This is despite Dickens's attempts to suggest it, by means of his allusion to the Good Samaritan, despite, too, the involvement of contemporary religious figures in the revision of the Poor Laws, which was particularly the object of his attack.

THE POOR LAWS

To understand and respond to this aspect of *Oliver Twist,* it is essential to clarify the immediately topical, historical situation which inspired the opening chapters. It may seem that this has been sufficiently expounded by, for instance, Humphry House, whose very thorough analysis in *The Dickens World* has been adopted by most later critics. But there is more to Dickens's attack upon the Poor Laws than has so far been made apparent. Dickens was tapping a specific contemporary source in the newspapers of the time for the views, even, to some extent, the techniques, adopted in his anti–Poor Law satire; and the way in which he transformed fact into fiction has not been fully accounted for, much less the relation of all this to a growing distrust of the religious establishment.

It is generally assumed that Dickens, as a young parliamentary reporter, must have heard, and so drawn on for *Oliver Twist,* the debates on the New Poor Law. In fact, debates on this new legislation during the period when he was actually in Parliament (1834–6) were relatively slight, since the Whig government hurried the reform through in a mere six months early in 1834, and thorough parliamentary discussion began only with the motion (proposed by John Walter of *The Times*) in February 1837 for a Select Committee to inquire into the working of the new law. This was the month in which *Oliver Twist* began appearing in *Bentley's Miscellany,* which reveals in what sense exactly Dickens's 'glance at the new poor Law Bill' was topical. The early months of 1837 marked the extension of the New Poor Law into the London metropolitan area, arousing great popular controversy, as the pages of the *Morning Chronicle* or *The Times* testify. It seems likely that it was these events, rather than the early debates on, or even the actual passing of, the new law, which directly inspired the writing of the novel. Dickens must have been very soon aware of the broader implications of the Bill: he later recalled how he and the editor of the *Morning Chronicle,* John Black, used to quarrel about its effects, the paper having been acquired in 1834 by the Whig John Easthope in order to support the Bill. His views were much closer to those of *The Times* which, under Walter's direction, consistently opposed the Bill and its results, becoming a veritable 'compendium of poor-law crimes', not all of them based on real evidence. A typical leader of February 1837 refers to the 'BENTHAMITE cant' then current according to which the policy designed to produce *'the greatest hap piness to the greatest number'* was 'unquestionably' the best, yet was 'most difficult to reconcile with Christianity or civilization'. This contrast between the utilitarian cant of the 'philosophers' and the claims of Christian civilisation runs right through *The Times*'s criticism, in leading articles, letters, even fiction—extracts from *Oliver Twist*'s opening chapters were published as soon as they appeared. Even if Dickens did attend some of the early debates on the new law, most of his information, as well as a confirmation of his basic position, was probably derived from *The Times.* The narrator who remarks of the members of the 'board' who bring in the new 'system' in *Oliver Twist* that they are 'very sage, deep, philosophical men' (ch. ii) shares the tone and attitude of the newspaper, which opened its extracts from the novel with the same words.

At the same time, Dickens is careful to purge his work of specific dates, places, or names—even the fictional 'Mudfog', used for Oliver's place of birth, he drops after its first appearance. He tries to avoid the accusation of bias and sensationalism inevitable when dealing with such a live issue, by avoiding the explicitness of a journalist—or of a typical 'social problem' novelist such as Frances Trollope, who clumsily attempted to deal with the renewed New Poor Law in her *Jessie Phillips* (1843). Dickens could not entirely avoid such accusations—*The Examiner* criticised his 'unworthy' use of the 'bugbears of popular prejudice'—but he was successful in preferring symbolic generalisation to detailed analysis in his treatment of the law. His art is an art of implication, not explication.

THE BASTARDY ISSUE

This does not mean that our reading of the novel cannot be helped by teasing out some of its more specific implications

—for instance, in relation to the bastardy issue, of obvious relevance to Oliver's plight. The new law set out to abolish the traditional duty laid on parishes since Elizabethan times to 'search for the father' of illegitimate children in their care. Oliver, it seems, is born before the passing of the new law, so 'the most superlative, and, I may say, supernat'ral exertions', if we can believe Bumble, have been made to discover 'who is his father, or what was his mother's settlement, name or con-dition' (ch. ii)—but in vain (a glance at the complicated unravelling of Oliver's family history towards the end of his story suggests a reason for this failure). However, the new 'system' which comes into being after Oliver's return from the branch workhouse introduces, in addition to the notorious dietary restrictions, regulations which 'instead of compelling a man to support his family, as they had heretofore done, took his family away from him, and made him a bachelor!' (ch. ii). Fathers need no longer be sought after, and so the 'natural' Christian ties between parents and children are denied. Dickens emphasises the sanctity of the family in such a way as to include illegitimate children such as Oliver—or Rose Maylie, who carries the 'shame' of illegitimacy despite the fact that, as we later learn, this was a mere slander (ch. li). When the truth about Oliver and Rose finally emerges, they share a 'sacred' embrace, for 'A father, sister, and mother, were gained, and lost, in that one moment' (ch. li). Dickens endorses Harry Maylie's sacrifice of parliamentary ambition in order to marry the apparently 'stained' Rose, just as he endorses Mr Brownlow's correction of Monks's use of the phrase 'bastard child' for Oliver, a reproach to those 'long since passed beyond the feeble censure of the world', reflecting 'disgrace on no one living, except you who use it' (ch. li). Not for Oliver or Rose—any more then for other illegitimates such as Esther Summerson in *Bleak House*—the stigma laid down by the Old Testament: 'A bastard shall not enter into the congregation of the Lord; even to his tenth generation shall he not enter into the congregation of the Lord' (Deuteronomy 23:2). Dickens consciously aligns himself against the contemporary puritan attitude to sexual morality which had developed since the seventeenth century, but which was given new force by the evangelicals, to the effect that children begotten in sin would inherit their parents' weakness. So he concludes *Oliver Twist* by having his two orphans visit a memorial stone 'within the altar' of the old village church, a stone hallowed to the memory of Oliver's mother, and where her 'shade' may hover, for all that she was 'weak and erring' (ch. liii). . . .

OLIVER'S "SIN"

Dickens's suspicion of the religious establishment's attitude towards the poor, whose spiritual guardian it was supposed to be, is clearly reflected in Oliver Twist, where it is a *sin* as well as a crime for an illegitimate pauper orphan to demand charity. Oliver's famous demand for more is followed by a passage generally overlooked: 'For a week after the commission of the impious and profane offence of asking for more, Oliver remained a close prisoner in the dark and solitary room to which he had been consigned by the wisdom and mercy of the board' (ch. iii).

'Impious', 'profane', 'wisdom', 'mercy': responsibility extends beyond the politicians and administrators; it is evidently an offence *against Christianity* to ask for more. Churchmen who nominally represented the interests of the poor on the Poor Law Commission and in the House of Lords were quite as eager as Benthamite 'philosophers' like Nassau Senior or Edwin Chadwick to transform workhouses from refuges for the needy and infirm into houses of correction in which unemployed and able-bodied paupers were treated as if they were depraved criminals. What happens to Oliver is an indication of wider social and religious attitudes, of the wider lack of sympathy and charity towards the poverty-stricken. . . .

Dickens was critical . . . of the whole structure of beliefs concerning the poor which underlay the legal system of his time: 'this ain't the shop for justice', as the Dodger remarks (ch. xliii). The link between the social philosophy of the utilitarian political economists and the religious outlook for the evangelicals, implicit in the new regulations, was forged long before their appearance, and not only among economists or evangelical ministers: it had long been the general conviction that the visible inequality of rewards was a part of the Providential plan; that vice and misery were God-given checks upon population growth; above all, that providing relief for the poor was simply interfering with the severe but necessary conditions for social, economic and moral progress. This is implicit in all that happens before the appearance of the board's new 'system'. Oliver's first cry in the workhouse advertises the fact of 'a new burden having been imposed upon the parish' (ch. i), a phrasing immediately suggestive of the prevailing attitude. Poverty is a vice to be cured by firmness, not compassion. Oliver's mother's death is brought about as much by the indifference of the authorities as by her fear of disapproval. Found lying in the street, and brought in by the overseer's order, her confinement has been attended by a pauper old woman 'rendered rather misty by an unwonted allowance of beer', and by the parish surgeon, who 'did such matters by contract' (ch. i). The ignorant inhumanity of the one, the uncaring professionalism of the other, are summed up in the surgeon's curt: 'It's all over, Mrs Thingummy!' (ch. i). Oliver's condition is that of a total outcast, illegitimate and naked, without identity; as such, he represents a fundamental challenge to the authorities to do something about him; they immediately ensure he is 'badged and ticketed' a 'parish child', henceforward to be 'despised by all, and pitied by none' (ch. i). Life at the branch workhouse to which he is farmed out confirms this prospect for him, as it does for the 'twenty or thirty other juvenile offenders against the poor-laws', rolling about the floor starving and naked (ch. ii). By appropriating the greater part of their weekly stipend for herself, the aptly named Mrs Mann proves herself 'a very great experimental philosopher', remarks Dickens, 'finding in the lowest depth a deeper still' (ch. ii). . . .

Oliver is the touchstone for the lack of mercy and charity in society. His plight absorbs the main force of the narrative, at times to a profoundly moving extent, as when he expresses the agony of his childish grief on being brought away by Bumble from the wretched baby-farm, associated only with deprivation, but containing also his companions in misery: he is, he cries, 'So lonely, sir! So very lonely!' causing even Bumble to lose his composure (ch. iv). Isolated from those who can offer him the compassion and security for which he so desperately longs, Oliver is a pitiful and largely passive object. He lacks the vitality of Bumble or even Noah Claypole. But his primary function is to reveal the neglect and corruption of those around him. . . .

APPEAL TO BROTHERHOOD

Dickens's reproaches to all those who fail to respond to the demands made by Oliver reach their climax with the boy's 'weary catalogue of evils and calamities' which 'hard men had brought upon him', to Mr Losberne and the Maylies. 'Oh!' exclaims the narrator,

if, when we oppress and grind our fellow-creatures, we be-
stowed but one thought on the evidences of human error,
which, like dense and heavy clouds, are rising, slowly it is true,
but not less surely, to Heaven, to pour their after-vengeance on
our heads; if we heard but one instant, in imagination, the deep
testimony of dead men's voices, which no power can stifle, and
no pride shut out; where would be the injury and injustice: the
suffering, misery, cruelty, and wrong: that each day's life
brings with it! (ch. xxx)

Fusing an almost evangelical earnestness of tone with his
Romantic vision of the day of judgement, Dickens utters an
appeal on behalf of our 'fellow-creatures', whose plight, he
suggests, we are finally unable to ignore. For the *truly* evangelical note, and perhaps the original source of Dickens's
imagery, one might compare John Newton's earlier observation of the cloud of smoke over London as suggestive of
the accumulated stock of human misery rising like 'that
cloud of sin which is continually ascending like a mighty cry
in the ears of the Lord of hosts'. Dickens holds to a more optimistic, Romantic, but nonetheless Christian notion, recog-
nised by the Boston *Christian Examiner,* according to which
'crime and depravity everywhere' come from 'our want of
sympathy with the poor, our small respect for man as man,
our violation of the natural pledge of brotherhood'. We have
to be brought to *see* (the visual metaphor is insistent), that
looking on 'nature' and our 'fellow-men' and crying 'that all
is dark and gloomy' is no more than a reflection of our own
'jaundiced eyes and hearts. The real hues are delicate and
need a clearer vision' (ch. xxxiv). This is confirmed in the
novel by the indestructibility of Oliver's goodness and, by
contrast, the self-destructiveness of evil, whether on the 'social' (e.g. Bumble) or more 'metaphysical' (Fagin) level.

CHAPTER 3

A Critical Selection

READINGS ON
OLIVER TWIST

The Purloined Handkerchief

John O. Jordan

In John O. Jordan's reading of *Oliver Twist,* the profuse references to handkerchiefs merit consideration. On one level, Jordan writes, the handkerchief is a function of plot: Oliver is, after all, part of a gang for which the theft of handkerchiefs is a common, everyday activity. On a deeper level, Jordan charts the social and historical significance of the handkerchief and how Dickens uses this motif to explore complex thematic material. The following essay originally appeared in *Dickens Studies Annual.*

> Handkerchief! confessions! handkerchief! To
> confess, and be hanged for his labor. First, to
> be hanged, and then to confess: I tremble at it.
>
> *Othello* IV.1.37–40.

The topic of this essay is a small but revealing aspect of Dickens' *Oliver Twist* (1837–39): namely, the motif of pocket-handkerchiefs in the book. The title, "The Purloined Handkerchief," aims not only at the scenes of pocket picking and handkerchief thieving in the novel but also, somewhat more obliquely, at Edgar Allan Poe's celebrated detective story of 1845, "The Purloined Letter," and at the important body of critical commentary that Poe's story has received in recent years, notably in essays by Jacques Lacan, Jacques Derrida, and Barbara Johnson. The term "purloined" derives largely from this critical tradition. The verb "to purloin" (from the Anglo-French *pur* + *loigner*) means to set aside or delay and hence, by extension, to steal; but as Lacan insists with respect to Poe, the word should properly retain something of its original sense of retardation and displacement in addition to the more straightforward notion of theft, and it is with this broader sense of its meaning that the word

Reprinted from "The Purloined Handkerchief," by John O. Jordan, *Dickens Studies Annual*, 1989. Reprinted with permission from AMS Press, Inc.

is used here. Like the letter in Poe's story, the handkerchiefs in *Oliver Twist* are displaced from their original location and made to circulate through the text and illustrations of the book along a complex network of communication and exchange. To describe some of the features of this network, its circuitry so to speak, will be a principal goal of this paper.

AN ABUNDANCE OF HANDKERCHIEFS

Pocket-handkerchiefs abound in *Oliver Twist.* Nearly every major character in the book handles, carries, or wears some form of handkerchief during the course of the narrative. Over fifty separate instances of the word "handkerchief" or its near-synonyms ("neckerchief," "cravat"; also the slang terms "fogle" and "wipe") occur in the text, and if we include references to other woven materials such as veils, shrouds, curtains, blankets, coverlets, and so forth, then the number is even greater. In addition, handkerchiefs figure prominently in Cruikshank's illustrations to the novel. At least half of the twenty-four plates in the book contain or suggest the presence of a handkerchief. Moreover, the novel appears at times deliberately to flaunt its preoccupation with handkerchiefs, presenting them not just singly but in astonishing profusion.

The abundance of pocket-handkerchiefs in *Oliver Twist* is of course in large part a function of the plot and of Dickens' decision to place his young protagonist in Fagin's gang of juvenile London pickpockets, for whom the theft of handkerchiefs represents a chief source of livelihood. The importance of handkerchiefs in the thieves' domestic economy is evident in the description of Oliver's first arrival at Fagin's den.

> [Fagin] was dressed in a greasy flannel gown, with his throat bare; and seemed to be dividing his attention between the frying pan and a clothes-horse: over which a great number of silk handkerchiefs were hanging. . . .
>
> "We are very glad to see you Oliver—very," said the Jew. "Dodger, take off the sausages; and draw a tub near the fire for Oliver. Ah, you're a-staring at the pocket-handkerchiefs! eh, my dear? There are a good many of 'em, ain't there? We've just looked 'em out, ready for the wash; that's all, Oliver; that's all. Ha! ha! ha!"

Oliver finds many things to wonder at in his new surroundings, but, as Fagin observes and as Cruikshank's illustration for this scene also suggests, what astonishes him most is the profusion of handkerchiefs. The reader immediately recognizes what Oliver fails to understand: namely, that the handkerchiefs are stolen. Oliver's failure to grasp this fact reveals more than just his naiveté, however. Ignorance here is a sign of goodness. Because his heart and mind are innocent, the idea of theft never occurs to him. Indeed, it is only much later, when he actually witnesses a crime, that the meaning of the handkerchiefs becomes clear. Until then, they remain morally neutral objects in what he mistakenly construes as a game.

A few chapters later, in a companion scene to the one just cited, the narrative follows Fagin through the streets of London to another point along the route traced by handkerchiefs through the text of the book.

> Near to the spot on which Snow Hill and Holborn Hill meet, there opens: upon the right hand as you come out of the city, a narrow and dismal alley leading to Saffron Hill. In its filthy shops are exposed for sale huge bunches of second-hand silk handkerchiefs, of all sizes and patterns; for here reside the traders who purchase them from pickpockets. Hundreds of these handkerchiefs hang dangling from pegs outside the windows, or flaunting from the door-posts; and the shelves, within, are piled with them. Confined as the limits of Field Lane are, it has its barber, its coffee-shop, its beer-shop, and its fried-fish warehouse. It is a commercial colony of itself: the emporium of petty larceny: visited at early morning, and setting-in of dusk, by silent merchants, who traffic in dark back-parlours; and who go as strangely as they come. Here, the clothesman, the shoe-vamper, and the rag-merchant, display their goods, as sign-boards to the petty thief; here, stores of old iron and bones, and heaps of mildewy fragments of woolen-stuff and linen, rust and rot in the grimy cellars.

Here we have the documentary urban journalist at work, the Dickens of *Sketches by Boz,* describing a real London street —Field Lane—for the benefit of middle-class readers who have presumably never seen it. Unlike Oliver in the preceding passage, the narrative voice here has no difficulty grasping the significance of the many handkerchiefs on display. They are "signboards" that advertise to both buyer and seller the particular form of commerce conducted within. As such, they belong to a larger class of cultural signs that the narrator records and interprets in conjunction with his project of documenting city life. As in the earlier passage, the very excess of pocket-handkerchiefs in the text calls attention to their status as signifiers in need of interpretation and thus reinforces the handkerchief motif in the book.

A FASHION ACCESSORY

In addition to documenting a particular class of petty criminals, the handkerchiefs in *Oliver Twist* are themselves part of a specific social and historical formation. During the 1820s and 30s, when the action of *Oliver Twist* presumably takes place, handkerchiefs continued, as they had throughout the eighteenth century, to be an important fashion accessory for well-to-do persons of both sexes. Fine handkerchiefs were considered articles of luxury, hence their value to thieves and receivers of stolen goods such as Fagin. Preferably made of silk, but also of cambric and fine muslin, dress handkerchiefs frequently bore the "marks" or initials of their owners embroidered into the fabric. Women's handkerchiefs were usually white, often with fancy face borders and other examples of fine needlework, while men's handkerchiefs, especially snuff handkerchiefs, were more likely to be dark and to bear a printed pattern or design.

Men's handkerchiefs of the period were quite large by modern standards, averaging more than thirty inches square; women's handkerchiefs, though somewhat smaller, also tended to be large. Since the eighteenth century, men generally carried handkerchiefs in the pockets of their trousers, waistcoats, or topcoats, bringing the term pocket-handkerchief into common parlance as a result. Ladies carried their handkerchiefs in a bag or reticule tied round the waist on top of the skirt. From a pickpocket's perspective, the most easily accessible place from which to take a handkerchief was probably the tail-pocket of a gentleman's long-tailed coat. It is from this location, as we see in Cruikshank's illustration, that the Artful Dodger and Charley Bates lift a handkerchief from the distracted Mr. Brownlow, while Oliver looks on in horrified amazement.

In addition to dress handkerchiefs of the kind I have been describing, the late eighteenth and early nineteenth century saw an increase in the use of handkerchiefs by people of the lower classes. The power loom and the availability of cheap cotton from America, together with improved dyeing techniques, made it possible for relatively inexpensive cotton handkerchiefs to be owned by all but the poorest members of society. Thus, although there are no handkerchiefs in the workhouse, when Oliver runs away from the undertaker's house, he does have a handkerchief in which to tie up his few articles of clothing. Likewise, the charity boy Noah Claypole arrives in London with his belongings tied in a hand-kerchief. Servants also have handkerchiefs. For example, we are told that Giles, the butler in Mrs. Maylie's house, wipes his eyes "with a blue cotton pocket-handkerchief dotted with white spots." This distinctive pattern identifies it as a "belcher" handkerchief, so named in honor of the early nineteenth-century prize righter, Jim Belcher, who wore neckerchiefs of this design.

The thieves also carry handkerchiefs—ordinary cotton ones worn characteristically around the neck rather than carried in the pocket. Bill Sikes, for example, wears "a dirty belcher handkerchief round his neck"; flash Toby Crackit wears an orange neckerchief; and Charley Bates explains the slang term "scragged" to Oliver by giving a "pantomimic representation" that involves holding the end of his necker-chief in the air and dropping his head on his shoulder so as to indicate "that scragging and hanging were one and the same thing." Only Fagin, whose throat is bare, lacks the dis-tinctive neckerchief that is virtually a badge of membership in the gang. Thus, although they steal silk handkerchiefs, the thieves do not normally wear them, the one exception to this rule being the occasion when Fagin dresses up like an old gentleman in order to teach Oliver the pocket-handkerchief "game." Fagin's own handkerchief, however, is an old cotton one in which he ties up his gold coins.

THE HANDKERCHIEF CODE

What begins to emerge from these examples is something like a rudimentary dress code in the book with respect to handkerchiefs. Silk handkerchiefs, carried in the pocket, are the property of the upper classes. Ordinary cotton handker-chiefs, often worn about the neck, belong to the lower classes, especially the thieves. Thieves wear neckerchiefs, the neckerchief being an article of working-class attire used for protection against the sun and for wiping away sweat. Sailors, agricultural laborers, and boxers wear neckerchiefs; gentlemen wear "neckcloths" and "cravats," ancestors of the present-day necktie. This code perhaps helps to explain why Mr. Bumble, a lower-class character whose role as beadle aligns him politically with the upper classes, should have two handkerchiefs: one in his pocket, which he daintily spreads over his knees when he takes tea with Mrs. Corney so as "to prevent the crumbs from sullying the splendour of his shorts"—a parodic imitation of upper-class gentility; and another that he takes from inside his hat to wipe his brow. There are, of course, exceptions to the handkerchief code. Both Grimwig and Monks, two upper-class characters, wear neckerchiefs, though the case of Monks is complicated by his close association with the thieves and by the special reason he has for covering his throat.

One other aspect of early nineteenth-century handkerchief history deserves mention at this point: a development that I shall call the "textualization" of the handkerchief. The invention of the roller or cylinder printing machine by Thomas Bell in 1785 was of tremendous importance for the British textile industry at the turn of the century. Printed handkerchiefs, which had previously been relatively difficult and expensive to manufacture, now became mass-produced articles. In addition to decorative patterns such as the blue and white belcher design, one finds an increasing number of utilitarian, commemorative, literary, and political motifs represented upon nineteenth-century handkerchiefs. Maps, statistical tables, poems, political caricatures, and scenes depicting important social and historical events appear with regularity. Handkerchiefs thus become texts as well as textiles, objects to be read and interpreted as well as used in connection with some bodily function.

The "textualization" of handkerchiefs of course begins long before the nineteenth century with the use of embroidered initials, names, and decorative motifs (like the strawberry pattern in *Othello*), but it is not until the Industrial Age that this practice becomes so elaborate or widespread. Dickens was well aware of these new developments in handkerchief production, as he was of nearly every commercial and technological innovation of the age. In *Nicholas Nickleby* (1838–39), for example, the novel that immediately followed *Oliver Twist*, he describes one of the boys who is about to leave with Squeers for Dotheboys Hall as sobbing and "rubbing his face very hard with the Beggar's Petition in printed calico." (*Nickleby*)

Likewise, in *Dombey and Son* (1846–48), a decade after *Oliver Twist*, he mentions something called "the Strangers' Map of London, . . . printed (with a view to pleasant and commodious reference) on pocket handkerchiefs" (*Dombey*). Although *Oliver Twist* contains no references to printed handkerchiefs of this sort, I believe that the idea of the handkerchief as a printed document or text is implicit in the novel and shall return to this point later in the paper.

THEMATIC SIGNIFICANCE

From the examples already cited, it will be clear that *Oliver Twist* is full of handkerchiefs to an extent that both reflects the tremendous increase in handkerchief production around and after the turn of the century and at the same time exceeds the requirements of any documentary or mimetic realism on Dickens' part. As they reappear and pass from one context to another, handkerchiefs take on increasing thematic and figural significance in the novel. Thus, although their importance as a commodity is evident, they seem as well to have symbolic or exchange value in the book, circulating like a form of currency in the thieves' underground economy. As we have seen, handkerchiefs also function as indicators of social class and gender in the book. Their distribution follows a semiotic system or dress code that may owe something to the philosophy of clothes elaborated in Carlyle's *Sartor Resartus* (1833–34) but that lends itself as well to analysis in terms of Roland Barthes' *Systeme de la mode.*

That Dickens was attempting to develop some kind of philosophy of clothing in the book is evident from a passage at the end of the opening chapter, in which the narrator moralizes upon the newly born Oliver's first entry into clothes:

> What an excellent example of the power of dress, young Oliver Twist was! Wrapped in the blanket which had hitherto formed his only covering, he might have been the child of a nobleman or a beggar; it would have been hard for the haughtiest stranger to have assigned him his proper station in society. But now that he was enveloped in the old calico robes which had grown yellow in the same service, he was badged and ticketed, and fell into his place at once—a parish child—the orphan of a workhouse—the humble half-starved drudge—to be cuffed and buffeted through the world—despised by all, and pitied by none.

Several important points concerning the "power of dress" emerge from this passage. First, clothes are a powerful way of marking social distinctions in a class society; second, power itself is often vested in clothing or social roles rather than in the person, as we see later on in the book from the example of Mr. Bumble, who loses every vestige of authority when he takes off his beadle's cocked hat, laced coat, and cane; and finally, dress codes function not just as a differential system of classification but as a means of social control whereby institutions like the workhouse identify and regulate ("badge" and "ticket") members of the lower classes. The exercise of this control begins in the workhouse with the naming, dressing, and subsequent selling of parish orphans as apprentices; it takes its ultimate form in the power of the state over life and death—that is, in the operation or the gallows, which, as Fagin notes, changes "strong and vigorous men to dangling heaps of clothes."

THE HANGING MOTIF

Not surprisingly, then, in a book so preoccupied with handkerchiefs, the power of the state in *Oliver Twist* extends to the absurd length of an attempt by the workhouse board of governors to forbid the possession of pocket-handkerchiefs by any inmate. When the gentleman in the white waistcoat predicts that one day Oliver will come to be hung, the narrator responds with the following ironic comment:

> It appears, at first sight, not unreasonable to suppose, that, if he had entertained a becoming feeling of respect for the prediction of the gentleman in the white waistcoat, he would have established that sage individual's prophetic character, once and for ever, by tying one end of his pocket-handkerchief to a hook in the wall, and attaching himself to the other. To the performance of this feat, however, there was one obstacle: namely, that pocket-handkerchiefs being decided articles of luxury, had been, for all future times and ages, removed from the noses of paupers by the express order of the board, in council assembled: solemnly given and pronounced under their hands and seals.

The connection between pocket-handkerchiefs and hanging that appears in this passage is another important aspect of the handkerchief motif in the book. The thieves of course all live in constant fear of the gallows. Their nervousness on this score is evident in their frequent joking references to public execution and in the colorful figurative language they use in order to avoid pronouncing the word "hanging." Instead, they say things like "scragged" and "dance upon nothing." Bill Sikes, who has more to fear than anyone at the hands of "Jack Ketch," betrays his anxiety by means of hostile attacks on other people's throats. He threatens to "stop [Oliver's] windpipe," takes his knife to Fagin's throat, and leaves bruises on Nancy's "neck and arms." "Wolves tear your throats!" is his most violent oath in the book, and he attempts to drown his dog by tying a stone to its throat with a handkerchief and throwing them in the river.

As these and other examples indicate, the throat is an extremely sensitive part of the anatomy in *Oliver Twist* precisely because it is the focus of so much physical and verbal aggression. It is little wonder then that the thieves make such efforts to protect their throats by wearing handkerchiefs around the neck. These neckerchiefs perform a double and almost contradictory function, however. In addition to protecting a sensitive part of the body, they also serve as a constant reminder of the noose that is figuratively always around the thieves' necks: the "cravat," as Fagin sardonically calls it at one point. Fagin's bare throat suggests his greater vulnerability to the danger that threatens them all, a danger reinforced linguistically throughout the novel by the pun lurking in the first syllable of the word "handkerchief." If handkerchiefs are "*hang*-erchiefs" and if petty larceny is a capital crime (as it was within recent memory, until the Larceny Act of 1808), then the game to which Oliver is introduced at Fagin's and in which Dodger and the other boys are old hands is one where they are invited to play with their own mortality.

The association between handkerchiefs and hanging is confirmed both verbally and visually in *Oliver Twist.* In the passage already discussed describing Oliver's first arrival at Fagin's den, the silk handkerchiefs are said to be "*hanging*" (emphasis mine) over a clothes-horse, and in the companion scene—describing Field Lane they "*hang dangling* from pegs outside the windows" (emphasis mine). The hanging motif is further reinforced in the illustration that accompanies the first of these scenes. On the wall adjacent to the cascade of handkerchiefs we can recognize a small popular print in which three bodies are shown hanging from a gallows. The hang/handkerchief pun is also apparent in Charley Bates's dumb-show explanation of the word "scragged." Here again, Cruikshank's illustration for the scene repeats and thus corroborates the evidence of the verbal text.

The thieves' obsessive fear of hanging may point toward other anxieties as well. Dianne Sadoff, for example, has argued that the thieves' tenderness about the neck represents the displacement upward of a repressed castration anxiety that structures the entire novel. For Sadoff, metaphors of castration at once repress and repeat Oedipal fantasies that underlie Oliver's story. Handkerchiefs and neckerchiefs can thus be understood as signifiers that mark the place of a conspicuous absence in the text—that of the phallus. Likewise, handkerchief stealing can be viewed as a defensive strategy whereby the original conflict is displaced but in which the substitute symptom—pocket picking—repeats in symbolic form the conflict it was intended to resolve.

OLIVER'S SEARCH FOR PARENTS

Castration anxiety is not the only motive for narration in *Oliver Twist.* If handkerchiefs signal a conspicuous absence in the text, then we should consider them as well in relation to Oliver's status as an orphan. Oliver's lack of parents, or rather the lack of any evidence as to their identity, is of course a central mystery that the plot works initially to obscure but ultimately to clear up to achieve narrative closure. The search for parents and for parental substitutes is thus an important motivating force behind the story. It is perhaps too much, however, to say that Oliver himself engages actively in this search. Indeed, he remains remarkably passive throughout the book, ready to attach himself to almost any adult figure that the plot tosses his way, but hardly ever an active participant in initiating such attachments. The search for his father, for example, is carried out on Oliver's behalf by a committee of (mostly) older men, all of them aligned in various ways with the paternal order and the rule of law. The place of Oliver's missing father is marked in the text by a series of written documents—the will, the letter, and the ring given by him to Oliver's mother with her name inscribed inside. All of these, along with other unnamed "proofs," have been either stolen or destroyed by Monks and his mother in their effort to conceal Oliver's paternal origin. They constitute what we might call the "purloined letters" of the novel, and they must be recovered before the plot can come to a close.

The place of Oliver's missing mother is marked in the text not so much by documents and inscriptions, although these exist, as by a series of woven materials such as blankets, curtains, shrouds, and of course handkerchiefs, that appear regularly throughout the novel. These materials are similar but not identical to what the psychoanalytic literature calls "transitional objects"—that is, objects that take the place of the absent mother and help the child to master the trauma of separation from her. Typically these include such things as the child's teddy bear or blanket—soft, malleable objects that recall the maternal breast and that the child can use as a comforting substitute when the mother is away. The transitional objects in *Oliver Twist* do not always provide comfort, however, but serve instead as reminders or premonitions of the mother's death.

The trail marked by these reminders of maternal death begins in the workhouse with the "patchwork coverlet" thrown over the body of his dying mother and continues with the "old blanket" that covers the corpse of the poor woman whose home Oliver visits in the company of the undertaker. It includes the curtain from behind which Mrs. Bedwin's "motherly" face appears at Mr. Brownlow's house, as well as the figurative "dusky curtain" or "shroud" that hangs over Brownlow's memory and keeps him from recognizing the resemblance between Oliver's face and the portrait of Agnes Fleming hanging on the wall. The portrait itself, painted on "canvas," is another instance of the motif, as is the rug that Bill Sikes throws over the body of the murdered Nancy. Less obvious examples include the wallpaper in Brownlow's house, whose "intricate pattern" Oliver traces with his eyes in the still of the night as if attempting to make out on the wall the image of his lost mother's face, an image that materializes for him the next morning when he sees the portrait. The white handkerchief that passes from Rose Maylie, who almost dies, to Nancy, who holds it up in an effort to ward off Bill Sikes' murderous assault, is another instance of the motif, the handkerchief here serving as a link among the three "sisters"—Rose, Nancy, and Agnes—each of whom briefly occupies the place of Oliver's mother in the book.

The signifying chain that unites these various examples comes to an end in the concluding image of the novel: the white marble tablet with the name "Agnes" inscribed upon it. White like the handkerchief and positioned like the portrait and the wallpaper patterns on the wall, the tablet achieves a permanency that the other objects lack and that promises therefore to bring the chain of substitutions to a close. The fact, however. that the inscription is incomplete —like the ring, it lacks a second name—and that it marks a grave without a corpse may indicate that the tablet is only a

temporary resting place in the endless process of significa-
tion. Indeed, the closure achieved here seems not only un-
stable but also transparently ideological in its motivation.
The marble tablet enshrines Agnes Fleming safely within
the bourgeois order that prevails at the novel's end. It thus
prevents the search for Oliver's mother from going back to
the anonymous pauper's grave at the workhouse where her
body presumably lies, and in this way it helps to shield the
institution—as well as Oliver's dead father—from any
charge of responsibility or neglect in the matter of her death.

NANCY'S HANDKERCHIEF

Among the many pocket-handkerchiefs that dot the text of
Oliver Twist none is so distinctive as the one that Nancy
holds aloft at the moment when Bill Sikes bludgeons her to
death. Nancy's handkerchief is memorable on several accounts, not the least of which is the strong contrast it presents to the phallic violence of Sikes. Hers is specifically a
female-gendered handkerchief—white, as if to suggest that
the purity of her womanly "nature" remains unstained despite the sordid conditions in which she lives. Moreover,
since it comes from Rose Maylie, the handkerchief signifies
the sisterly bond that unites two women of different social
classes who are nevertheless alike in their devotion to
Oliver. The handkerchief also seems imbued with religious
significance, for as she lifts it "towards Heaven" Nancy
"breathe[s] one prayer for mercy to her Maker."

It is important to recall that Nancy acquires the handkerchief from Rose Maylie not as a simple gift but in exchange
for the information about Oliver that she provides to the
Maylie group. Nancy will not sell her story, refusing the
money that they offer as a reward, but requests from Rose
instead some personal memento—a glove or handkerchief.
The fact that it is exchanged for a story suggests that the
handkerchief has story value of its own, as a female subtext
or intertext in a narrative ostensibly about the progress of a
parish boy. When Sikes strikes through the handkerchief
with his club, he is attempting to cancel the woman's story,
but he succeeds only in driving it underground. He re-
presses it (just as he covers Nancy's body with the rug), but
it will not stay hidden. The story dogs him, literally, in the
form of the mongrel that follows and finally betrays him to
the mob. Even the handkerchief returns to haunt him. In

Cruikshank's illustration of the scene in which Sikes falls to his death, we see not only the belcher handkerchief around his neck and the hangman's noose that awaits his fall, but in the background, hanging from a pole, a large white square cloth, mentioned in the text only as an absence—"the linen that is never there"—but traceable nonetheless back to Nancy and to Rose. Although repressed, the female subtext returns to assert its power in the end.

SHAKESPEARE REVISED

One further suggestion concerning Nancy's handkerchief merits consideration at this point. The scenes between Sikes and Nancy in the final one-quarter of the novel represent, I believe, Dickens' attempt to retell the story of *Othello*, with Bill Sikes in the role of the murderer, Nancy as Desdemona, and Fagin as the cunning, manipulative Iago who drives Sikes to commit the deed. "You won't be—too—violent, Bill?" he says after confronting Sikes with the evidence of Nancy's betrayal. The handkerchief that Nancy lifts toward Heaven in the murder scene is thus, I would suggest, an intertextual allusion to the lost or purloined handkerchief that serves as the focus of Othello's sexual jealousy. Nancy's unexpected and futile gesture with the handkerchief has its motive partly at least in Shakespeare's play, in Desdemona's equally futile wish to prove her innocence by returning to her husband the missing object that has come to symbolize for him her sexual infidelity.

The hypothesis that Dickens may have been attempting a Newgate *Othello* in *Oliver Twist* is not entirely without foundation. Dickens was of course familiar with all of Shakespeare's work, both as a reader and as a theatergoer. His friend Macready often played the part of Othello and was in fact performing it in 1838, just as Dickens was putting the finishing touches to his novel. Moreover, Dickens appears to have taken a particular interest in *Othello* during the 1830s. We know that in 1833, for example, at the age of 21, he wrote and produced a burlesque theatrical version of *Othello* entitled *O'Thello*, in which his father took a leading role. Only a few manuscript fragments of this burlesque have survived. Similarly, the satirical sketch of 1834 entitled "Mrs. Joseph Porter," reprinted two years later in *Sketches by Boz,* deals with the hilarious and unsuccessful attempt to mount an amateur theatrical production of *Othello*. The scenes between Sikes and Nancy in *Oliver Twist* thus may well be another effort to revise Shakespeare's tragedy, this time as melodrama rather than burlesque or farce. If this hypothesis is correct, it may also help to explain the shift in narrative perspective that takes place toward the end of the book, when the novel's point of view moves inside the guilty consciousness of Sikes, creating greater sympathy for him and making him, if not a tragic hero, at least briefly the protagonist of a Victorian melodrama.

Finally, and at the risk of giving an overly figural reading to the book, I would submit that Oliver himself is a purloined handkerchief circulating through the text of the novel and waiting to be claimed by his rightful owner. To view Oliver in this way is to consider him not so much a character as a narrative function—a small but valuable piece of portable property shuttled about the story by forces outside of his control, including the narrator, until he settles more or less permanently in the Maylie household.

Certainly, from the hour of his birth onward. Oliver is treated more like an object than a human child. " 'You needn't mind sending up to me, if the child cries, nurse' said the surgeon. . . . 'It's very likely it will be troublesome. Give it a little gruel if it is!' " The narrator himself ironically adopts the language of the workhouse in order to satirize its treatment of people as commodities, calling Oliver an "item of mortality" and "an article direct from the manufactory of the Devil himself." If at times Oliver figures as a small piece of manufactured goods, he is also, in Bumble's delightfully mixed metaphor, a strange species of neckerchief: "a porochial 'prentis, who is at present a dead-weight; a millstone, as I may say; round the porochial throat."

OLIVER'S CHARACTER

Like a handkerchief, Oliver seems at first to be little more than a blank space on which others can inscribe their mark of ownership. Bumble gives him the memorable name by which be is known, using the arbitrary, impersonal rule of the alphabet as one guide and his own inadvertent talent for metaphor as another. The police officer who brings Oliver before Mr. Fang, the magistrate, gives him his other name: Tom White. Both names reflect in different ways the namegiver's attempt to classify the boy and insert him in a narrative. "Twist" suggests the hangman's rope and thus the often-repeated prediction that "this boy will be hung." "Tom White" is of course a generic name (recalling Tom Jones), used here to indicate obscure origin and social inconsequence. At the same time, the name suggests that whiteness is an important quality in the boy. Its connotations include both moral purity and genteel birth, both of which Oliver turns out to possess in ample amounts, as well as the inviting and somewhat feminized blankness that leads so many characters to try and leave their mark on him. White, we recall, is also the color of women's handkerchiefs.

Fagin too attempts to impose an identity on Oliver, but not by giving him a name. Rather, he seeks to inscribe a narrative of crime on Oliver's blankness by telling him exciting stories about robbery and giving him the Newgate Calendar to read. In this way he hopes to "blacken" Oliver's soul—an echo of Dickens' blacking factory experience, perhaps. Oliver appears to be a *tabula rasa* unmarked by experience, and he is often described as having a face of perfect innocence. His body is physically unmarked as well. The proof of his identity does not depend, like that of Fielding's Joseph Andrews, on the discovery of a strawberry mark upon his breast. Instead, it his brother Monks who bears the identifying mark, in this case of evil—a birthmark located, significantly, on his throat.

MARKED CHARACTERS

Although he seems at first to be a blank handkerchief, Oliver in fact turns out to be a printed one. In the opening chapter of the book, Oliver's mother "imprint[s] her cold white lips passionately on [his] forehead" only a moment before she dies, and this mark apparently remains with him through the rest of the novel. A crucial scene for this reading of Oliver's character is the one in which he is set to work by Fagin "picking the marks out of the pocket-handkerchiefs." The task that Fagin assigns him is in fact the same one that Fagin is engaged to perform upon the boy—to remove the mark of origin from his soul. Oliver is a pocket-handkerchief that bears the mark of its owner, the dead mother whose spirit serves as Oliver's guardian angel. The question of whether that mark is indelible or can be effaced and another printed in its place is raised by the terms of the father's will. Oliver can inherit only if it can be shown that in his minority he should never have "stained" his name with any public act of dishonor, meanness, cowardice, or wrong.

The question of "marks" and "stains," of genetic traits and environmental determinants, arises in connection with other characters in the book. Rose, Nancy, Sikes, and Monks are all "marked" characters in one way or another. Indeed, the novel seems to revert at times to an almost literal understanding of the idea of "character" as a graphic sign or glyph. For example, the female pauper who announces the death of Old Sally in the workhouse has a face that "resembled more the grotesque shaping of some wild pencil, than the work of Nature's hand." Character in this sense is something written or printed on the body, a textual effect like the designs and patterns printed upon nineteenth-century handkerchiefs.

The handkerchiefs in *Oliver Twist* belong both to a material economy of production and exchange and to a symbolic economy of representation. I have tried to show the presence of both economies in the book as well as some of the connections between them. The history and sociology of handkerchiefs in Britain from the eighteenth through the early nineteenth century provides a useful context for understanding the different kinds of handkerchiefs that appear in the book. In particular, the dramatic increase in handkerchief production at the end of the century, brought about by the new industrial technology, may help to explain the presence of so many handkerchiefs in *Oliver Twist* as well as their availability for the complex thematic treatment that Dickens gives to the handkerchief motif.

Handkerchiefs are integral to the plot and to the narrative project of documenting London's criminal classes. They carry a range of thematic significance, especially in relation to hanging and to issues of power and social control. They are also one of the chief means by which the novel represents its own text-making practice. The circulation of handkerchiefs, like the regular displacement of the letter in Poe's story, is a figure for the process of narration itself. So long as handkerchiefs remain in circulation, the story continues. When they stop, the story ends.

In his "Seminar on 'The Purloined Letter,'" Lacan draws the conclusion that "a letter always arrives at its destination." One might argue similarly with respect to *Oliver Twist* that a purloined handkerchief always reaches its destination as well. Indeed, the story of Oliver, suggests that a handkerchief usually ends up back in its owner's pocket. The story of Oliver's mother, however, suggests otherwise. If the marble tablet on the church wall provides a fitting emblem of closure and containment, refiguring Rose Maylie's white handkerchief after its violent passage through the scene of Nancy's murder, this image of reconciliation is offset by the figure of Agnes Fleming's restless "shade" hovering about the church, and even more so, in the final words of the novel, by the narrator's memory of the living woman as "weak and erring." Despite his evident wish to recover and redeem the fallen woman, the narrator's language here recalls the transgressive sexual desire that generated the entire story as well as the weary, footsore vagrant who gives birth to Oliver in the novel's opening chapter. "Erring"—that is, wandering—she remains an outsider to the final scene of domestic bliss.

The novel's effort to reach closure thus contains the elements of its own undoing, an undoing that Derrida would attribute to the process of "dissemination" and that he views as inherent in the structure of the signifier. To paraphrase Derrida's reformulation of Lacan, it is not that the handkerchief never arrives at its destination, but that it belongs to the structure of the handkerchief to be capable, always, of not arriving. In *Oliver Twist*, the handkerchief that arrives, but at the same time does not fully arrive, is female.

The Evil Triumvirate

Juliet McMaster

Juliet McMaster describes *Oliver Twist*'s three main villains—Fagin, Sikes, and Monks—as an evil triumvirate based on the ideological pattern that traditionally delineates power, knowledge, and love as the three aspects of God. As a diabolic inversion of these qualities, then, Fagin represents demonic knowledge, while the ferocious Sikes embodies the inversion of power. Completing the triumvirate is Monks, who, consumed by hatred, represents the inversion of love. McMaster, a professor of English, has written several books on well-known authors, including *Jane Austen on Love* and *Thackeray: The Major Novels.*

Most readers and critics of *Oliver Twist* agree that the villains steal the show. Fagin with his gang of prostitutes and pickpockets, part demon, part engaging domestic crony; Bill Sikes in his brute strength and surliness; even Monks, with his scar and his sensational epilepsy, have a vital presence and an imaginative power that the Brownlows and Maylies never achieve. Oliver, whom Dickens called "the principle of good surviving through every adverse circumstance," has for good reason latched onto the world's imagination as a victim, an object of compassion, a vehicle for pathos. But his virtues are of necessity mainly passive. The evil figures are the more evil for their roles vis-à-vis Oliver, in exploiting, terrorizing, and seeking to corrupt him; but in himself he can present no positive force for good. And the virtuous adults who range themselves on his side are colourless and ineffectual in comparison with their villainous antagonists. If in the outcome these faintly imagined forces are to triumph over such figures as Fagin, Sikes, and Monks, it is only by some very visible string-pulling on the part of the author, and some rather contradictory suggestions that the forces of

Excerpted from "Diabolic Trinity in *Oliver Twist*," by Juliet McMaster, *Dalhousie Review,* Summer 1981. Reprinted with permission from the author and *Dalhousie Review.*

law and order in this society are better and juster than the rest of the novel has led us to believe.

"This world of Dickens is a world without God," says Graham Greene; "and as a substitute for the power and the glory of the omnipotent and omniscient are a few sentimental references to heaven, angels, [and] the sweet faces of the dead." The backing of any sense of conviction in a powerful deity may be absent from the presentation of the good characters; but there is instead an almost theological authority for the conception of the evil triumvirate of Fagin, Sikes, and Monks. For Dickens has as it were taken God to hell, and transformed his attributes to a diabolic inversion of divine knowledge, power, and love. For omniscience, we have Fagin, the informer, with his endless knowledge of what will hang his associates fastest. For omnipotence, we have Sikes, the brutal murderer whose mode is violence. For benevolence, there is Monks, motivelessly malignant, consumed with a desire to corrupt and destroy his brother. This "knot of . . . associates in crime," as Dickens called them, forms a tight ideological pattern which reinforces, if it does not create, the authenticity and extraordinary vitality of the characters in the "dark" half of the novel.

THREE ASPECTS OF GOD

The classification of knowledge (or wisdom), power, and love (or goodness) as the principal aspects of God (and hence of the best faculties of man, made in God's image) was a commonplace of nineteenth-century Christian thought, with a long and respectable tradition going back as far as Augustine. Even the merely carnal sense of man, Calvin observed, confronted with the Creation, cannot but be aware of "the wisdom, power, and goodness, of the Author in producing such a work." The concept was given renewed vigour and publicity in Dickens's day by the publication of the Bridgewater Treatises. When he died in 1829, the Earl of Bridgewater left £8000 in the hands of the Royal Society for the publication of a series of works "On the Power, Wisdom and Goodness of God, as Manifested in the Creation"; a number of prominent scholars, including theologians like Thomas Chalmers and scientists like William Whewell, were duly commissioned to write the treatises, and they appeared with some éclat between 1833 and 1840. The tripartite formulation of the aspects of God, together with their reflection in man, was familiar and useful to several of Dickens's contemporaries. The concept is central to Browning's thought, and elaborated particularly in *Paracelsus* and "A Death in the Desert": and it was of more than passing interest to Wordsworth and Tennyson.

Theologians, philosophers, and even scientists, no less than artists, have delighted in the number three, and the three qualities we have been discussing turn up, with variations, in a number of different contexts. Ficino, the neo-Platonist reconciler of pagan philosophy with Christian thought, pronounces authoritatively, "No reasonable being doubts . . . that there are three kinds of life: the contemplative, the active, and the pleasurable (*contemplativa, activa, voluptuosa*). And three roads to felicity have been chosen by men: wisdom, power, and pleasure (*sapientia, potentia, voluptas*)." Over the centuries many correspondences have been elaborated between the aspects of God and the tripartite soul of man; the physical, passional, and rational modes of being; the three principal organs of the body, the liver, the heart and the brain, which are respectively the seats of appetite, passion and reason (a set of correspondences between physiology and psychology most memorably laid out by Burton in *The Anatomy of Melancholy*); his study of Browning, has found it possible to devise a whole table of correspondences.

A frequent connection in classical mythology was with the iconographic subject of the Judgement of Paris: Hera, Athene and Aphrodite, the queen of heaven and the goddesses of wisdom and beauty, offer Paris the rewards that are theirs to give, power, knowledge and love. Tennyson's "Oenone" of 1833 was a recent treatment of this subject. Dickens was familiar with at least one parodic version of the Judgement of Paris, the second plate of Hogarth's *Rake's Progress*. Here young Tom Rakewell chooses among the modern temptations of dancing and music, fencing and the martial arts, and sport, while a neo-classical painting on the wall depicts Paris choosing among the goddesses.

THE TRINITY

The three aspects of God were often, though not invariably, aligned with the persons of the Trinity: God the Father, God the Son, and God the Holy Spirit stood for omnipotence, benevolence, and omniscience respectively. In Donne's devotional poem "The Litanie" the first three stanzas are addressed separately to the Father, the Son, and the Holy Ghost; then follows the prayer to the Trinity:

As you distinguish'd undistinct
By power, love, knowledge bee,
Give mee a such selfe different instinct
Of these: let all mee elemented bee,
Of power, to love, to know, you unnumbered three.

The formulation of power, knowledge and love as the three aspects of God, then, was quite familiar in Dickens's day; and with variations the same configuration has formed a strong archetype in mythology and Christian doctrine. It was Dickens's inspiration in *Oliver Twist* to invert these qualities and to make them the dominant aspects of the evil beings in his world. To this extent his vision is indeed Manichaean, as Greene calls it. Evil has its equal and opposite existence and power that are symmetrically opposed to the good. We are shown the kingdom of Satan as the dark reflection of the kingdom of God, and the Devil as being also a trinity figuring forth the diabolic inversions of "the Power, Wisdom and Goodness of God."

FAGIN

Fagin, as has been often pointed out, is a devil, and made recognizable by many features traditionally ascribed to the devil: he wields a toasting-fork, he crouches over a fire, he hates the daylight, he is red-haired, and he leaves no footprints. Moreover, the other characters, like Sikes and Nancy, frequently refer to him as the devil.

But Fagin, though the most obvious incarnation of the devil in the book, is not the only one. Monks too leaves no footprints, and is called "a born devil," and boasts of burning in "hell's fire." The devil imagery is not so insistently connected with Bill Sikes, though he too is set apart from mankind in being "utterly and irredeemably bad." But he is still part of the knot of associates: the hands of the enterprise, so to speak, the necessary doer of the dirty work. All three are committed to the devil's task of the temptation and corruption of mankind—mankind in this case being represented by Oliver. But they need to specialise. Monks has the hatred and the will to destroy Oliver, but not the power ("I won't shed blood," he declares, although he would be happy to have him dead [1941]); Fagin collects the information and mediates;

Bill enacts the burglary with Oliver and the murder of Nancy, but without an understanding of what he is doing.

If Fagin in this trinity stands for knowledge, it is not for knowledge as light and enlightenment. He works characteristically in the dark, and he deals in mysteries and secrets. The knowledge he most covets is knowledge of crime and misdoings, and that which is unknown to anyone else and which will consequently give him most power. As the narrative follows him on his undefined errands, stalking in dark labyrinths that none but he can thread, he is presented as wrapped in mystery, some dark primaeval force secretly on the prowl.

> The mud lay thick upon the stones, and a black mist hung over the streets. . . . It seemed just the night when it befitted such a being as the Jew to be abroad. As he glided stealthily along, creeping beneath the shelter of walls and doorways, the hideous old man seemed like some loathsome reptile, engendered in the slime and darkness through which he moved: crawling forth, by night, in search of some rich offal for a meal.

We seldom see Fagin eating or drinking—Bill Sikes is disgusted by his abstinence—and the "offal" on which he wants to feast is less likely to be food than some decaying piece of information that he can turn to account. The best repository for knowledge, so far as he is concerned, is in dead men, because they tell no tales. The soliloquy that Oliver overhears is almost a hymn to knowledge safely deposited, knowledge used to destroy the dangerous people, his enemies, and to preserve himself.

> 'Clever dogs! Clever dogs! Staunch to the last! Never told the old parson where they were. Never peached upon old Fagin! And why should they? It wouldn't have loosened the knot, or kept the drop up, a minute longer. . . . What a fine thing capital punishment is! Dead men never repent; dead men never bring awkward stories to light. Ah, it's a fine thing for the trade! Five of 'em strung up in a row, and none left to play booty, or turn white-livered!'

Among his many activities as gang leader, miser, and receiver of stolen goods, his main business is the getting and using of other people's secrets. There is something of the cannibal or the vampire about him in this activity. He lives and thrives on the deaths of others. As J. Hillis Miller observes, the denizens of Fagin's world live in "general fear of the unseen look that steals one's secret," and so jeopardizes one's identity and even one's life. In an underworld society of spies, Fagin is the chief. He is always on the alert for more information, incriminating if possible. He has "a restless and suspicious manner habitual to him." And he is sharply aware of the nuances and fluctuations of Nancy's feelings for Oliver, in spite of all her efforts to disguise them. "I shall have it out of you, my girl, cunning as you are," he promises himself.

FAGIN'S *MODUS OPERANDI*

We see in detail the process by which he gains power over Noah Claypole, and again it is by stealing his secret. First he spies on him through the dark window at the Three Cripples, described in detail as a convenient arrangement for watching customers without their knowledge.

> Mounting a stool, he cautiously applied his eye to the pane of glass, from which secret post he could see Mr. Claypole. . . .
>
> 'Aha!' he whispered, looking round to Barney, 'I like that fellows looks. He'd be of use to us. . . . Don't make as much noise as a mouse, my dear, and let me hear 'em talk—let me hear 'em.'
>
> He again applied his eye to the glass, and turning his ear to the partition, listened attentively: with a subtle and eager look upon his face, that might have appertained to some old goblin.

That is Fagin's *modus operandi,* watching and listening unseen, in a characteristic pose. Presently he overhears some incriminating words from Noah about the till he has robbed and the further robberies he intends, and then he has him where he wants him. He goes in and treats Noah and Charlotte to a drink.

> 'Good stuff that,' observed Mr. Claypole, smacking his lips.
>
> 'Dear!' said Fagin.' A man need be always emptying a till, or a pocket, or a woman's reticule, or a house, or a mail-coach, or a bank, if he drinks it regularly.'
>
> Mr. Claypole no sooner heard this extract from his own remarks than he fell back in his chair, and looked from the Jew to Charlotte with a countenance of ashy paleness and excessive terror.

Thereafter Noah is utterly under Fagin's control.

Fagin revels in the power over his associates that his cunningly acquired knowledge gives him. He proudly refers to himself as "*I,* that know so much, and could hang so many besides myself!" And he contemptuously refers to his associates as "a drunken gang that I could whistle away the lives of!" Being offered Phil Barker as ripe for the taking, by the landlord of the Three Cripples, he enjoys the opportunity to play fate, to propose and dispose on the lives and deaths of his creatures. "Aha! But it's not Phil Barker's time," he responds. ". . . Phil has something more to do, before we can afford to part with him; so go back to the company, my dear, and tell them to lead merry lives—*while they last.* Ha! ha! ha!" If the right evil secret does not yet exist for his purposes, he does what he can to bring it about: so he has corrupted his gang of pickpockets and prostitutes; he tries to make a thief out of Oliver, and a murderess out of Nancy, and he succeeds in making a murderer out of Bill. In his relations with Nancy, particularly, we see him hungry for a determining knowledge of evil. "'With a little persuasion,' thought Fagin, 'what more likely than that she would consent to poison him [Bill]? . . . There would be the dangerous villain: the man I hate: gone; . . . and my influence over the girl, with a knowledge of this crime to back it, unlimited.'" This is the demonic inversion of divine omniscience.

As one who exists by spying and informing, Fagin is particularly sensitive to being spied upon, to having his own secret stolen, as we learn early from the scene where Oliver overhears his soliloquy and watches his miserly gloating over his trinkets. As soon as he is aware that Oliver is awake, and watching and listening,

> He closed the lid of the box with a loud crash; and, laying his hand on a bread knife which was on the table, started furiously up. He trembled very much though; for, even in his terror Oliver could see that the knife quivered in the air.

> 'What's that?' said the Jew. 'What do you watch me for? Why are you awake? What have you seen? Speak out, boy! Quick—quick! for your life!'

It is a charged moment. The creature of the slime and darkness, the unseen watcher, the dealer in other people's guilty secrets, cannot endure to be watched himself. He shows similar symptoms of panic when he has exposed more than he intends of himself and his motivation to Nancy. To be observed and understood is to be undone, unmade, destroyed.

OVERCOMING EVIL

And here we come to the question of the defeat of evil in *Oliver Twist*, the harrowing of hell. Graham Greene observes that the good, as inadequately conceived in the novel, is too weak and ineffectual to overcome the evil convincingly, and thus that we cannot believe in the quenching of these dark forces. "We read of the defeat of Monks, and of Fagin screaming in the condemned cell, and of Sikes dangling from his self-made noose, but we don't believe." And yet, although it is hard to conceive of Brownlow and the Maylies as powerful and triumphant, we do believe it—the deaths of Sikes and Fagin have an imaginative force that matches that of their lives. It is not that good triumphs, but that evil, of its very nature, ultimately destroys itself. It is inverted, perverted, monstrous; and as such is bound to explode or collapse, by the same laws of moral physics that make Mrs. Clennam's house fall, in hideous ruin and combustion down, in *Little Dorrit.*

Fagin's end has a dire appropriateness for the diabolic inversion of divine knowledge. He is arrested as the result of a relentless series of self-generating acts of revelation. Fagin the informer employs another spy, Noah Claypole, to spy on another informer, Nancy. With the same obsessive fear that he had shown in other scenes when too much has been brought to light about him, he informs on the informer, letting Bill understand much more than the truth of what Nancy has told Rose Maylie. (In fact she had refused to betray either Bill or Fagin.) It is Bill's brutal murder of Nancy, as instigated by Fagin, and its coming to light as the sun at last rises on the criminal world, that leads to the exposure and collapse of the whole dark fabric, the arrest of Fagin and the pursuit of Sikes.

Fagin at the trial and in the condemned cell is the informer informed on, the peacher peached against. He is suffering a punishment that tellingly matches his crime, and his function as diabolic knowledge. As the workings of his mind are described in detail, it is clear that he is suffering a kind of torture of consciousness, as of fronting the sun with lidless eyes. He is achingly, agonizingly, infinitely aware: aware at the same time of the huge fact of his impending horrible death, the death to which he had sent so many others, and of the minutest distracting detail of the scene surrounding him.

> Not that, all this time, his mind was, for an instant, free from one oppressive overwhelming sense of the grave that opened at his feet; it was ever present to him, but in a vague and general way, and he could not fix his thoughts upon it. Thus, even while he trembled, and turned burning hot at the idea of

> speedy death, he fell to counting the iron spikes before him,
> and wondering how the head of one had been broken off, and
> whether they would mend it, or leave it as it was.

With this burden of appalling knowledge already piled on
him, he is nevertheless stuck in his old pose of eager spying
and listening, as though forever doomed to go on knowing
more and more: "He stood there, in all this glare of living
light, with one hand resting on the wooden slab before him,
the other held to his ear, and his head thrust forward to enable him to catch with greater distinctness every word that
fell from the presiding judge." There he is the watcher from
dark places, the listener, the gatherer of guilty secrets; but
now the secrets being exposed are his own, the knowledge
he is to gain that of his own condemnation to death. And he
is himself exposed, utterly and defencelessly, to the total and
terrible scrutiny of the universe:

> The court was paved, from floor to roof, with human faces.
> Inquisitive and eager eyes peered from every inch of space.
> From the rail before the dock, away into the sharpest angle of
> the smallest corner in the galleries, all looks were fixed upon
> one man—Fagin. Before him and behind: above, below, on
> the right and on the left: he seemed to stand surrounded by a
> firmament, all bright with gleaming eyes.

"It is a universe which has become all eyes," as Miller says,
"eyes which see into every corner of one's soul, and do not
have leave any recess which is free or secret." Fagin's role as
knowledge of evil in Dickens's presentation of the diabolic
trinity is not just part of an abstract ideological pattern: it
gives an informing dramatic force to some of the most powerful passages in the novel.

BILL SIKES

The divine power of creation finds its demonic inversion in
the violence and destructiveness of Bill Sikes, the housebreaker and brutal murderer. It is hardly necessary to document his violence and ferocity—he acts them out at every
appearance. He has "the kind of legs, which . . . always look
in an unfinished and incomplete state without a set of fetters
to garnish them." His living quarters are furnished with
"two or three heavy bludgeons" and an ironically named
"life-preserver," and his favourite playthings are a crowbar
and a boxed set of housebreaking tools. His speech is largely
made up of oaths, threats, and abuse. Here is a sample, from
his exclamations when he is on the run and pursued by

dogs: "'Wolves tear your throats!' muttered Sikes, grinding his teeth. 'I wish I was among some of you; you'd howl the hoarser for it.' . . . Sikes growled forth this imprecation, with the most desperate ferocity that his desperate nature was capable of." His mind, what there is of it, can linger over fantasies of violent cruelty. Asked what he would do to Noah if he turned informer, Bill responds, "I'd grind his skull under the iron heel of my boot into as many grains as there are hairs upon his head." In the running heads to the chapter on his pursuit and death, he is twice called "the wild beast." In short, as Fagin tells Nancy, "he's a brute, Nance, a brute-beast."

BULL'S-EYE

One can learn more about Bill Sikes from his dog, who also habitually "growls." For Bill's dog is like Miss Havisham's wedding-cake, a metaphoric extension of the character, and a commentary on it. Bill and his dog both have white coats, they show the same signs of getting into violent fights, and when Bill drinks hard, the dog gets red-eyed. The dog's name, Bull's-eye, suggesting "Bill's eye," is useful here, as Bull's-eye does indeed act as his master's organ and instrument. When he is tired of a tirade from Nancy, Bill threatens, "if I hear you for half a minute longer, the dog shall have such a grip on your throat as'll tear some of that screaming voice out." And when he has recaptured Oliver from the Brownlow household, he can similarly use his dog as an extension of his own power. "Here, Bull's-eye, mind him, boy! Mind him!" So Bull's-eye enacts for Bill what Bill enacts for Fagin. One might call them both cat's-paws, but that the term is inappropriately feline.

This technique of extension, quite common in Dickens, is psychologically interesting here. For Bull's-eye, while being identified with Bill, is also separate from him, and so their relation is a correlative for Bill's self-estimate, and for his relation with himself. Considering the degree to which their interests and characters seem to be identified, the relation between the man and his dog is stormy and hostile. This is their first entry:

> 'Come in, d'ye hear?' growled this engaging ruffian. . . . 'Why didn't you come in afore? . . . You're getting too proud to own me afore company, are you? Lie Down!'
>
> This command was accompanied with a kick, which sent the animal to the other end of the room. He appeared well used to it, however.

If Bill assumes the dog is ashamed of him, it appears to be because he is on no very good terms with himself. This suggestion is reinforced by an apparently gratuitous scene of startling ferocity on their next appearance. Dickens plays upon his readers' sentimental preconceptions about the unquestioning devotion expected of man's best friend. Bill, drunk and surly, has just delivered a kick and a curse on the dog, for no particular reason:

> Dogs are not generally apt to revenge injuries inflicted upon them by their masters; but Mr. Sikes's dog, having faults of temper in common with his owner, . . . made no more ado but at once fixed his teeth in one of the half-boots. Having given it a hearty shake, he retired, growling, under a form; just escaping the pewter measure which Mr. Sikes levelled at his head.

> 'You would, would you?' said Sikes, seizing the poker in one hand, and deliberately opening with the other a large clasp knife, which he drew from his pocket. 'Come here, you born devil! Come here! D'ye hear?'

> The dog no doubt heard; because Mr. Sikes spoke in the very harshest key of a very harsh voice; but, appearing to entertain some unaccountable objection to having his throat cut, he remained where he was, and growled more fiercely than before: at the same time grasping the end of the poker between his teeth, and biting at it like a wild beast.

This scene of escalating ferocity is the more suggestive for the fact that we have been shown Bill and Bull's-eye as being identified. What we have is a scene of fiercely dramatised self-hatred. Bill's generalised brutality and savagery against the whole external world is an extension of his self-distrust, and so eventually turns back upon himself. The first person that he murders is the one being in the world who loves him, the woman who is closest to being flesh of his flesh and bone of his bone. After that he tries again to kill Bull's-eye, this time by drowning. Then, as he had feared, the crowd tracks him down by following his dog, so that Bull's-eye in a sense betrays him. The next being he kills is inevitably himself, in that memorable scene of self-execution. And, in case his own weight has not been enough to break his neck at the end of the noose, the dog leaps down to reinforce it, and thereby destroys also his other self.

So Bill Sikes, the diabolic inversion of divine power, by a kind of inner necessity, turns his brutal power against himself, and is destroyed by it. This aspect of evil, like Fagin's evil knowledge, has been monstrous, ingrown, and must eventually self-destruct.

MONKS

Monks is clearly not so successful a creation as Fagin or Sikes, and his part in *Oliver Twist* has been much criticized. Dickens has quite unabashedly endowed him with all the conventional marks of the melodramatic villain: he is tall, dark and haggard, and scarred. He even wears a cloak, and uses, among others, the standard villain's oath of "Curses." Moreover, he is inextricably involved in the elaborate mechanism of what Arnold Kettle derogatorily calls "the plot," the final explanation involving Oliver's real parentage, the burned will, and the explanation of Monks's and his cohorts' attempt to corrupt Oliver. (In fact the real plot of *Oliver Twist* is surely much greater and more comprehensive than this mechanical piece of it, and comprehends the whole action of the novel.)

Some weaknesses in the conception of this character being conceded, Monks nevertheless remains a figure of some power. He does not collapse for being recognized as in large part conventional. He has at least one hauntingly memorable scene of almost apocalyptic dimensions, in which he confronts the trembling Mr. Bumble and his wife during a storm. His epileptic seizures, which Dickens uses to suggest some horrible communion with the dark powers, make him more sinister and frightening than the usual moustache-curling villain. And in completing a pattern his presence also enhances the conceptions of the more powerful creations of Fagin and Sikes. Monks is one of Fagin's secrets, and in being unknown is the more effective in precipitating the uncomprehending violence of Sikes.

Until the ending we cannot fathom Monks's motive for his obsessive loathing of Oliver. And to Oliver too he is an inexplicable emanation, a surreal apparition, horrifying, as Magwitch is to Pip, for apparently starting up from nowhere and having no rhyme or reason. Oliver bumps into a stranger, by accident, when he is intent on another errand; and finds he has unwittingly awakened a malignity far in excess of the cause. The man curses him "in a horrible passion"; shakes his fist, and tries to strike him; and then falls down impotently, "writhing and foaming, in a fit." The episode has considerable power, and the more for being unexplained at the time.

Even when we do get the explanation, in the laborious last chapters, it doesn't provide Monks with any very sufficient reason for his hatred of his half-brother Oliver. According to their father's will, the younger brother was to inherit the fortune only if he had behaved himself: hence Monks's pact with Fagin to make a thief of Oliver. But that will, we are further told, was burned, and no evidence remains that it had ever existed. So though Monks's hatred comes across convincingly enough, it remains essentially unmotivated, really an emanation from a being whose whole existence is hatred.

Monks completes the trinity, embodying the diabolic inversion of love as Fagin embodies that of knowledge and Sikes that of power. In his case his allegorical function as hatred is made most explicit. He received as a bequest from his mother, he says, "her unquenchable and deadly hatred," and swears to pursue his infant brother "with the bitterest and most unrelenting animosity; to vent upon it [the child] the hatred that I deeply felt; and to spit upon the empty vaunt of that insulting will by dragging it, if I could, to the very gallows-foot." As Sikes's violence is significantly turned against the woman who loves him, his other half, so Monks's hatred is against his brother.

Unlike Fagin and Sikes, Monks is left alive at the end. But his life also is to be his defeat, the logical self-annihilation that their deaths are, as a prolonged existence of generalised loathing at last centres in himself: he is to go on, we are to suppose, "mutter[ing] curses on himself in the impotence of baffled malice." He is to be like Spenser's Malbecco, Jealousy, or love turned into hatred, forever trying to destroy himself, and never succeeding.

Oliver Twist: An Autobiographical Reading

Steven Marcus

Steven Marcus describes Oliver Twist as a completely passive figure, seemingly incapable of shaping his own destiny. Albeit ineffectual, Oliver is inherently good and of strong moral character. According to Marcus, Dickens casts the incorruptible Oliver as a "vessel of grace"—and ultimately, the recipient of grace—partly because he identified with the neglected orphan. Without a doubt, writes Marcus, Oliver's experiences record agonizing events in Dickens's past—namely his separation from family and banishment to a blacking factory. Marcus is the author of *Dickens: From Pickwick to Dombey*, from which the following is excerpted.

One of the criticisms of Dickens that was most confidently put forward by the later Victorians was that he could not manage a plot. Few critics today, however, are likely to regard even the absence of a plot—let alone its mismanagement—as particularly disabling, for the attenuation of plot has been one of the most notable tendencies in the novel during the twentieth century. Although the chief origins of the nineteenth-century novel's typically complex plot are probably to be found in the drama, and then secondarily in romance (the linear progression of the picaresque novel being inadequate to an intricate and exhaustive organization of experience) plot in the novel does not function quite as it does in the drama. Plot represents, it may be suggested, an active principle of coherence wherever it appears; its very presence seems to assert the coherent nature of experience, which is why its attenuated role in contemporary fiction is of such significance. But the traditional esthetic of the novel permits a far greater flexibility of organization than is allowed the drama. Furthermore, unlike the drama, the novel has consistently tended to regard itself as taking for its subject nothing less than society itself: one of its conscious historic aims has been to describe what it is like to be alive in a particular kind of world at a particular time, under particular material and spiritual circumstances. The novel is that form of art in which the documentary impulse becomes an imaginative power. In the era before modern sociology was invented, the novel was an indispensable agent in the understanding of society; the complicated, intertwining narrative of the nineteenth-century novel was one of its chief means of discovering and dramatizing the facts of life. And among the English novelists of the century, Dickens had the strongest instinct for elaborate and intricate plots in whose unfolding there would be revealed his complex experience of the world. Nevertheless, for late-nineteenth-century readers and even for some modern ones, Dickens's handling of plot represents his greatest vulnerability. The coincidences he seemed always to be feverishly working up in his novels have been judged as irrefutable evidence of his inability to "tell a story," [according to Frederick Harrison].

On closer inspection, however, these coincidences, especially in *Oliver Twist,* are entirely appropriate to the kind of reality Dickens is concerning himself with, and to the sense is trying to communicate. The coincidences in *Oliver Twist* are of too cosmic an order to belong in the category of the fortuitous. It is no accident, for instance, that on his very first visit to London Noah Claypole finds his way, like a homing pigeon, to "The Three Cripples"—it is the place toward which wicked people naturally gravitate. And it is no "mere" coincidence that as soon as Mr Bumble arrives in London, enters an inn and picks up a newspaper, "the very first paragraph upon which . . . [his] eye rested" is an advertisement for information about Oliver. Nor can any of Oliver's adventures be supposed to be fortuitous: we cannot take it as an accident that the first time Oliver is sent out with the Dodger and Charley, the person whom they choose to rob turns out to be the man who was the closest friend of Oliver's father; it is no coincidence that the first time he walks out of Mr Brownlow's house he is recaptured by the thieves; and the fact that the house the thieves break into, again when Oliver is first sent out, happens to be his aunt's beggars the very notion of accident. For the population of *Oliver Twist* consists only of persons—the wicked and the beneficent—involved with the fate of the hero. There are, almost, no other sorts of people in it; and in a world where there is no accidental population, no encounter can be called a coincidence. In effect there is also no reality, no existence in *Oliver Twist* other than the parabolic one the characters inhabit and serve; and where the world is thus circumscribed, the ordinary tests of fortuitousness do not apply. The controlling view of society at large in *Oliver Twist* is that of a "great beaste", the mob, which, featureless and materializing out of nowhere, is always ready to pursue, surround and inflict its casual, impersonal outrage upon whoever is being pursued, whether it be Oliver or Sikes or Fagin.

THE HELPLESS CHILD

Naturally, one of the effects of such a relentless circumscription of society is a field of action so confined that the force which both parties exert in their contention for Oliver seems as concentrated and intense as a nightmare—or the struggle for a soul. It also eliminates the possibility of Oliver's ever escaping into something else: for there is nothing else. But although Oliver shares with Bunyan's Christian, that other hero of a moral tug-of-war, this experience of a claustral universe, there is a conspicuous difference in the two contests. However inadequate Christian may feel in his struggles with the giants and demons of the world, and however urgently he petitions for the assistance of Evangelist and his ministers, he makes a resolute stand whenever he must, does battle with Appolyon, and even wounds him. He is an active, positive heroic figure whose behavior, though a necessity of Bunyan's art, contradicted Bunyan's predeterminist theology. But in Dickens's conception it is indispensable that Oliver virtually be unable to do anything, that he be incapable of fighting for or winning a birthright—and in this respect Oliver is the archetypal hero of Dickens's early novels. Being a child, he is naturally helpless; everything seems done to him and for him, and almost nothing is done by him. When he is adopted by Mr Brownlow his workhouse clothes are removed and he is dressed in the clothes of a young gentleman, and when he is recaptured by the thieves they promptly strip him of his new suit and give him back his old clothes. He is active in the way that a ball batted back and forth between opposing sides is active: he is moved through space. Oliver is essentially the incarnation of a moral quality, and the particular virtue he represents requires that he appear all but defenseless. For he is ideal and incorruptible innocence.

OLIVER'S VIRTUES

Furthermore, the sources of Oliver's character are mysterious, for there is nothing in his experience to account for what he is. His disposition and moral character are so unlike everything he has known, so apart from all external influence, that it almost seems as if he, like Mr Pickwick, might have come from another world. In effect, Oliver is the vessel of Grace, but a grace that has been secularized and transformed into a principle of character. This is why he and the other outcast but favored children in Dickens's novels speak, in defiance of all probability, exquisitely well-bred English unlike, say, the young Heathcliff, "a dirty, ragged, black-haired child", who, discovered by Mr Earnshaw "starving and houseless" in the streets of Liverpool, speaks only "some gibberish that nobody could understand". *Wuthering Heights* has its changeling, too, but unlike Dickens's Oliver, Heathcliff is a demon cast into human form, and so originally speaks the language of demons. Oliver is very much an angel, and so speaks the language of angels, "correct" English: it is Dickens's way of showing that grace has descended upon him.

IN DICKENS'S IMAGE

Speech is the recognized sign of class and status, and when Dickens uses a well-bred speech as indication of inborn virtue he would seem clearly to be implying a connection between grace and the ascent into a better social class. The bearing this matter has upon Dickens's own experience in the blacking warehouse cannot, I think, be missed. The young Dickens had possessed, he said, "some station" among the rough boys there. "Though perfectly familiar with them, my conduct and manners were different enough from theirs to place a space between us. They, and the men, always spoke of me as 'the young gentleman'. . . . Poll Green uprose once, and rebelled against the 'young gentleman' usage; but Bob Fagin settled him speedily." And although the young Charles was treated "as one upon a different footing from the rest", he never uttered "to man or boy, how it was that I came to be there", and never "gave the least indication of being sorry that I was there. That I suffered in secret, and that I suffered exquisitely, no one ever knew but I. How much I suffered, it is, as I have said already, utterly beyond my power to tell. No man's imagination can overstep the reality. But I kept my own counsel, and I did my work. I knew from the first, that if I could not do my work as well as any of the rest, I could not hold myself above slight and contempt. I soon became at least as expeditious and as skilful with my hands, as either of the other boys."

In one important respect this is not at all like Oliver Twist, who—even if he had had the ambition—would have made the world's most incompetent pickpocket. Oliver, the first youthful example of the passive central figure so recurrent in Dickens's novels, is obviously not conceived in Dickens's own character image. There have been few men capable of more potent self-assertion than Dickens, or more confident in their aggressive will; he was unembarrassed by his genius and loved to celebrate his power of command. Oliver, and all the other passive young men in Dickens's novels, are idealized representations of some other side of their author's being. What this side is, it is not difficult to discover. Here, again, we are inevitably directed toward the religious influences which played upon Dickens. In associating grace with the inability to do anything on behalf of one's destiny except endure and watch it unfold, and freeing it of the taint of willful or self-interested participation in one's fate, it would seem clear that Dickens was revealing a more primitive Protestant tendency than Bunyan. For Oliver's salvation depends solely on his ability to withstand passively the seductions of Fagin; that he has this ability is never truly in doubt —the strength of his inner light is sufficient to last for ten inheritances.

THE YOUNG DICKENS'S DEGRADATION

Oliver is the *lusus naturae*, a Christian boy. If there is something in all of this that seems touched with self-deception and self-congratulation, it is only fair to add that it didn't take Dickens very long to discover that one cannot finally put aside or cancel out one's time in the workhouse by coming into a long-lost inheritance. The experiences of Oliver

Twist without doubt record Dickens's memory of the central episode in his own childhood and the neglect he suffered at the hands of his parents. As we have seen, these early circumstances—the prison, the breaking up of the family, the agony of being deserted and forgotten, the public exposure and the rough companionship of the boys at the blacking factory—had excited in him an extreme and ineradicable feeling of humiliation, of having been violated, degraded and declassed. In his autobiographical sketch he wrote:

> It is wonderful to me how I could have been so easily cast away at such an age. It is wonderful to me, that, even after my descent into the poor little drudge I had been since we came to London, no one had compassion enough on me—a child of singular abilities, quick, eager, delicate, and soon hurt, bodily or mentally—to suggest that something might have been spared, as certainly it might have been, to place me at any common school. . . . No one made any sign. My father and mother were quite satisfied. They could hardly have been more so, if I had been twenty years of age, distinguished at a grammar-school, and going to Cambridge. . . .
>
> No words can express the secret agony of my soul as I sunk into this companionship; compared these everyday associates with those of my happier childhood; and felt my early hopes of growing up to be a learned and distinguished man, crushed in my breast. The deep remembrance of the sense I had of being utterly neglected and hopeless; of the shame I felt in my position; of the misery it was to my young heart to believe that, day by day, what I had learned, and thought, and delighted in, and raised my fancy and my emulation up by, was passing away from me, never to be brought back any more; cannot be written. My whole nature was . . . penetrated with the grief and humiliation of such considerations. . . .
>
> No advice, no counsel, no encouragement, no consolation, no support, from any one that I can call to mind, so help me God. . . .
>
> I know that I worked, from morning to night, with common men and boys, a shabby child. . . . I know that I have lounged about the streets, insufficiently and unsatisfactorily fed. I know that, but for the mercy of God, I might easily have been, for any care that was taken of me, a little robber or a little vagabond.

The autobiographical sketch was written in 1847, almost twenty-five years after the events it recalls. The man who wrote it was the greatest and most famous English novelist of his time. Yet those events were as vivid to him as if they had just happened: "Even now," he continued, "famous and caressed and happy, I often forget in my dreams that I have a dear wife and children; even that I am a man; and wander desolately back to that time of my life". Those events were indeed alive—as alive as his immense success, which by then had begun to fail of its redemptive powers.

Nevertheless, in *Oliver Twist* suffering has no consequences in the character of the child; it is Oliver's self-generated and self-sustaining love, conferred it would seem from Heaven alone, that preserves him from disaster and death. This is perhaps an accurate indication of how Dickens was inclined to remember his own childhood at that time; it was as if those dreadful months of loneliness and servitude were not to be of ultimate account. Only success, only the achievement of one's birthright—whether that involved becoming a famous writer, or a gentleman, or both—was the conclusive judgment on one's being.

Chronology

1812

Charles Dickens born February 7, to John and Elizabeth Dickens; War of 1812 begins with United States.

1814

John Dickens transferred to London.

1817

John Dickens transferred to Chatham.

1821

Charles Dickens starts school.

1822

John Dickens transferred to London.

1824

John Dickens arrested for debt and sent to Marshalsea Prison; Charles Dickens begins work at Warren's Blacking Factory.

1824–1826

Attends Wellington House Academy in London.

1827

Works as law clerk; improves his education at the British Museum Reading Room.

1830

Meets Maria Beadnell.

1831

Becomes reporter for the *Mirror of Parliament.*

1832

Becomes staff writer for the *True Sun.*

1833

First published piece appears in the *Monthly Magazine;* slavery abolished in British Empire.

1834

Becomes staff writer on the *Morning Chronicle;* street sketches published in the *Evening Chronicle;* meets Catherine Hogarth; Poor Law of 1834 enacted.

1836

Sketches by Boz published in book form; marries Catherine Hogarth; plays *The Strange Gentleman* and *The Village Coquettes* produced at St. James's Theater; meets John Forster, a lifelong friend and biographer; Ralph Waldo Emerson publishes *Nature.*

1836–1837

Pickwick Papers published in monthly installments.

1837

Pickwick Papers published in book form; begins installments of *Oliver Twist* in *Bentley's Miscellany;* play *Is She Your Wife?* produced at St. James Theater; first child, Charles, born; Catherine's sister Mary Hogarth dies suddenly; Victoria becomes queen of England; Thomas Carlyle publishes *The French Revolution.*

1838

Nicholas Nickleby appears in installments; *Oliver Twist* published in book form; first daughter, Mary, born; first railroad train enters London.

1839

Nicholas Nickleby published in book form; second daughter, Kate, born; People's Charter, stating six demands for voting and representation for the poor; Chinese-British Opium Wars begin; end 1860.

1840

Dickens edits *Master Humphrey's Clock,* a weekly; *The Old Curiosity Shop* appears in installments and in book form; England annexes New Zealand; Queen Victoria marries Prince Albert; James Fenimore Cooper publishes *The Pathfinder.*

1841

Barnaby Rudge appears in *Master Humphrey's Clock* and in book form; Dickens's second son, Walter, born; the magazine *Punch* founded; Ralph Waldo Emerson publishes *Essays.*

1842

Dickens tours America with Catherine; *American Notes* published; Alfred, Lord Tennyson publishes *Poems;* anesthesia first used in surgery.

1843

Martin Chuzzlewit appears in monthly installments; "A Christmas Carol" published for Christmas; William Wordsworth becomes poet laureate.

1844

Dickens tours Italy and Switzerland; *Martin Chuzzlewit* published in book form; "The Chimes" published for Christmas; Dickens's third son, Francis, born; first message by Morse's telegraph.

1845

Dickens produces the play *Every Man in His Humour;* "The Cricket on the Hearth" published for Christmas; Dickens's fourth son, Alfred, born; Edgar Allan Poe publishes *The Raven and Other Poems.*

1846

Dickens creates and edits the *Daily News; Dombey and Son* appears in monthly installments; *Pictures from Italy* published in book form; "The Battle of Life: A Love Story" published for Christmas; Irish potato famine results in mass immigration to United States; repeal of Corn Laws, which regulated grain trade and restricted imports; Elias Howe invents sewing machine.

1847

Dickens starts a theatrical company and takes *Every Man in His Humour* on a benefit tour; Dickens's fifth son, Sydney, born; Charlotte Brontë publishes *Jane Eyre;* Emily Brontë publishes *Wuthering Heights;* Henry Wadsworth Longfellow publishes *Evangeline.*

1848

Theatrical company performs for Queen Victoria; theatrical company performs *The Merry Wives of Windsor* to raise money for preservation of Shakespeare's birthplace; *Dombey and Son* published in book form; "The Haunted Man" published for Christmas; Dickens's sister Fanny dies.

1849

David Copperfield appears in monthly installments; Dickens's sixth son, Henry, born; Henry David Thoreau publishes "Civil Disobedience."

1850

David Copperfield published in book form; Dickens establishes and edits *Household Words;* Dickens's third daughter,

Dora Annie, born, dies in infancy; Elizabeth Barrett Browning publishes *Sonnets from the Portuguese;* Tennyson becomes poet laureate; Nathaniel Hawthorne publishes *The Scarlet Letter.*

1851

Dickens and theatrical company perform charity plays; Dickens's father, John, dies; Nathaniel Hawthorne publishes *The House of the Seven Gables;* Herman Melville publishes *Moby-Dick.*

1852

Bleak House appears in monthly installments; *A Child's History of England* published in book form; Dickens's seventh son, Edward, born; Harriet Beecher Stowe publishes *Uncle Tom's Cabin.*

1853

Bleak House published in book form; Dickens gives first public reading from the Christmas books; travels to France and Italy.

1854

Hard Times appears in installments in *Household Words; Hard Times* published in book form; Henry David Thoreau publishes *Walden;* Crimean War begins; ends 1856.

1855

Little Dorrit appears in monthly installments; Dickens and family travel to Paris; Walt Whitman publishes *Leaves of Grass.*

1856

Dickens purchases Gad's Hill.

1857

Little Dorrit published in book form; Dickens spends year on theatrical productions.

1858

Dickens separates from Catherine; Dickens gives public readings; Henry Wadsworth Longfellow publishes *The Courtship of Miles Standish.*

1859

Dickens ends *Household Words;* begins *All the Year Round; A Tale of Two Cities* appears in *All the Year Round* and in book form.

1860

Great Expectations appears in weekly installments.

1861

Great Expectations published in book form; *The Uncommercial Traveller,* a collection, published; George Eliot publishes *Silas Marner;* U.S. Civil War begins; ends 1865.

1862

Dickens gives many public readings; travels to Paris; Victor Hugo publishes *Les Misérables;* Lincoln issues Emancipation Proclamation, freeing slaves.

1863

Dickens gives public readings in London and Paris; mother, Elizabeth, dies; Lincoln delivers Gettysburg Address.

1864

Our Mutual Friend appears in monthly installments.

1865

Dickens suffers a stroke, leaving him lame; *Our Mutual Friend* published in book form; *The Uncommercial Traveller,* a second collection, published; Lewis Carroll publishes *Alice in Wonderland;* Leo Tolstoy publishes *War and Peace;* rapid postwar industrialization in United States.

1866

Dickens gives public readings in Scotland and Ireland; Fyodor Dostoyevsky publishes *Crime and Punishment.*

1867

Dickens travels to America to give public readings; England grants dominion status for Canada.

1868

Dickens gives public readings in England; Louisa May Alcott publishes *Little Women.*

1869

Dickens begins *The Mystery of Edwin Drood;* Mark Twain publishes *Innocents Abroad;* imprisonment for debt abolished; Suez Canal opened.

1870

Dickens gives farewell public reading in London; *The Mystery of Edwin Drood* appears in monthly installments; becomes seriously ill, June 8; dies, June 9; buried in Poet's Corner, Westminster Abbey, June 14.

FOR FURTHER RESEARCH

ABOUT CHARLES DICKENS AND *OLIVER TWIST*

Peter Ackroyd, *Dickens*. New York: HarperCollins, 1990.

G.K. Chesterton, *Charles Dickens: The Last of the Great Men*. New York: Readers Club, 1942.

A.O.J. Cockshut, *The Imagination of Charles Dickens*. New York: New York University Press, 1962.

Philip Collins, ed., *Dickens: Interviews and Recollections*. London: Macmillan, 1981.

Robert James Cruikshank, *Charles Dickens and Early Victorian England*. New York: Chanticleer, 1949.

Richard J. Dunn, *Oliver Twist: Whole Heart and Soul*. Boston: Twayne, 1993.

John Forster, *The Life of Charles Dickens*. 3 vols. Philadelphia: J.B. Lippincott, 1874.

Edgar Johnson, *Charles Dickens: His Tragedy and Triumph*. 2 vols. New York: Simon & Schuster, 1952.

Fred Kaplan, *Dickens: A Biography*. New York: William Morrow, 1988.

——, *Oliver Twist: A Norton Critical Edition*. New York: W.W. Norton, 1993.

Stephen Leacock, *Charles Dickens: His Life and Work*. London: Peter Davies, 1933.

Harlan S. Nelson, *Charles Dickens*. Boston: Twayne, 1981.

Angus Wilson, *The World of Charles Dickens*. London: Martin Secker and Warburg, 1970.

WORKS BY THE AUTHOR

Charles Dickens, *Oliver Twist*. Enriched Classics Series with a reader's supplement to the text. New York: Washington Square Press, 1975.

——, *Oliver Twist*. In Heron Books Series *Books That Have Changed Man's Thinking*. With an introduction by Arthur Calder-Marshall. Geneva: Heron Books, 1970.

——, *Oliver Twist.* Doris Dickens, ed. London: Michael Joseph, 1962.

——, *Oliver Twist.* Peter Fairclough, ed. Penguin English Library Edition. Harmondsworth, Middlesex, England: Penguin, 1966.

——, *Oliver Twist.* The Oxford Illustrated Dickens with an introduction by Humphry House. London: Oxford University Press, 1949.

——, *Oliver Twist.* With an introduction by Irving Howe. Toronto: Bantam Books, 1982.

——, *Oliver Twist.* The Heritage of Literature Series. With an afterword by Edward LeComte. New York: New American Library, 1961.

——, *Oliver Twist.* With an introduction by J. Hillis Miller. New York: Holt, Rinehart and Winston, 1962.

——, *Oliver Twist.* With an introduction and notes by Ian Ousby. London: Pan Books, 1980.

——, *Oliver Twist.* Kathleen Tillotson, ed. Oxford: Clarendon, 1966.

——, *Oliver Twist.* With an introduction by Kathleen Tillotson. Oxford: Oxford University Press, 1982.

ABOUT DICKENS'S TIMES

S.G. Checkland and E.O.A. Checkland, eds., *The Poor Law Report of 1834.* Harmondsworth, Middlesex, England: Penguin 1974.

Kellow Chesney, *The Anti-Society: An Account of the Victorian Underworld.* Boston: Gambit, 1970.

Amy Cruse, *The Victorians and Their Reading.* Boston: Houghton Mifflin, 1935.

John W. Derry, *A Short History of Nineteenth-Century England.* London: Blandford, 1963.

Norman Longmate, *The Workhouse.* London: Maurice Temple Smith, 1974.

Michael E. Rose, *The English Poor Law 1780–1930.* Newton-Abbot: David and Charles, 1971.

R.J. White, *The Horizon Concise History of England.* New York: American Heritage, 1971.

ORGANIZATION TO CONTACT

Dickens Society (DS)
Department of Humanities and Arts
Worcester Polytechnic Institute
Worcester, MA 01609-2280

Phone: (508) 831-5572
Fax: (508) 831-5878

The society conducts and supports research and general interest in the life, times, and works of Dickens. Its scholarly journal, the *Dickens Quarterly,* includes an annual index and bibliographies.

INDEX